Horr
from Gothic to Post-Modern

Horror Literature
from Gothic to Post-Modern

Critical Essays

Edited by MICHELE BRITTANY *and*
NICHOLAS DIAK

Foreword by Lisa Morton
Afterword by Becky Spratford

McFarland & Company, Inc., Publishers
Jefferson, North Carolina

ASSOCIATION

The essays contained in this volume were adapted from presentations given at the 2017 and 2018 Ann Radcliffe Academic Conferences. The conference is part of the Horror Writers Association's academic outreach programming and is held in conjunction with HWA's annual convention, StokerCon. The Bram Stoker Award for Superior Achievement in Non-Fiction and StokerCon are registered trademarks of the Horror Writers Association.

LIBRARY OF CONGRESS CATALOGUING-IN-PUBLICATION DATA

Names: Brittany, Michele, 1965– editor. | Diak, Nicholas, 1982– editor. |
   Morton, Lisa, 1958– writer of foreword. | Spratford, Becky Siegel,
   writer of afterword. | Horror Writers Association. Ann Radcliffe
   Academic Conference (1st : 2017 : Long Beach, Calif.) | Horror
   Writers Association. Ann Radcliffe Academic Conference (2nd :
   2018 : Providence, R.I.)
Title: Horror literature from Gothic to post-modern : critical essays /
   edited by Michele Brittany and Nicholas Diak ; foreword by Lisa Morton ;
   afterword by Becky Spratford.
Description: Jefferson, North Carolina : McFarland & Company, Inc.,
   Publishers, 2020 | "The essays contained in this volume were adapted
   from presentations given at the 2017 and 2018 Ann Radcliffe Academic
   conferences." | Includes bibliographical references and index.
Identifiers: LCCN 2019051447 | ISBN 9781476674889 (paperback : acid free paper) ∞
   ISBN 9781476637914 (ebook)
Subjects: LCSH: Horror tales—History and criticism—Congresses. |
   Horror in literature—Congresses.
Classification: LCC PN56.H6 H66 2020 | DDC 809/.9164—dc23
LC record available at https://lccn.loc.gov/2019051447

BRITISH LIBRARY CATALOGUING DATA ARE AVAILABLE

ISBN (print) 978-1-4766-7488-9
ISBN (ebook) 978-1-4766-3791-4

Front cover image © 2020 Shutterstock

Printed in the United States of America

McFarland & Company, Inc., Publishers
   Box 611, Jefferson, North Carolina 28640
   www.mcfarlandpub.com

Acknowledgments

This collection would not have been possible without the support of Lisa Morton, former president of the Horror Writers Association, who championed the Ann Radcliffe Academic Conference. We'd also like to express gratitude to the HWA board, and to Kate Jonez, Kevin J. Wetmore, Jr., and James Chambers who chaired StokerCon 2017 and 2018 and who helped make the Ann Radcliffe Academic Conference a success for its first two years. Thanks also goes to Lee Murray who advocated the conference and to our editor at McFarland, Layla Milholen.

We'd also like to recognize the original presenters at AnnRadCon 2017 and 2018: Emily Anctil, James Anderson, Elizabeth Bobbitt, Naomi Borwein, Karen Bovenmyer, Allison Budaj, Elsa Carruthers, Mathias Clasen, J. Rocky Colavito, Caitlin Duffy, Audrey Fessler, Anthony Gambol, Eric Guignard, Janet Holden, Daniel Holmes, Gavin Hurley, Rhonda Jackson Joseph, Melissa Kaufler, Bridget Keown, Frazer Lee, Jennifer Loring, Khara Lukancic, Erica McCrystal, Johnny Murray, Jamil Mustafa, Holly Newton, Joanna Parypinski, Shawn Pendley, Kent Pettit, Michelle Reinstatler, Danny Rhodes, Rahel Sixta Schmitz, Maya Thornton, John Tibbetts, Michael Torresgrossa, Amanda Trujillo, and Kevin J. Wetmore, Jr.

Table of Contents

Foreword

The Truth of Horror: A Brief History of the Genre's Nonfiction Works ... and Why We Need Them

LISA MORTON

"Terror and horror are so far opposite, that the first expands
the soul, and awakens the faculties to a high degree of life;
the other contracts, freezes, and nearly annihilates them."
—From "On the Supernatural in Poetry"
by Ann Radcliffe[1]

It is perhaps appropriate that Ann Radcliffe's 1826 piece "On the Supernatural in Poetry"—which might be considered the first serious work of critical horror analysis—was seemingly penned from beyond the grave, since
Radcliffe died three years prior to its publication. Radcliffe, whose importance
in the development of the Gothic tale and, by extension, horror fiction, cannot
be overstated (John Keats even referred to her as "Mother Radcliff"[2] [sic]).
Radcliffe had originally intended the essay to occupy a place in her novel
Gaston de Blondeville (1826), but decided against its inclusion. Fortunately,
the piece was discovered posthumously among her papers and placed in *The
New Monthly Magazine and Literary Journal*, and thus was the study of horror
born. Now, nearly two centuries later, it is fitting that the Horror Writers
Association (HWA) has recognized Radcliffe's work by naming their annual
academic conference in her honor, a conference that continues the fine ancestral line of nonfiction within the horror genre.

But what is that ancestral line? What are the major markers in the study
of horror? Do we really need detailed study of the horror genre? What purpose does horror nonfiction (including academic papers, popular magazine

1

2   Foreword

articles, bestselling biographies, histories, and detailed critical analyses) really serve?

Genre specialist Daniel Chandler argues, "Genre analysis situates texts within textual and social contexts, underlining the social nature of the production and reading of texts…. As well as locating texts within specific cultural contexts, genre analysis also serves to situate them in a historical perspective."[3] Horror's most prolific purveyor in the 20th century, Stephen King, asked a slightly different question: "Why are people willing to pay good money to be made extremely uncomfortable?"[4] King spent all of one entire book, *Danse Macabre* (1981), trying to answer that question, and finally came up with a somewhat lyrical conclusion:

[handwritten: Productive or creative]
[handwritten: seller/vendor.]
[handwritten: NON FICTION]

> Here is a chance to bust that tunnel vision wide open, bricks flying everywhere so that, for a moment at least, a dreamscape of wonders and horrors stands forth as clearly and with all the magic reality of the first Ferris wheel you ever saw as a kid, turning and turning against the sky…. It's a way of awakening the child inside, who never dies but only sleeps ever more deeply. If the horror story is our rehearsal for death, then its strict moralities make it also a reaffirmation of life and good will and simple imagination—just one more pipeline to the infinite.[5]

[handwritten left margin: helpful too assignment]
[handwritten left margin: causes wonder + imagination]

A cynic might suggest here that horror writers should study King in order to sell as many books as possible, or that academics should study obscure Gothic novels only to attain tenure. However, the study of the horror genre provides other, deeper satisfactions, to writer, academic, and fan alike. A look back at some of the key works shows exactly why the nonfiction side of the genre must be preserved, cherished, and encouraged to continue forward.

Possibly the first book-length study of horror literature was Edith Birkhead's 1921 *The Tale of Terror: A Study of the Gothic Romance.*[6] Birkhead, a British lecturer and author, wrote near the end of the first chapter of her book, "the tale of terror appeals to deeply rooted instincts, and belongs, therefore, to every age and clime."[7] Birkhead's book may have sparked a revival of interest in the Gothic classics during the 1920s, although other critics have noted a concurrent rise in popularity of both psychoanalysis and surrealism.[8]

Six years after the appearance of Birkhead's work, H.P. Lovecraft published his own overview, "Supernatural Horror in Literature." Lovecraft extended his study beyond the Gothic to cover writers like Arthur Machen, Lord Dunsany, and M.R. James, and he offered a simple yet elegant defense of horror at the beginning of the piece:

> The oldest and strongest emotion of mankind is fear, and the oldest and strongest kind of fear is fear of the unknown. These facts few psychologists will dispute, and their admitted truth must establish for all time the genuineness and dignity of the weirdly horrible tale as a literary form.[9]

[handwritten bottom: suitable way of showing horror ← weird fiction + also documents]

It's interesting to note that both Birkhead and Lovecraft are noting the genre's deeply rooted place in human consciousness as a way of arguing the importance and value of the genre.

The 1950s and '60s saw yet another revival of interest in Gothic literature, led by a number of important critical works like Devendra P. Varma's *The Gothic Flame: Being a History of the Gothic Novel in England: Its Origins, Efflorescence, Disintegration, and Residuary Influences* (1957). In the book's foreword, the esteemed art historian, literary critic, and philosopher Herbert Read comments, "now, after reading Dr. Varma's revealing account of the origins and development of the Gothic novel, I feel more convinced than ever that our neglect of this phase of English literature is unjust."[10] Is there a better argument in favor of the existence of horror nonfiction than restoring a neglected corner of the genre to its rightful place in literary history?

The 1970s saw an explosive rise of interest in horror, both in bookstores and theaters, with titles like *The Other, The Exorcist*, and *Jaws* occupying slots first on bestseller lists and then box-office charts. This rise in dark fiction/film was accompanied by a wave of biographies and bibliographies archiving the horror authors of the past. Readers looking for the next thrill beyond the contemporaries could learn more about Edgar Allan Poe (Peter Haining's *The Edgar Allan Poe Scrapbook* [1977]), Lovecraft (L. Sprague de Camp's *Lovecraft: A Biography* [1975]), Robert E. Howard (Glenn Lord's *The Last Celt: A Bio-Bibliography of Robert E. Howard* [1977]), Dunsany (Mark Armory's *Lord Dunsany: A Biography* [1972]), Ray Bradbury (William F. Nolan's *The Ray Bradbury Companion* [1975]), and Robert Bloch (Graeme Flanagan's *Robert Bloch: A Bio-Bibliography* [1979]). The wealth of information and analysis to be found in biographies of key horror writers was further underscored in 1987, when Muriel Spark's *Mary Shelley* became the first recipient of the Horror Writers Association's Bram Stoker Award for Superior Achievement in Non-Fiction in 1987.[11]

In 1981, the reference publisher Bowker published a book that, in its own preface, called itself "the first reference book compiled for horror fiction, poetry, and the pulp magazines"[12]: *Horror Literature: A Historical Survey and Critical Guide to the Best of Horror* by Marshall B. Tymn. At over 550 pages and fully indexed, this volume provided fans and scholars with a much-needed reference work to key authors and titles in the genre. In his foreword, Haining discusses how this volume bridges the critical gap between the ghost story and the horror story, noting, "despite the view sometimes expressed that horror literature is a rather narrow and limited field, over the years it has explored many areas of interest from the depths of the unconscious mind to those primitive, but still potent, fears of the dark."[13] The burgeoning field → beginning to grow or increase rapidly of horror references was continuing (from Birkhead and Lovecraft) to promote the genre's ever-increasing breadth and depth.

Horror continued to gain sales and fans throughout the 1980s; in bookstores, mass-market paperbacks featuring embossed covers proliferated, while theaters were dominated by slasher films. Meanwhile, horror nonfiction also became increasingly popular, with a number of notable authors producing works that dominated awards lists and sold well: Stephen Jones (*Horror: The 100 Best Books* [1988], *Clive Barker's Shadows in Eden* [1991]); Kim Newman (his seminal 1985 *Nightmare Movies* would be reprinted for almost thirty years); the aforementioned Haining; and, moving into the 1990s, S.T. Joshi (who provided the first serious study of weird fiction in 1990, and the definitive biography of Lovecraft in 1996) and David J. Skal, whose 1993 *The Monster Show: A Cultural History of Horror* (revised in 2001) placed horror films within the context of their times and political landscapes, and coined the phrase "monster culture" to describe "a phenomenon of horror-movie hoopla that began in the late fifties and continued into the mid-sixties."[14]

In the 1990s, academic appreciation of the genre produced a number of important texts. Carol Clover's *Men, Women, and Chainsaws: Gender in the Modern Horror Film* (1992) approached slasher movies via feminist theory and textual analysis, expanding on ideas Clover had first explored in a 1987 paper called "Her Body, Himself." In that work, she had created the term "Final Girl" (which she most simply describes as "the female victim-hero" found in horror films[15]), but Clover's term soon moved well beyond scholarly circles to become a pop culture catch phrase (and granting some horror film and fiction—for example, Wes Craven and Kevin Williamson's 1996 *Scream*—the ability to become "meta," or self-referential, one of the few times when nonfiction had a direct impact on horror fiction). Noël Carroll's *The Philosophy of Horror: Or, Paradoxes of the Heart* (1990) examined the genre's aesthetics via philosophy. And *The Dread of Difference: Gender and the Horror Film* (1996) offered breakdowns of horror's use of gender from nearly two dozen academics, including such important figures as Clover, Barbara Creed, Linda Williams, Vivian Sobchack, and Tony Williams.

Academics weren't the only ones being educated in the 1990s: those who aspired to write horror were fully catered to as the art of creating horror was commodified. Nolan dissected one of his own stories to explain the craft in *How to Write Horror Fiction* (1991), Stanley Wiater provided a wealth of valuable advice gathered in interviews with 50 horror writers for 1997's *Dark Thoughts*; and in 1997, HWA released its own how-to, *Writing Horror: A Guidebook*, edited by Mort Castle (a revised second edition followed in 2006).

In the new millennium, the internet became a first source of information for many, and the Non-Fiction Bram Stoker Awards nominees reflected that.[16] Websites and electronic newsletters that have provided a boon to those seeking knowledge have included Ralan.com (a market source for writers), Hell-Notes (a general horror information newsletter), the Jobs in Hell Newsletter (which provided market and publishing news for writers, artists, and poets), and the RA for All: Horror blog (a major source for librarians looking to build their horror sections). HWA now hosts a forum for academics looking to exchange information.

But the printed hard copy was still alive and well by 2017, when Michele Brittany (a Non-Fiction Bram Stoker Award nominee for her anthology *Horror in Space: Critical Essays on a Film Subgenre*) and Nicholas Diak organized the first Ann Radcliffe Academic Conference as part of HWA's yearly StokerCon. For the first time, horror's academics were part of a larger event designed for writers and fans alike. In 2018, HWA's Board of Trustees voted unanimously (for the first time in the thirty-plus-year history of the awards) to recognize Short Non-Fiction as a Bram Stoker Award category.

The essays collected in this volume amply convey the extraordinary range of modern horror studies. There are pieces on American horror authors ranging from Stephen King to Richard Laymon; international authors like Koji Suzuki and L.T.C. Rolt; children's books and zombie novels; weird fiction and mythology.

There's even an essay dealing with Ann Radcliffe.

Surely Mother Radcliffe would have been pleasantly shocked to find that the study of dark literature, which she gave birth to with an unfinished piece of 482 words, has grown to encompass an entire world of terror … and even its more vulgar cousin horror.

NOTES

1. Ann Radcliffe, "On the Supernatural in Poetry," *The New Monthly Magazine and Literary Journal* 16.1 (1826), 150.
2. John Keats, "To George and Georgiana Keats (Sunday Morng. February 14, 1819)," *Poems by John Keats (1795–1821)*, accessed October 5, 2018, http://keats-poems.com/to-george-and-georgiana-keats-sunday-morng-february-14-1819/.
3. Daniel Chandler, "An Introduction to Genre Theory," *Stanley Kubrick*, http://visual-memory.co.uk/daniel/Documents/intgenre/chandler_genre_theory.pdf.
4. Stephen King, *Danse Macabre* (New York: Everest House, 1981), 10.
5. *Ibid.*, 379–380.
6. Edith Birkhead, *The Tale of Terror: a Study of the Gothic Romance* (Project Gutenberg, 2004), http://www.gutenberg.org/cache/epub/14154/pg14154-images.html.
7. *Ibid.*
8. See, for example, Kimberly Marwood, "Imaginary Dimensions: Women, Surrealism and the Gothic," in *Women and Gothic*, ed. Maria Purves (Newcastle Upon Tyne: Cambridge Scholars Publishing, 2014).
9. H.P. Lovecraft, "Supernatural Horror in Literature," *The Recluse*, no. 1 (1927), 23.
10. Herbert Read, foreword to *The Gothic Flame: Being a History of the Gothic Novel in England: Its Origins, Efflorescence, Disintegration, and Residuary Influences*, by Devendra P. Varma (London: Arthur Baker Limited, 1957), vii.
11. "1987 Bram Stoker Award Nominees and Winners," *The Bram Stoker Awards*, accessed October 5, 2018. http://www.thebramstokerawards.com/uncategorized/1987-bram-stoker-award-nominees-winner/.
12. Marshall B. Tymn, *Horror Literature: An Historical Survey and Critical Guide to the Best of Horror* (New York: R.R. Bowker Company, 1981), xi.

13. Peter Haining, foreword to *Horror Literature: An Historical Survey and Critical Guide to the Best of Horror,* by Tymn B. Marshall (New York: R.R. Bowker Company, 1981), ix.

14. David J. Skal, *The Monster Show: a Cultural History of Horror,* Revised Edition (New York: Farrar, Straus and Giroux, 2001), 266.

15. Carol J. Clover, "Her Body, Himself: Gender in the Slasher Film," *Representations* No. 20, Special Issue: Misogyny, Misandry, and Misanthropy (Autumn, 1987), 189.

16. "Category: Non-fiction," *The Bram Stoker Awards,* accessed October 5, 2018, http://www.thebramstokerawards.com/category/non-fiction/.

Bibliography

Armory, Mark. *Lord Dunsany: A Biography.* London: Collins, 1972.

Birkhead, Edith. *The Tale of Terror: A Study of the Gothic Romance.* 1921. Project Gutenberg, 2004. http://www.gutenberg.org/cache/epub/14154/pg14154-images.html.

Brittany, Michele. *Horror in Space: Critical Essays on a Film Subgenre.* Jefferson, NC: McFarland, 2017.

Carroll, Noël. *The Philosophy of Horror: Or, Paradoxes of the Heart.* New York: Routledge, 1990.

Castle, Mort. *On Writing Horror: A Handbook by the Horror Writers Association,* 2nd ed. Cincinnati, OH: Writers Digest, 2006.

"Category: Non-Fiction." *The Bram Stoker Awards.* Accessed October 5, 2018. http://www.thebramstokerawards.com/category/non-fiction/.

Chandler, Daniel. "An Introduction to Genre Theory." *Stanley Kubrick,* http://visual-memory.co.uk/daniel/Documents/intgenre/chandler_genre_theory.pdf.

Clover, Carol J. "Her Body, Himself: Gender in the Slasher Film," *Representations* 20, Special Issue: Misogyny, Misandry, and Misanthropy (Autumn, 1987), pp. 187–228.

_____. *Men, Women, and Chainsaws: Gender in the Modern Horror Film.* Princeton: Princeton University Press, 1993.

Conley, Ralan. *Ralanwww.* Accessed October 5, 2018. http://www.ralan.com.

de Camp, L. Sprague. *Lovecraft: A Biography.* Garden City: Doubleday & Co., 1975.

Flanagan, Graeme. *Robert Bloch: A Bio-Bibliography.* Canberra City, AUS: Graeme Flanagan, 1979.

Grant, Barry Keith. *The Dread of Difference: Gender and the Horror Film.* Austin: University of Texas Press, 1996.

Haining, Peter. *The Edgar Allan Poe Scrapbook.* New York: Schocken Books, 1978.

Jones, Stephen. *Clive Barker's Shadows in Eden.* San Francisco: Underwood Miller, 1991.

Jones, Stephen, and Kim Newman. *Horror: The 100 Best Books.* Philadelphia: Running Press, 1993.

Joshi, S.T. *H.P. Lovecraft: A Life.* West Warwick, RI: Necronomicon Press, 1996.

_____. *The Weird Tale.* Austin: University of Texas Press, 1990.

Keats, John. "To George and Georgiana Keats (Sunday Morng. February 14, 1819)." *Poems by John Keats (1795–1821).* Accessed October 5, 2018. http://keats-poems.com/to-george-and-georgiana-keats-sunday-morng-february-14-1819/.

King, Stephen. *Danse Macabre.* New York: Everest House, 1981.

Lord, Glenn. *The Last Celt: A Bio-Bibliography of Robert E. Howard.* Hampton Falls, NH: Donald M. Grant, 1976.

Lovecraft, H.P. "Supernatural Horror in Literature," *The Recluse* 1 (1927), 23–59.

Newman, Kim. *Nightmare Movies.* London: Proteus, 1985.

"1987 Bram Stoker Award Nominees and Winners" *The Bram Stoker Awards.* Accessed October 5, 2018. http://www.thebramstokerawards.com/uncategorized/1987-bram-stoker-award-nominees-winner/.

Nolan, William F. *How to Write Horror Fiction.* Cincinnati, OH: Writers Digest, 1991.

_____. *The Ray Bradbury Companion.* Farmington Hills, MI: Gale, 1975.

Olson, Paul F., Garrett Peck, Judi Rohrig, and David B. Silva. *Hellnotes.* Accessed October 5, 2018. http://hellnotes.com/.

Radcliffe, Ann. "On the Supernatural in Poetry," *The New Monthly Magazine and Literary Journal* 16.1 (1826), 145–152.

Read, Herbert. Foreword to *The Gothic Flame: Being a History of the Gothic Novel in England: Its Origins, Efflorescence, Disintegration, and Residuary Influences*. Devendra P. Varma. London: Arthur Baker Limited, 1957.

Skal, David J. *The Monster Show: A Cultural History of Horror*. New York: W.W. Norton, 1993.

Spark, Muriel. *Mary Shelley*. New York: Dutton, 1987.

Spratford, Becky. *RA for All: Horror*. Accessed October 5, 2018. http://raforallhorror.blogspot.com/.

Tymn, Marshall B. *Horror Literature: An Historical Survey and Critical Guide to the Best of Horror*. New York: R.R. Bowker, 1981.

Varma, Devendra P. *The Gothic Flame: Being a History of the Gothic Novel in England: Its Origins, Efflorescence, Disintegration, and Residuary Influences*. London: Arthur Baker Limited, 1957.

Wiater, Stanley. *Dark Thoughts: On Writing: Advice and Commentary from Fifty Masters of Fear and Suspense*. San Francisco: Underwood Books, 1997.

Lisa Morton is a screenwriter and nonfiction and fiction book writer whose work was described by the American Library Association's Readers' Advisory Guide to Horror as "consistently dark, unsettling, and frightening." She is the author of four novels and more than 130 short stories, a six-time winner of the Bram Stoker Award, a world-class Halloween expert, and the president of the Horror Writers Association.

Introduction

MICHELE BRITTANY *and* NICHOLAS DIAK

The catalyst for this collection of essays began in 2016 when interest in an academic conference was broached by Horror Writers Association (HWA) leadership. As two academic members of the organization and having past experience presenting and chairing at the Southwest Popular/American Culture Association, we proposed a brand new, horror-centric academic conference to run in tandem with the newly created StokerCon. Thus, the first Ann Radcliffe Academic Conference was held with StokerCon 2017 at the Queen Mary in Long Beach, California. The conference, whose namesake pays homage to Radcliffe and her contributions to early horror academia, featured 14 presentations by HWA members and non-members covering horror from a variety of popular culture mediums: books, comics, video games, films, and television shows. Spurred by its success the first year, the conference returned in 2018 with StokerCon held in Providence, Rhode Island. The conference doubled in size! Given that many fine presentations from the first two conferences focused on horror literature, the idea of collecting essays that centered on the medium was born and hence pursued.

HWA President Lisa Morton, who has long been a supporter of and writer of nonfiction provided a fascinating foreword that traces the history of horror studies commencing with 18th century horror writer Ann Radcliffe, right through to the contemporary writers who are shaping the genre for tomorrow. The afterword is from librarian Becky Spratford, who reminds all of us who identify with the genre that we have a role to play in bringing about and promoting horror as a legitimate course of study. In between these two exceptional pieces are four sections to guide the reader through 14 insightful essays.

Section One, "Horror Writers Who Forged New Ground," focuses on three writers who have engaged with horror in new ways. Elizabeth Bobbitt's "'The mist of death is on me': Ann Radcliffe's Unexplained Supernatural in

9

Gaston de Blondeville" explores the creative motivations behind horror studies' pioneer Ann Radcliffe as she defines horror as a new and modern genre. In the next essay, Erica McCrystal argues how Robert Louis Stephenson's split personality character has become a multifaceted popular culture media term that has transcended its original good/evil dichotomy in "Jekyll and Hyde Everywhere: Inconsistency and Disparity in the Real World." To finish up this section, J. Rocky Colavito's "ScatterGories: Class Upheaval, Social Chaos and the Horrors of Category Crisis in *World War Z*" exposes a problematic humanity and class issues in Max Brooks' apocalyptic novel, *World War Z: An Oral History of the Zombie War.*

In Section Two, "Spotlighting Horror Writers," John C. Tibbetts introduces readers to British author Margaret Gabrielle Vere Long, better known as Marjorie Bowen, in his essay, "Marjorie Bowen and the Third Fury." Bowen used many pseudonyms while churning out over 150 volumes that included supernatural horror stories. Danny Rhodes introduces and argues that British writer L.T.C. Rolt modernized the ghost story genre in "'When the cage came up there was something crouched a-top of it': The Haunted Tale of L.T.C. Rolt." Hopping across the Atlantic to America, Gavin F. Hurley analyzes the use of negative space and power of the English language with his essay, "Richard Laymon's Rhetorical Style: Minimalism, Suspense and Negative Space" while in "Four Quadrants of Success: The Metalinguistics of Author Protagonists in the Fiction of Stephen King," James Arthur Anderson evaluates King's writer characters and how their critical or commercial acclaim translate to what King himself sees as success.

Section Three, "Exploring Literary Theory in Horror," opens with Bridget E. Keown's "'The symptoms of possession': Gender, Power and Trauma in Late 20th Century Horror Novels" which focuses on teenage girls who are disenfranchised by masculine hegemony in possession genre horror novels such as William Peter Blatty's *The Exorcist* and Paul Tremblay's *A Head Full of Ghosts.* Emily Anctil argues the importance of children's horror picture books, a medium that is mostly neglected in children's literature studies, in her essay "'Not a Bedtime Story': Investigating Textual Interactions Between the Horror Genre and Children's Picture Books." Naomi Simone Borwein breaks new ground with "Synchronic Horror and the Dreaming: A Theory of Aboriginal Australian Horror and Monstrosity" as she explores Australian-indigenous monster mythology. Johnny Murray closes out this section by evaluating and clarifying concepts in "weird" genre in "'Gelatinous green immensity': Weird Fiction and the Grotesque Sublime."

Essays in the last section, "Disease, Viruses and Death in Horror," tackle pandemics in the horror genre. In "*Night of the Living Dead, or Endgame*: Jan Knott, Samuel Beckett and Zombies" Kevin J. Wetmore, Jr., explores the bleak nihilism through a close reading of both George A. Romero's classic 1968 film through Samuel Beckett's *Endgame* and Jan Kott's reading of *King Lear*. Frazer Lee provides an in-depth retrospective of the franchise that has been fueled by its literary and filmic outputs in his essay, "Koji Suzuki's *Ring*: A World Literary Perspective." Finally, Rahel Sixta Schmitz's "Mapping Digital Dis-Ease: Representations of Movement and Technology in Jim Sonzero's *Pulse* and Stephen King's *Cell*" discusses how the representation of movement, disease, and technology in contemporary horror fiction negotiates a growing unease, or dis-ease, regarding the potentially hazardous effects of digital technologies on human life.

Currently, the horror genre is experiencing a resurgence, both critically and commercially, most visible with television shows such as *Stranger Things* (2016–present) and *The Walking Dead* (2010–present) and films such as *It* (2017, Andy Muschietti), *Bird Box* (2018, Susanne Bier), *Hereditary* (2018, Ari Aster) and *Annihilation* (2018, Alex Garland). Horror literature is becoming rejuvenated as readers rediscover both old masters such as H.P. Lovecraft and Edgar Allan Poe, and contemporary writers such as Josh Malerman, Victor LaValle, Jeff VanderMeer and Caitlín R. Kiernan. With such an upswing in interest, the need for academic assessment on such texts becomes even more essential. It is the hope that the essays in this collection continue the dialogue illustrated in Morton's foreword that examines, contextualizes, redefines, and most importantly, underscores the significance of the horror genre.

Horror Writers
Who Forged New Ground

"The mist of death is on me"

Ann Radcliffe's Unexplained Supernatural
in Gaston de Blondeville

Elizabeth Bobbitt

Ann Radcliffe's last novel, *Gaston de Blondeville or, The Court of Henry III Keeping Festival in Ardenne* represents a significant shift in Radcliffe's creative trajectory which is only beginning to be fully explored by Radcliffean scholars today.[1] Published in 1826, *Gaston de Blondeville* is the first text in William Radcliffe's four-volume collection of his wife's posthumously-published works. Set approximately ten years before the Second Barons' War (1264–67), Radcliffe's novel tells the tale of a duplicitous knight, Gaston de Blondeville, who is a favorite of Henry III (1207–72). During the royal court's removal to Kenilworth Castle for Blondeville's lavish wedding to Barbara of Huntingdon, Hugh Woodreeve, a merchant, comes forward to accuse Blondeville of murdering his kinsmen, Reginald de Foleville. Upon making this accusation, Woodreeve is unjustly imprisoned by Henry III. The novel is followed in the collection by two lengthy verse narratives: *St. Alban's Abbey; A Metrical Tale*, which outlines the events of the First Battle of St. Alban's in 1455, a conflict which sparked the Wars of the Roses (1455–85), and *Salisbury Plains: Stonehenge*, in which Radcliffe imagines a mystical origin story for the construction of Stonehenge.[2]

In looking more closely at Radcliffe's depiction of her first "unexplained" ghost, this essay will suggest specific ways in which scholars might begin to understand Radcliffe as a "Romantic Antiquary," fascinated by the material relics of Britain's deep past, local history, practices of touristic viewing, and the varied (and often contested) cultural inheritances which such inquiry often exposed. Placing Radcliffe's later work beyond the familiar and well-charted territory of the Female Gothic, and within the context of the surge

15

of antiquarian interest which occurred within the second half of the 18th and early 19th centuries will allow scholars to examine the ways in which Radcliffe's last novel gestures towards a renewed excavation of the Gothic. In doing so, readers can begin to understand Radcliffe as an author deeply invested in re-situating the Gothic within its original context. That is, as a genre deeply concerned with Britain's ancient, or medieval past, and the disturbing—often horrific—ramifications when that past resurfaces or returns. It is here, then, that the motivations behind Radcliffe's first truly supernatural ghost in *Gaston de Blondeville* can begin to be traced and further understood. After contextualizing Radcliffe's last novel as a work which is concerned to highlight the Gothic's earlier historical roots, the remainder of this essay will focus on a closer examination of the armored specter of Reginald de Foleville, and his climactic confrontation with Henry III at the conclusion of *Gaston de Blondeville*.

As is evident from a cursory examination of the titles and subjects of the main works in this collection, Radcliffe's later imagination became increasingly "overwhelmed by an antiquarian impulse."[3] This impulse sets her later works apart from her 1790s romances, which by the publication of *The Italian* in 1797, had become synonymous with their Mediterranean settings, persecuted heroines, and tyrannical villains. Not only are Radcliffe's post–1797 texts deeply self-conscious examinations of Britain's past, but they are also intimately locked to historical place. Significantly, Radcliffe's last novel rehearses a creative return from the balmy climes of Southern Europe to Britain, a setting she had not used since her first novel set in the Highlands of Scotland, *The Castles of Athlin and Dunbayne* (1789). *Gaston de Blondeville* also privileges a diverse range of literary and historical sources, including contemporary works of popular history such as David Hume's *History of England* (1754–61), the studies of local antiquaries such as William Dugdale's *The Antiquities of Warwickshire* (1656), contemporary literary works such as Sophia Lee's *The Recess* (1783), and the Gothic ruins emblematic of the nation's past such as Kenilworth Castle in Warwickshire. By featuring such a varied range of historical, literary, and physical sources in *Gaston de Blondeville*, Radcliffe explores contemporary questions regarding the validity of different types of historical inquiry, and ensuing questions regarding the problematic establishment of authorial identity, textual transmission, historical authenticity, and the potential irrecoverability of the national past. *Gaston de Blondeville* is presented to the reader as an authentic 13th-century manuscript entitled the "Trew Chronique" composed first by Grimbald, a Norman monk at the Priory of St. Mary at Kenilworth in 1256, and then by an unnamed monk during the reign of Richard II. Radcliffe's text, then, is a determined pastiche of medieval syntax and orthography, divided into a chronicle-like structure which details the events of the eight days in which Henry III's court resides at Kenilworth.[4] Through this pastiche, Radcliffe ironically foregrounds the potentially apocryphal nature of the Trew Chronique.

In the present-day introductory frame narrative to *Gaston de Blondeville*, Radcliffe introduces a fictional antiquary named Mr. Willoughton, who discovers the Trew Chronique during his tour of Kenilworth's ruins, and who is subsequently inspired to "translate" the Norman text into "modern" English. At the conclusion to Willoughton's translation of the text, however, Radcliffe suggests that "long before [Willoughton] had finished [translating the manuscript], he had some doubts as to its origin" and that "one better versed in antiquities would have found out, that several of the ceremonies of the court here exhibited, were more certainly those of the fourth Edward than the third Henry...."[5] It is this playful and rhetorically-complex retrospect on the constructive processes of historical narrative which distinguishes Radcliffe's "antiquarian impulse" in her later works, not only serving to separate them from her wildly successful 1790s romances, but also underpinning the creative impetus behind her first truly supernatural ghost in *Gaston de Blondeville*, the most significant innovation which her post–1797 works effect on her previous romances.

Until the publication of *Gaston de Blondeville*, Radcliffe's 1790s romances had become typified by her controversial use of the explained supernatural, in which apparently supernatural occurrences are eventually explained away by rational causes. In *The Mysteries of Udolpho* (1794), for instance, the mysterious noises from the northern apartments of Chateau le Blanc are revealed to be the distant sounds heard from a hidden passage connecting the chateau to a cave occupied by banditti.[6] Contemporary critics argued that upon the completion of her 1790s romances, her readers are left to feel hoodwinked, or disappointed, as her narratives conclude with explanations which appear even more improbable than the supernatural ones her works originally put forward. Radcliffe's Gothic romances were often associated with a ritualization of aroused, although never satisfied suggestion. She titillates her readers, allowing them to dabble in a dangerous world of sexual transgression and excess, while doing her duty as a "proper" female novelist by firmly re-situating readers within a world of domesticity, decorum and propriety by the end of the novel.[7] In his biographical preface to Radcliffe's works for *Ballantyne's Novelists Library* (1824), Sir Walter Scott comments on the detrimental effects of this disappointment:

> Her heroines often sustain the agony of fear, and her readers that of suspense, from incidents which, when explained, appear of an ordinary and trivial nature. In this we do not greatly applaud her art. A stealthy step behind the arras may ... have no small influence upon the imagination; but if the conscious listener discovers it to be only the noise made by the cat, the solemnity of feeling is gone, and the visionary is at once angry with his senses for having been cheated....[8]

Coleridge, similarly notes the disappointing pattern of Radcliffe's explained supernatural, arguing, "curiosity is raised oftener than it is gratified, or rather, it is raised so high, that no adequate gratification can be given it...."[9] Barbauld's sentiments resonate with Scott and Coleridge, who wrote in her prefatory memoir of Radcliffe for *The British Novelists* in 1810, that Radcliffe's proffered explanations for the supernatural in her 1790s romances "are not all, however, well accounted for," and that "the mind experiences a sort of disappointment and shame at having felt so much from appearances which had nothing in them...."[10] While Radcliffe's use of the explained supernatural was often criticized for its inefficacy as a rhetorical technique, it also provides evidence of Radcliffe's savvy handling of her delicate position as a female novelist of the late 18th and early 19th centuries. Her use of the explained supernatural allowed her readers to experience all the suspense of terror, without having to "degrade" their moral sense with a truly superstitious tale. As a result, Radcliffe managed to evade charges of moral and sexual corruption with which other female novelists of the day such as Charlotte Smith, Mary Hays, and Eliza Haywood were charged. For T.J. Mathias, for example, Radcliffe was set apart from such "unsex'd revolutionaries," being "bred among the paler shrines of Gothic superstition."[11]

Contemporary reviews of *Gaston de Blondeville* register the perplexing creative shift which the novel has come to represent in critical evaluations of Radcliffe's canon. In registering this shift, contemporary critics focus specifically on her first overt representation of the unexplained supernatural. *The London Literary Gazette*, for instance, recognizes how, "in this romance, Mrs. Radcliffe has abandoned the principle to which she confined herself in her former works, and has taken advantage of ghostly aid...."[12] While *The London Literary Gazette* appears to have generally approved of Radcliffe's radical reversal in her handling of the supernatural, venturing to "anticipate that this unearthly being will be pronounced one of the most solemn creatures of the language," other critical reviews disapproved of it.[13] The *Monthly Review* argues, for example, that "tales of this description may startle in the nursery, and amuse the vulgar, but they cannot attract the attention of those whose judgement is of any value in matters of literature."[14] Contemporary critical opinions concerning Radcliffe's last novel, then, are decidedly contradictory and unstable. While they register a sense of the startling difference between *Gaston de Blondeville* and Radcliffe's earlier 1790s romances, they do not adequately define the exact nature or motivation behind this difference. This is a critical commonplace which has survived today, and this essay attempts to redress this imbalance in Radcliffean scholarship.

Critics today have tended to consign *Gaston de Blondeville* and Radcliffe's other post–1797 works to what they see as her relatively unproductive "later life," despite the fact that Radcliffe was only thirty-eight when she began her composition of *Gaston de Blondeville*. E.J. Clery for instance, only cursorily alludes to the existence of *Gaston de Blondeville* and *St. Alban's Abbey* in her study entitled *Women's Gothic* (1995), framing their composition as a rather uninspiring bookend to Radcliffe's 1790s Gothic romances, having "none of the magic of her famous works."[15] Other critics, such as Sue Chaplin, have obliquely commented on the inherent "strangeness" of the novel, and the ensuing difficulty in attempting to situate it comfortably within Radcliffe's accepted oeuvre, characterizing the novel as a "strangely supplemental work" in relation to Radcliffe's 1790s romances.[16] Here are some of the most intriguing, yet unanswered questions of Radcliffe's life and publishing career. Why did she suddenly retire from the literary scene at the height of her popularity in 1797 with the publication of *The Italian*? Why did she choose to stop composing her successful Gothic romances in favor of historical narratives, which take as their subjects rather obscure, and little-known episodes from Britain's past? Thomas Noon Talfourd, Radcliffe's "official" biographer, commissioned by Radcliffe's husband after her death to write a preface to *Gaston de Blondeville*, characterizes Radcliffe as, "a figure of delicate apprehensiveness," who preferred to live "in unbroken retirement," never even intending to publish her last novel, which was solely meant for the amusement of herself and her husband.[17] This essay suggests that Talfourd's biography, carefully proof-read and edited by William Radcliffe, does not provide readers with the entire story. Instead, an examination of Radcliffe's last novel (and her other post–1797 works) can help to shed light on the true motivations behind this sudden and unexplained decision in Radcliffe's publishing career. For example, what motivations can be assigned to Radcliffe's later work, in order to explain her radical shift in creative trajectory from an author of Gothic romance, to a writer of proto-historical metafiction, complete with her own truly supernatural specter? And how is this sudden shift in creative trajectory reflected in her radically different portrayal of horror and haunting in her last novel?

A closer examination of Radcliffe's post–1797 work serves to complicate and interrupt traditionally held critical notions of Radcliffe's career as an author and resulting body of work. She is an author whose writerly persona has been entirely constructed from her five most popular Gothic romances, serving to locate her work within the realm of the strictly Female Gothic put forward by critics such as Diane Long Hoevler and Carol Davison, while her post–1797 texts have been relatively ignored by critics today. Radcliffe's later imagination indicates a growing fascination with antiquarian works, research, and enquiry—a field which was understood by Radcliffe's contemporaries to be firmly situated within the male sphere.

Gaston de Blondeville should be understood as a dynamic repositioning of Radcliffe's authorial intentions. It marks her purposeful return to earlier iterations of the Gothic from the mid–18th century such as Thomas Leland's

Longsword, Earl of Salisbury (1762), Clara Reeve's *The Old English Baron* (1777), Anne Fuller's *Alan Fitz-Osborne* (1787), and the anonymously published *Edwy, Son of Ethelred the Second, An Historical Tale* (1791). Radcliffe re-privileges the historical epochs and medieval settings of earlier Gothic novels in *Gaston de Blondeville* which, as Anne Stevens charts, had generically developed alongside the historical novel, in which Gothic simply denoted the medieval.[18] While Radcliffean scholars can only speculate at the motivation behind this shift in Radcliffe's re-excavation of the Gothic genre's literary origins, her decision to set her novel during the rather obscure reign of Henry III should be seen as a statement of intent for her later work, clearly setting her apart from contemporary female Gothic writers such as Mary Wollstonecraft, whose work, at the beginning of the 19th century, was becoming heavily politicized. Wollstonecraft's *Maria: or, The Wrongs of Woman* (1798), for instance, openly criticizes late 18th century patriarchal marital laws, allowing George Venables, Maria's husband in the novel, to commit his wife to an insane asylum without appeal. *Gaston de Blondeville*, on the other hand, eschews the most central figure in her Gothic romances, the persecuted heroine, and decentralizes the familiar plight of the female character, setting a clear boundary between *Gaston de Blondeville* and other contemporary writers of the Female Gothic.

Radcliffe's likely desire to distance herself from these female authors, and her re-privileging of the historical themes, settings, and narratives of earlier "Historical Gothic" romances, should not simply be characterized as Radcliffe's attempt to shy away from politically engaging with her readers. While Radcliffe's side-stepping of directly political themes may at first glance appear to indicate a somewhat conservative ideological stance, it is important to recognize the ways in which Radcliffe was adept at engaging with political themes in a way which registered their complexity without reducing them to a radical or conservative stance. Thus, in setting *Gaston de Blondeville* ten years before the Second Barons' War, led by Simon de Montfort, Henry III's brother-in-law, Radcliffe obliquely gestures towards the conflict without providing readers with a straightforward reading of its historical significance to a broader history of Britain's feudal past and its political implications for early 19th-century Britain. Similarly, allegorical attempts to read Henry III's poor governance in the novel are similarly stymied by Radcliffe's text. Drawing on Anne Fuller's representation of Edward I (Henry III's son) in *Alan Fitz-Osborne*, set during the Second Barons' War, Radcliffe instead chooses to focus on depicting the political complexity of civil conflict, rather than presenting her readers a straightforward "good" or "bad" side in the rebellion. While her novel ultimately condemns the Second Barons' War as the result of de Montfort's crucial lack of loyalty to the institution of the crown, Radcliffe allows the radical notions of the barons to remain active as a destabilizing force within the text. While it celebrates Edward I as "the restorer of general order" and the "queller of rebellion," readers are repeatedly provided with examples of Henry III's weak will and corrupt reign.[19] He is, for example, easily manipulated by the corrupt Prior of St. Mary. Thus, according to Radcliffe, "it was above all, the weakness of the King which subjected him to the sway of designing men, [causing him] to be drawn aside from the administration of justice...."[20] Here, as Deborah Russell argues, "Radcliffe's return to an earlier conception of the Gothic genre paradoxically provoked a sense of experimentation; the interest of *Gaston de Blondeville* lies not in its formulation of a political statement, but in the productive working through of different, even conflicted, attitudes to the nation's Gothic heritage...."[21]

Radcliffe's last novel, then, can be understood as a backward-looking text, both in terms of the contemporary literary market in which it appeared, and also in terms of its literary inspirations and antecedents. It is a text which draws attention to the various methods of textual mediation which earlier authors of the Gothic and historical romance employed in their attempts to authentically depict the nation's past. Radcliffe purposefully utilizes familiar rhetorical structures and tropes which explicitly recall earlier proto-Gothic texts, such as the generic, stock opening of the historical romance, which works to establish a specific historical context. The opening to *Gaston de Blondeville* strikingly recalls Thomas Leland's opening to *Longsword, Earl of Salisbury* (1762) not only in its use of the same historical epoch, the reign of Henry III, but also in its word-for-word re-formulation of Leland's introduction, asserting, "It was at the feast of St. Michel, that King Henry, the third of his name ... came to keep court at Kenilworth."[22] Radcliffe's depiction of her first supernatural ghost is similarly influenced by earlier ghostly representations in mid–18th century novels of the Historical Gothic.

Radcliffe's text is haunted by the ghostly presence of Reginald de Foleville, the murdered kinsmen of Hugh Woodreeve, who, dressed in a full suit of armor, periodically appears to the court at Kenilworth during the celebration of Gaston de Blondeville's wedding, "pointing with his sword to the Baron de Blondeville."[23] Her depiction echoes the use of supernatural armor imagery in Horace Walpole's *The Castle of Otranto* (1764), which depicts the bizarre and sudden appearance of a giant helmet which falls from the sky and kills Manfred's sickly son, Conrad, on his wedding day.[24] Similarly, a ghostly suit of armor which had belonged to Lord Lovel haunts the abandoned apartments of Lovel Castle in Reeve's *The Old English Baron*. It appears to two men of the castle, "in complete armour ... with one hand extended, pointing to the outward door,"[25] just as Radcliffe's apparition appears to the Baron de Blondeville. Radcliffe blatantly lifts Walpole's use of blood imagery as a symbol of incontrovertible guilt when Blondeville's robe becomes inexplicably "covered ... with crimson," after three drops of blood which had previously fallen on the Barons' mantle as he walked by the ghost of Foleville spread across his garment.[26] This is taken directly from Walpole's text, in which "three drops of blood fall from the nose of Alfonso's statue," revealing Manfred's guilt.[27] The appearance of the supernatural within these texts, embodied by ghostly suits of armor, or unexplainable drops of blood, is figured as evidence of divine retribution, and acts as the catalyst which unveils the secret machinations of characters within each novel who have perverted the course of justice. As George Dekker argues, "crude though they may appear, [these] materializations of divine justice" work to "[authenticate] the story as the product of a bygone age of Gothic superstition."[28]

Radcliffe's decision to depict her first truly supernatural spirit is sanctioned by the morality of Reginald de Foleville's cause, and also by the literary precedent of similar specters depicted in earlier works of the Historical Gothic, which "used strikingly similar ... plots which dealt with the exorcism of corruption and the restoration of property to legitimate heirs."[29] Radcliffe's theme of supernatural retribution is carried to its conclusion at the end of the novel, when Gaston de Blondeville falls from his horse as a "dead weight" at a tournament after being confronted by the armored appearance of Reginald de Foleville.[30] Her treatment of the miscarriage of justice plot from earlier Historical Gothic novels is also likely influenced by Fuller's *Alan Fitz-Osborne*. Alan's maternal grandfather in the novel is Hubert de Burgh, Henry III's justiciar (a Norman administrator of justice) who became embroiled in a bitter political dispute with Henry III over his lack of success in subduing the attacks of Llewellyn of Wales. This is a dispute which is implicitly referred to by Radcliffe in connection to Henry III's loss of a "precious ring" which made its wearer impervious to the dangers of battle.[31] Radcliffe follows Fuller in highlighting this episode as a particular example of the poor judgement of Henry III. As the offspring of Hubert's familial line, Fuller's hero, Alan, comes to embody the "sword of justice" in a multi-generational blood feud between the descendants of the de Burghs and Henry III's followers; Radcliffe appears to have borrowed this phrase from Fuller's novel in which he is designated as the divine "avenger" of his blood-line.[32]

In looking more closely at Radcliffe's depiction of her first use of the unexplained supernatural, one begins to see Radcliffe as a "Romantic Antiquary." Susan Manning argues that "antiquarian activity reaches right into the quiddity of Romantic writing," through the ways in which the antiquary and his pursuits came to represent differing notions concerning the proper collection of historical artifacts, and how such objects might be assimilated into coherent historical narratives of British nationhood.[33] Often satirized as indiscriminate material collection, antiquarian study was seen to run the risk of being unorganized or "unarticulated into a cohesive trajectory of national identity."[34] *Gaston de Blondeville* playfully embodies the intellectual approach of the antiquary in order to exploit the essential ideological malleability of antiquarian study, allowing her to excavate the differing strands of Britain's cultural heritage without presenting straightforward allegorical readings of the nation's (dis)unity. In presenting *Gaston de Blondeville* to her readers as an authentic "small quarto [manuscript], printed in black letter and bound in real boards, which had been guarded in the corner with brass" discovered alongside two ancient romances entitled "A Trew Historie of Two Mynstrells" and a "Boke of Sprites," Radcliffe plays on the "considerable slippage" inherent in the connotations of ancient romance.[35] This "slippage" wavers "between a version of romance as fiction … and a historicist version, locating it at various moments in a stadialist sequence which linked the barbarous past to modernity."[36]

The minutely material description of the Trew Chronique, situates Radcliffe's text as a physical relic of the nation's feudal past, serving as a historical record of the manners and customs of the thirteenth century. However, by constructing this elaborate framework which conflates the textual and the material remains of the past, Radcliffe deftly shields herself from being charged with any uses of the supernatural which are improper for a proper lady-author. For, it is not Radcliffe, but Grimbald who relates the tale of the ghostly Reginald de Foleville, stalking through Henry III's court in demand of divine retribution. Radcliffe introduces another layer of authorial transmission into the structuring of her text through her use of Willoughton as another "mouthpiece" such as Grimbald. An examination of the notes which Radcliffe took on her visit to Kenilworth with her husband in 1802, published in Talfourd's prefatory biography, demonstrates that portions of the introductory section in the novel are directly paraphrased from her own observations. Willoughton's particular fascination with Kenilworth's great hall, with its "arched doorway, so appropriately and elegantly sculptured with vine leaves,"[37] is in fact an echo of Radcliffe's personal observations. She comments that the room "forming the third side of the court, is the most picturesque remainder of the castle … where three beautiful pointed window-frames are there still," and the "'arch of a Gothic door' is elegantly twined with vine leaves."[38] Here, Radcliffe deftly lays claim to an area of intellectual pursuit traditionally associated with men, couching this appropriation in terms of what appears to be a familiar and socially accepted exploration of proper male historical feeling. It is through Radcliffe's assumption of Willoughton's leisured male persona that Radcliffe is able to legitimate her depiction of Reginald de Foleville on which the plot of *Gaston de Blondeville* turns. In doing so, Radcliffe displaces associations of superstition onto the figure of the male antiquary and his practice, away from the female novel reader or writer, and related charges of sexual impropriety.

Radcliffe's ghost makes one of his first appearances at the wedding ceremony of Gaston de Blondeville and Barbara of Huntingdon, recorded on the third day of the Trew Chronique. One of the most significant aspects of this early visitation of the ghost is the setting in which it occurs. Drawing on William Dugdale's *Antiquities of Warwickshire*, Radcliffe relates how:

> King Henry, during his visits to Kenilworth, had newly repaired and adorned the chapel of the castle, and there the marriage was to be solemnized. By his command, the walls had been painted with the story of King Edward the Confessor, giving the ring off his finger to a poor stranger…. The lights were all a-blaze, so that they overcame the perpetual tomb lights of Geoffrey de Clinton, the founder of the castle, interred in the chapel here.[39]

During the ceremony, Blondeville catches sight of the ghostly knight standing by the tomb of Geoffrey de Clinton and falls into a terrified stupor, while the "stranger," as the specter is supposed to be by Blondeville, stands by in "gloomy sternness."[40] When the wedding guests turn to look in the direction of the tomb where the Baron's eyes are riveted in fear, all they can perceive is the "extended marble image of the dead one within. The stranger was no longer there."[41] Radcliffe's staging of this moment is telling and worth examining more closely. Rather than introducing the scene by focusing on a description of the more traditional aspects of the ceremony, such as the bride's wedding dress. Grimbald eschews such details, writing, "I say not now more of her appearance at this time."[42] Radcliffe chooses instead to introduce the scene by focusing on the history of the chapel's early foundations and renovations. By first drawing attention to the original founder of the chapel, and then proceeding to chart the restorations which Henry III made to the chapel, readers are given a carefully stadial sense of the historical and architectural progression of Kenilworth Castle and its surrounding compound. In doing so, Radcliffe evokes a conception of the nation's past which is essentially palimpsestic. Thus, in choosing the tomb of Geoffrey de Clinton as the site in which the ghost of Reginald de Foleville first appears, Radcliffe conjures a purposeful layering of Kenilworth's past and present epochs. Indeed, Radcliffe's complex understanding of the national past as a palimpsest mirrors the larger structure of *Gaston de Blondeville* itself, mediated as it is by different translators of the Trew Chronique from the 13th, 14th, and 19th centuries.

Radcliffe is also at pains to couch the ghost's appearance in a space which subtly emphasizes the various strands of cultural identity which can be identified in an early 19th century English (and more broadly British) national identity. Henry III, the son of King John, was a Plantagenet King, descended from William the Conqueror. His decision to paint a famous scene from the Saxon King, Edward the Confessor's life, demonstrates his awareness of the importance of presenting the Plantagenet dynasty as continually descended from the ancient kings of Britain, rather than as foreign, French invaders. Here, Henry III's decision to name his son Edward, can be seen as another strategic decision to evoke this same sense of continuity with England's Saxon past. Radcliffe's foregrounding of these issues resonates with the contemporary radical tradition of the "Norman yoke," an idea which Chiu makes much of her introduction to *Gaston de Blondeville* in order to read Radcliffe's last novel as evidence of her radical political stance in the wake of the Treaty of Amiens in 1802. The theory of the Norman yoke associates the foundation of English liberty with early Anglo-Saxon parliamentary assemblies and common law, destroyed by the Norman Conquest and their imposition of feudalism.[43] While Radcliffe anticipates Scott's *Ivanhoe* (1820), by inviting such readings in key moments in the text, such as in her description of the Provençal Queen Eleanor's entrance into the castle, when the on-looking crowd shouts "Away with foreigners," her invocation of the Norman Yoke theory is inherently complicated.[44] The ghost of Reginald de Foleville, for example, who acts in the text as a mechanism of divine justice, appears by his name to be of Norman origin himself, thereby troubling the "Norman versus Saxon" formulation of British national identity which the Norman Yoke theory puts forward.

At the climax of the novel, after a succession of failed attempts to reveal Blondeville as the murderer that he is, the ghost pays a visit to Henry III's bedchamber in the dead of night. When the ghost appears before him, the King asks, "What art thou? Wherefore art thou come?"[45] The specter pleads for the innocent Woodreeve, answering, "give me rest … the mist of death is on me…. Release an innocent man."[46] Here, the ghost implicitly threatens the King's life, warning, "if [Woodreeve] perish for my sake, he shall not fall alone…."[47] Significantly, it is only after this threat that Henry III is finally convinced of Blondeville's guilt. Radcliffe's leaves her readers with a deeply troubled sense of England's medieval governance, despite looking towards the wiser rule of Edward I. Radcliffe's first use of the unexplained supernatural, functions as "as a narrative reflection of the haunting aesthetic power of the past" and as a "device for engaging with and commenting on earlier superstitious belief systems."[48] Thus, in relocating her last novel back to Britain, Radcliffe challenges her readers to acknowledge a most fundamental haunting: the violence and injustice of Britain's own medieval past.

NOTES

1. Some of the most recent critical examinations of *Gaston de Blondeville* can be found in *Ann Radcliffe, Romanticism and the Gothic*, edited by Dale Townshend and Angela Wright in 2014. See also Frances Chiu's annotated edition of *Gaston de Blondeville* for Valancourt Books (2006) and Fiona Price's *Reinventing Liberty: Nation Commerce and the Historical Novel from Walpole to Scott* (2017).

2. This collection also contains twenty-six miscellaneous poems, including a three-part fairy poem entitled *Edwy*, set on the grounds of Windsor Castle.

3. Rictor Norton, *The Mistress of Udolpho: The Life of Ann Radcliffe* (Leicester, UK: Leicester University Press, 1999), 119.

4. A good example of Radcliffe's self-conscious medieval pastiche, in which she borrows synthetic medieval vocabulary from Thomas Chatterton's falsely attributed *Rowley Poems* (1777), comes during the description of the court's procession to Kenilworth, in which, "amongst the damsels attending the Queen, none were so fair as the Lady Isabel ... and the lady Barbara [of Huntingdon] ... Ychon of them were beautiful beyond doubt..." Ann Radcliffe, *Gaston de Blondeville*, ed. by Frances Chiu (Chicago: Valancourt Books, 2006), 30.

5. Radcliffe, *Gaston de Blondeville*, 205. All citations from *Gaston de Blondeville* in this essay are taken from Frances Chiu's edition of Radcliffe's novel: Ann Radcliffe, *Gaston de Blondeville*, ed. Frances Chiu (Chicago: Valancourt Books, 2006).

6. Ann Radcliffe, *The Mysteries of Udolpho* (Mineola, NY: Dover Publications, 2004), 568–9.

7. Here I adopt Ina Ferris's distinction between the "proper" and "ordinary" female novel of the period. Ferris argues that contemporary reviews "tended to cohere in beginning their organization of novelistic discourse by dividing contemporary fictional practice into two kinds of novel under two different female signs: that of female reading, which is identified as the origin of the 'ordinary novel'; and that of feminine writing, which is credited with generating the superior, morally edifying mode of the 'proper novel.'" Ina Ferris, *The Achievement of Literary Authority: Gender, History and the Waverley Novels* (Ithaca, NY: Cornell University Press, 1991), 35.

8. Sir Walter Scott, "Memoir of Mrs. Radcliffe," in *Ballantyne's Novelist's Library*, vol. 10 (Edinburgh, 1824), xxvi. Scott singles out Ludovico's discovery of banditti as an example of Radcliffe's good use of the explained supernatural.

9. Samuel Taylor Coleridge, *The Critical Review* (1794), 361–72.

10. Anna Laetitia Barbauld, *The British Novelists; with an Essay, and Prefaces, Biographical and Critical by Mrs. Barbauld*, vol. 43 (London: 1810), i–viii.

11. T.J. Mathias, *Pursuits of Literature: a Satirical Poem in Four Dialogues* (London: 1798), 58.

12. *The London Literary Gazette* (London: 1826), 321–3.

13. *Ibid.*, 321–3.

14. *Monthly Review* (London: 1826), 280–93.

15. E.J. Clery, *Women's Gothic* (Tavistock, UK: Northcote House Publishers, 2004), 67.

16. Sue Chaplin, *The Gothic and the Rule of Law 174–1820* (New York: Palgrave Macmillan, 2007), 120.

17. T.N. Talfourd, "Memoir of the Life and Writings of Mrs. Radcliffe," in *Gaston de Blondeville, of the Court of Henry III Keeping Festival in Arden, a Romance; St. Alban's Abbey: a Metrical Tale, with Some Poetical Pieces by Ann Radcliffe, to Which Is Prefixed a Memoir of the Author with Extracts from Her Journals* (London: 1826), 90.

18. Anne Stevens, *British Historical Fiction Before Scott* (New York: Palgrave Macmillan, 2010), 49.

19. Radcliffe, *Gaston de Blondeville*, 169.

20. *Ibid.*

21. Deborah Russell, "Domestic Gothic: Narrating the Nation in Eighteenth Century Women's Gothic Fiction" (Dissertation, University of York, 2011), 126.

22. Radcliffe, *Gaston de Blondeville*, 28.

23. *Ibid.*, 94.

24. Horace Walpole, *The Castle of Otranto, a Gothic Story* (London: 1791), 5.

25. Clara Reeve, *The Old English Baron: A Gothic Story* (London: 1789), 114.

26. Radcliffe, *Gaston de Blondeville*, 52–3.

27. Walpole, *The Castle of Otranto, a Gothic Story*, 193.

28. George Dekker, *The Fictions of Romantic Tourism: Radcliffe, Scott, and Mary Shelley* (Stanford, CA: Stanford University Press), 54.

29. James Watt, *Contesting the Gothic: Fiction, Genre, and Cultural Conflict 1764–1820* (Cambridge: Cambridge University Press, 1999), 64.

30. Radcliffe, *Gaston de Blondeville*, 185.

31. *Ibid.*, 129.

32. Anne Fuller, *Alan Fitz-Osborne* (London: 1791), 60.

33. Susan Manning, "Antiquarianism, Balladry, and the Rehabilitation of Romance," in *The Cambridge History of English Romantic Literature*, ed. James Chandler (Cambridge: Cambridge University Press, 2009), 45.

34. *Ibid.*

35. *Ibid.*, 68.

36. *Ibid.*

37. Radcliffe, *Gaston de Blondeville*, 7.

38. T.N. Talfourd, "Memoir of the Life and Writings of Mrs. Radcliffe," 37.

39. Radcliffe, *Gaston de Blondeville*, 70. Compare Radcliffe's description of the chapel at Kenilworth to Dugdale's description of the chapel: "In 26. H. 3. much cost in building, and repaires, was bestowed here;… in seeling the Chappell with Wainscote, and painting it, making seats for the King and Queen, handsomly adorn'd; repairing the Tower where the bells hung; making all the walls new on the South-side…" William Dugdale, *Antiquities of Warwickshire* (London: 1656), 161.

40. Radcliffe, *Gaston de Blondeville*, 72.

41. *Ibid.*, 73.

42. *Ibid.*, 70.

43. Christopher Hill, *Intellectual Origins of the English Revolution Revisited* (Oxford: Oxford University Press, 1997), 57.

44. Radcliffe, *Gaston de Blondeville*, 33.

45. *Ibid.*, 195.

46. *Ibid.*

47. *Ibid.*

48. Deborah Russell, "Domestic Gothic: Narrating the Nation in Eighteenth Century Women's Gothic Fiction," 101.

BIBLIOGRAPHY

Ann Radcliffe, Romanticism and the Gothic. ed. by Dale Townshend and Angela Wright, Cambridge: Cambridge University Press, 2014.

Barbauld, Anna Laetitia. "Mrs. Radcliffe." *The British Novelists; with an Essay, and Prefaces, Biographical and Critical by Mrs. Barbauld*, vol. 43, London: 1810.

Chaplin, Sue. *The Gothic and the Rule of Law, 1764–1820.* New York: Palgrave Macmillan, 2007.

Chiu, Frances. Introduction to *Gaston De Blondeville Or, the Court of Henry III Keeping Festival in Ardenne* by Ann Radcliffe, vii–xxxix. Chicago: Valancourt Books, 2006.

Clery, E.J. *Women's Gothic.* Tavistock, UK: Northcote House Publishers, 2000.

Coleridge, Samuel Taylor. "The Mysteries of Udolpho." *The Critical Review.* August 1794. 361–72.

Dekker, George. *Fictions of Romantic Tourism: Radcliffe, Scott, and Mary Shelley.* Stanford, CA: Stanford University Press, 2005.

Dugdale, William. *The Antiquities of Warwickshire Illustrated; from Records Ledger-Books, Manuscripts, Charters, Evidences, Tombs and Arms.* London: 1730. 2 vols.

Ferris, Ina. *The Achievement of Literary Authority: Gender, History and the Waverley Novels.* Ithaca, NY: Cornell University Press, 1991.

Fuller, Anne. *Alan Fitz-Osborne, an Historical Tale.* London: 1787.

"Gaston De Blondeville." *London Literary Gazette*, 488, London: 27 May 1826, 321–323.

"Gaston De Blondeville." *Monthly Review*, London: 1826, 280–93.

Hill, Christopher. *Intellectual Origins of the English Revolution Revisited.* Oxford: Oxford University Press, 1997.

Manning, Susan. "Antiquarianism, Balladry, and the Rehabilitation of Romance" in *The Cambridge History of English Romantic Literature*, edited by James Chandler, 45–70. Cambridge: Cambridge University Press, 2009.

Mathias, T.J. *Pursuits of Literature: A Satirical Poem in Four Dialogues*, London: 1798.

Norton, Rictor. *The Mistress of Udolpho: The Life of Ann Radcliffe.* Leicester: Leicester University Press, 1999.

Radcliffe, Ann. *Gaston De Blondeville*. Chicago: Valancourt Books, 2006.

Reeve, Clara. *The Old English Baron: A Gothic Story*. London, 1789.

Russell, Deborah. "Domestic Gothic: Narrating the Nation in Eighteenth Century Women's Gothic Fiction." Dissertation, University of York, 2011.

Scott, Walter. "Memoir of Mrs. Radcliffe" in *Ballantyne's Novelist's Library*, vol. 10, Edinburgh: 1824.

Stevens, Anne. *British Historical Fiction Before Scott*. New York: Palgrave Macmillan, 2010.

Talfourd, Thomas Noon. "Memoir of the Life and Writings of Mrs. Radcliffe" in *Gaston De Blondeville, of the Court of Henry III Keeping Festival in Arden, a Romance; St. Alban's Abbey: A Metrical Tale, with Some Poetical Pieces by Ann Radcliffe, to Which Is Prefixed a Memoir of the Author with Extracts from Her Journals*. London: 1826.

Walpole, Horace. *The Castle of Otranto: A Gothic Story*. London: 1791.

Watt, James. *Contesting the Gothic: Fiction, Genre, and Cultural Conflict 1764–1820*. Cambridge: Cambridge University Press, 1999.

Jekyll and Hyde Everywhere

Inconsistency and Disparity in the Real World

ERICA MCCRYSTAL

Robert Louis Stevenson's iconic double character, Dr. Jekyll and Mr. Hyde, has evolved from a Victorian villain to become a timeless signifier of disparity in the real world. *The Strange Case of Dr. Jekyll and Mr. Hyde* (1886) allowed Victorian readers to think about the dangers of science, psychological instability, and the potential for degeneration. In the novella, the character represents good in contrast to evil, but over time, Jekyll and Hyde has developed connotations beyond these polarized oppositions. The phrase "Jekyll and Hyde" has even become adopted into regular lexicon. It can be a descriptor of any person, situation, or concept. While "Jekyll and Hyde" is a recognizable phrase, the understanding of Jekyll and Hyde as both a character and a concept has become increasingly difficult to encapsulate. This essay will analyze the various manifestations of Jekyll and Hyde in adaptations and news media, which continue to illustrate the ways in which the character has a deeply rooted and evolving reciprocal relationship with the real world.

In his classic novella, Stevenson created a Gothic villain that visibly illuminates polarized oppositions through a transformation that is the result of scientific manipulation, psychological instability, and the supernatural. But the character was actually inspired by the activities of a real man. In the 18th century, William Brodie was a master cabinet maker and skilled locksmith in Edinburgh, Scotland. He was named Deacon of the Incorporation of Wrights (woodworking guild) and gained a seat on the town council.[1] Brodie was a well-respected socialite and seemed to be a trustworthy individual. Outwardly, he maintained the appearance of an honorable, upright citizen, but inwardly, Brodie had criminal intentions. He made wax impressions of wealthy clients' keys in order to make copies for himself. At night, he would sneak into their houses to rob them. He offered his sympathies to friends

29

who he robbed and even sat on city council meetings and helped make plans to catch the crook.[2] Brodie was also a gambler, betting on cock-fighting and trick dice, and he had two mistresses and five kids with them.[3] In 1786, Brodie planned an armed robbery of Edinburgh's Excise Office, which failed, and an accomplice betrayed him to the authorities. Brodie fled the country but was caught and executed by public hanging in 1788.[4] Brodie was not an obvious suspect for criminality because he had gained social respectability. His double life showed the ways that a man's character and intentions can be inconsistent and deceptive, which serves as a terrifying verification that man cannot truly be known.

Brodie was a fitting inspiration for a Gothic villain, as doubling is a common trope found in 19th-century Gothic fiction. Stevenson was creatively inspired by Brodie's double nature, and he also had a physical connection to this duplicitous figure. Stevenson grew up in Edinburgh, and in his childhood bedroom, he had a mahogany veneer cabinet that was built by Brodie. A creation of Brodie's, situated in the domestic space, a space that is supposed to be safe, inspired Stevenson's own creativity. Stevenson co-wrote, with W.E. Henley, the play *Deacon Brodie, or the Double Life: A Melodrama*, which was produced in 1882. In the play, Brodie's character says, "On with the new coat and into the new life! Down with the Deacon and up with the robber!"[5] Brodie's language imagines the ways in which an upright citizen transforms into a deceitful criminal. Brodie chooses his path deliberately, which contrasts with Dr. Jekyll, who loses control of his good self. Brodie's morality is inconsistent with his outward appearance. Human agency involved with identity instability raises questions about an individual's true nature. Stevenson suggests that not only is man deceptive but also that anyone could be corrupted. Although the play was not successful, four years later *The Strange Case of Dr. Jekyll and Mr. Hyde* was published, and a new Gothic version of Brodie emerged.

Stevenson's novella, with its predominant focus on doubling, finds polarized oppositions of identity contained within an individual's body. Henry Jekyll declares, "man is not truly one, but truly two."[6] Essentially, the truth of human nature, according to Jekyll, is that a single body can house two distinct and separate identities. Jekyll further qualifies man's dual nature: "all human beings, as we meet them, are commingled out of good and evil."[7] The notion of Manichaean forces existing within a single person suggests that any sort of in-between or attempt at balance is a source of constant tension; one self pushes upon another in an ongoing battle for dominance. As the novella progresses, Jekyll notes that Hyde becomes increasingly harder to suppress. He says, "I was slowly losing hold of my original and better self, and becoming slowly incorporated with my second and worse."[8] Jekyll is aware of the power of evil within oneself to dominate over the good. His second self is a force that resists restraint and control. Morality is also lost when Hyde takes over his body. Hyde exists as an animalistic brute who is void of a moral compass or respect for humanity. While Jekyll initially chooses to separate his two selves, he does not realize that doing so will unleash a villain. To rationalize Hyde's crimes and immorality, Jekyll finds that his body must contain two opposing forces: evil in contrast to moral goodness. In this way, Hyde becomes an excuse for criminality.

Adaptations of Stevenson's novella have led to further discussions on duplicity and identity and suggest that anyone is corruptible. Hyde's connection to immorality and criminality has also influenced the perceptions that people have of criminals in the world. Shortly after publication, *The Strange Case of Dr. Jekyll and Mr. Hyde* was adapted by Thomas Russell Sullivan into a play called *Dr. Jekyll and Mr. Hyde* with Richard Mansfield appearing as the lead. The play maintained the characterizations of Jekyll and Hyde as good in contrast to evil but made changes, such as giving Jekyll a love interest. This was possible because the Jekyll/Hyde character has the versatility to believably exist under any circumstances. The play opened in Boston in May of 1887 and then premiered in London on August 4, 1888. Mansfield's transformation occurred on stage right in front of the audience, which raises questions about how people can trust appearances.[9] The terrifying reality that audiences faced was that an ordinary-looking man could be a heinous criminal underneath.[10] Audiences viewing the transformation had to confront the reality of it happening to anyone. This suggestion ended up spilling from the stage into the real world, demonstrating the direct impact of fiction to affect public perceptions of real people.

A few weeks after the play opened in London, the first murder credited to Jack the Ripper was committed. The Whitechapel murders created anxiety for Londoners, especially because the murderer eluded the authorities. *The New York Times* published an article on September 8, 1888, stating: "There is a bare possibility that it may turn out to be something like a case of Jekyll and Hyde."[11] The cold-blooded killer could be someone who appears to be an upright citizen, which means that anyone could be a suspect. Londoners were therefore on watch. In fact, because Richard Mansfield so impressively transformed from respectable man to menacing murderer on stage, some patrons considered him a suspect for the Whitechapel murders. One individual, disturbed by Mansfield's performance, sent an anonymous letter to the authorities detailing suspicions. The letter includes some deductions to show the police this is a valid claim.[12] The anxieties about crime in the real world made audiences wary of everything and everyone around them, and even pure acting talent was enough to arouse suspicions.

Largely due to the anxious climate, *Dr. Jekyll and Mr. Hyde* did not last very long on stage. On October 12, 1888, *The Daily Telegraph* reported: "Experience has taught this clever young actor [Mansfield] that there is no taste in London just now for horrors on the stage. There is quite sufficient to make us shudder out of doors."[13] The idea of Jekyll and Hyde is so powerful and so terrifying that individuals project the character into the real world. They imagine real people taking on the qualities of the fictional villain, a villain who was inspired from a real man who led a double life. Through such a circular chain, the real world informs the fiction, and the fiction informs the real world. The idea of a criminal leading a double life was not new, but Stevenson provided a name for it. Jekyll and Hyde became the signifier of duplicity and inconsistency and it remains so today.

Early film adaptations of *The Strange Case of Dr. Jekyll and Mr. Hyde* maintain much of the characterizations within the novella but adapt plot elements from the play. In these adaptations, such as those released in 1920 starring John Barrymore, in 1931 starring Fredric March in an Oscar-winning performance, and in 1941 starring Spencer Tracy, Hyde is still an aggressive murderer who increasingly emerges from a respectable Jekyll. The figure continues to represent pure evil in contrast to good. But, as with the play's adaptation, the plot may change and not damage the familiarity of the character. Audiences know who Jekyll and Hyde are and what Hyde is capable of no matter what the context. The terrifying reality is that a Gothic villain can emerge from within any individual in any place and at any time.

However, the characterization of Hyde shifted greatly in 1962, expanding the character's capacity to represent more than just duality. The Hyde figure could also raise awareness about the true locations of threats to humanity. Stan Lee and Jack Kirby created a comic book series inspired by *The Strange Case of Dr. Jekyll and Mr. Hyde* about a scientist, Bruce Banner, who transforms into a monstrous beast, the Hulk. The cover of *The Incredible Hulk* #1 says, "the strangest man of all time!!" and "Is he man or monster or … is he both?"[14] This version of Hyde is not a villain but an unconventional hero. The creation of a Hyde figure that could be a hero and save lives disrupts the novella's declaration that man's dual nature is polarized expressions of good and evil. *The Incredible Hulk* presents the notion that monsters are not necessary evil, and heroes are not necessarily ideal. Even though the Hulk is a volatile figure, there are larger threats that plague the world. The Hulk serves as a powerful hero who can combat true villains. Instead of raising anxieties about man's criminal nature and the potential for degeneration, the comics are concerned with Cold War era military technology and nuclear power.[15] The Hulk may be viewed as representative of the atomic bomb and its destructive abilities.[16] Therefore, *The Incredible Hulk* raises questions about whether the U.S. military needs atomic power since it can be an effective weapon, but it is also incredibly destructive.[17] *The Incredible Hulk* comics simultaneously consider the defensive need for and the dangers of monstrous power. Lee and Kirby essentially created a monster-hero,[18] which is a major altering of the original evil villain. The comics show how Jekyll and Hyde need not have oppositional intentions but still be definitive of inconsistency in behavior.

When a reference is made to Jekyll and Hyde, people understand the connotation even if they have never read the original novella. The popular understanding is that he represents two contrasting sides of a single entity. Stevenson's character has inspired the creation of other characters who share a similar trait of having a dual identity. In the film *The Nutty Professor* (1963, Jerry Lewis), a nerdy professor (Jerry Lewis) creates a potion that allows him to turn into sexy and charming Buddy Love. The film's remake (1996, Tom Shadyac) follows an overweight professor (Eddie Murphy) who similarly drinks a solution to transform into a thin obnoxious alter ego. Also, for the sake of comedy, Dr. Jekyll was adapted into Steve Urkel (Jaleel White) in the television series *Family Matters* (1989–1998). In the episode "Dr. Urkel and Mr. Cool," Steve develops "cool juice," which transforms him into the charming dreamboat Stefan Urquelle. But Stefan has faults, as Laura Winslow (Kellie Shanygne Williams) says that Steve "had feelings" and "cared about people," while the only person Stefan cares about is himself.[19] The distinctions within the dichotomous body greatly have to do with ego and sympathy. In *Family Matters* and in *The Nutty Professor* films, the Hyde figure has more sex appeal in contrast to the nerdy Jekyll figure. But Jekyll proves to be the more appealing individual at the end as others reject Hyde in favor of the original Jekyll. As these are comedies, they do not arouse the Gothic terror under which Hyde was initially conceived, but they further demonstrate the malleability of the Jekyll/Hyde figure into any context and within any atmosphere. The films and TV show teach about beauty within, so Jekyll and Hyde become appropriated to deliver a moral lesson. There is some consistency, though, as the suave Hyde figures do not seem a part of the original Jekyll figures; they only share the portal for releasing their identities: a human body.

While adaptations have certainly allowed Stevenson's dual character to evolve and permeate various contexts. Today, the phrase "Jekyll and Hyde" is frequently applied to a vast variety of entities. It can signify a single person, but it can also refer to something less tangible or concrete. Journalists often use the phrase in headlines because it provides a recognizable association for readers. Stevenson's fiction continues to inform an understanding of the world. The most similar connections to Stevenson's creation are associations with criminals who lead a double life. In these cases, there is no moral ambiguity as found with the Hulk. Criminality is clearly intrinsic to Hyde but masked by a respectable Jekyll, and this characteristic has been repeatedly found in real criminals. A headline from *The Guardian* dated November 20, 2017, reads: "Man who murdered adopted daughter was 'Jekyll and Hyde character.'"[20] In court, the judge specifically used the language quoted in the headline to describe the convicted man. This also occurred in a case in California, where the judge said of a man who murdered his three children and attempted to murder his wife: "You are a Jekyll and Hyde. You were a loving father and husband, and then you were a murderer."[21] Within the legal institution, then, there is an understanding of a "Jekyll and Hyde" criminal, an individual who seems a good, loving person but has a darker, violent side that, when unleashed, is incredibly dangerous and life-threatening. Legal circles have adopted the literary reference to put a name upon a criminal who commits this type of behavior. This makes Stevenson's character come to life in new ways as he penetrates institutions that uphold society. "Jekyll and Hyde," then, is an understanding, a form of legal jargon, a method of characterization, and a means for the rationalization of behavior.

The "Jekyll and Hyde" qualifier may also help determine sentencing and treatment of criminals who fall under such characterization. An article published in *The News* titled "Suspended sentence for 'Jekyll and Hyde' stalker" quotes the victim of the stalking: "He strikes me as a Jekyll and Hyde character projecting the front of an elderly and kind gentleman while actually he is a lonely and controlling man."[22] The defense barrister even said: "He is sorry for what happened and ashamed of himself. He is a really charming, caring man when he is not infatuated by someone."[23] This real-life version of Jekyll and Hyde has a trigger, the infatuation with a woman, that drives him into stalker mode. In addition to a prison sentence, the court also ordered that the man attend a stalking clinic. In the real world, duplicity is treated, and criminals are given chances to reform. Stevenson's novella presents a bleaker outlook, where human degeneration occurs as Jekyll continues to lose control of the transformations into Hyde. Society today acknowledges that similar criminal characters exist, but that does not signify that people are reverting to a primitive, more bestial state. These individuals can be disciplined, educated, and treated in hopes of conditioning the Jekyll side to suppress the Hyde.

While the association with duplicitous criminals is the most directly related connection to Stevenson's character, "Jekyll and Hyde" has become a term that signifies volatility or inconsistency within other entities. Journalists often use the term to describe politicians and political activity. "Jekyll and Hyde" is used as an insult that claims that there is no stability to individuals and policies. Since the term has criminal originations, its association with politics creates a negative impression of the person or policy under critique. In *The New York Times'* article "The Republicans' Jekyll-and-Hyde Health Care Plan," Drew Altman describes the details of the health care plan, delineating specific points under the category of Mr. Hyde and others under Dr. Jekyll. Within the policy itself, the favorable terms are deemed Jekyll, while the concerning conditions are designated Hyde.[24] This piece takes a pros and cons list and applies the recognizable cultural reference for emphasis of discrepancy. This is a clever persuasive writing strategy to demonize the points that the author dislikes.

In other media outlets, President Trump has been compared to Stevenson's character. Headlines from *Politico Magazine* and *The Spokesman-Review* read, "Trump's Jekyll and Hyde Foreign Policy"[25] and "President Jekyll, Mr. Hyde,"[26] respectively. Journalists have the widespread reach of the media to project political opinion through an iconic cultural reference. "Jekyll and Hyde" is not only used in discussing Americans or American politics. A journalist for *VUE Weekly* penned an article about the Canadian government, "A tale of Jekyll and Hyde."[27] Journalists have frequently used the term to discuss their political opinions. Such an appropriation is different from the criminal association with Hyde because it is based upon opinion. An individual with contrasting political views may designate the terms of policies and behaviors of politicians differently than the writers of such articles. What is a Jekyll for one individual may be a Hyde for another. This means that there is no agreed upon standard for Jekyll or Hyde. The term is applicable to any positive and negative list with the understanding that such designations are discretionary.

As a descriptor of policies, "Jekyll and Hyde" is not limited to the confines of the human body. "Jekyll and Hyde" has permeated the real world through its ability to qualify ideas and entities. In this vein, "Jekyll and Hyde" has been used to describe business and the economy. Economist John Rizzo uses the term in his headline for *Long Island Business News:* "Real estate issues loom in a Jekyll and Hyde economy." In his piece, Rizzo describes the economy as both "rosy" and "sinister."[28] The Jekyll side includes upticks in employment and wages, whereas the Hyde side is the stagnant real estate market. In this case, Jekyll and Hyde are descriptors of the current status of the economy, which could easily shift and then change its association. While "Jekyll and Hyde" in an individual clearly demarcates hidden criminal nature, in the economy, it signifies the condition during the present moment. It is also dependent upon many external factors, which can affect the state of any sector to become positive or negative. "Jekyll and Hyde" is more complicated than two selves trapped within one body. Instead, it is a construct of influences, factors, and trends that are perpetually in flux.

Business activity is also volatile enough to warrant "Jekyll and Hyde" designation. The *Union of Concerned Scientists* blog published the article "ExxonMobil's Jekyll-and-Hyde Act: A Year in Holding Fossil Fuel Companies Accountable."[29] The author, Kathy Mulvey, refers to Jekyll and Hyde as two "corporate personas" that are made visible by company behavior. When fossil fuel companies negatively impact the climate, or if they vocally deny the findings of climate science, they are Hydes. When they take action toward climate health, they are Jekylls. Bosses have also been compared to Stevenson's double-character. Business professor Joel Brockner describes Jekyll and Hyde "characters" who "behaved very morally in some situations and very immorally in others."[30] Brockner reviews a study about the ethical behavior of bosses in the workplace that found that "bosses who behaved more ethically on the first day were *more* likely to behave abusively toward their subordinates the next day."[31] This was explained first as a result of "moral licensing," where bosses who behaved ethically felt their actions "gave them moral credits."[32] This explanation suggests that bosses permit Hyde behavior and rationalize it based on their previous Jekyll behavior. Another explanation for "Jekyll and Hyde" behavior in bosses is "ego depletion, which assumes that people have a limited amount of self-control resources."[33] This seems more aligned with Stevenson's creation, as Jekyll gradually loses control over his other self. The position of power seems to enable the release of Hyde. Power as a trigger removes association with science or the supernatural and instead places human constructed hierarchies as potential threats to stimulate volatile or inconsistent behavior.

"Jekyll and Hyde" may also be a clever marketing tactic. *Boise Dev* published an article about the upcoming opening of Jekyll and Hyde Bagel Company, which will be a bagel bakery during the day and a greasy spoon bar at night.[34] This eatery intends to use the popular cultural reference to entice patrons. The establishment's uniqueness (and association with Stevenson's novella) is based on its change from day to night. The Hyde parallel is not criminality or immorality but perhaps an environment that is edgier than the Jekyll bagel joint and encourages indulgence of unhealthy food and beverages. The hopes are that people will be intrigued by the adaptation of a classic character to a physical space, which is a major transformation from its initial containment within the human body. This example shows the way that Jekyll and Hyde can be descriptors of space depending upon the activities that occur within the space.

Other entities that are also compared to Jekyll and Hyde include sports teams and their performances. "Jekyll and Hyde" signifies inconsistencies in play and is often used by journalists to describe both teams and individual athletes. For example, in *Evening Standard,* an article titled "Roy Hodgson frustrated by Crystal Palace's Jekyll and Hyde show" describes how the British soccer team played poorly the first half of the game (Hyde), but after halftime, played much better (Jekyll).[35] *NBC Sports* also uses the term to describe the hockey team the Wild, who plays well at home (Jekyll) but struggles on the road (Hyde).[36] Individual athletes can also display Jekyll and Hyde sports performances. *Dream Team*'s article "Serge Gnabry had a Jekyll and Hyde 15 minutes against parent club Bayern Munich" describes how the German soccer player missed a penalty kick (Hyde) but shortly after, he scored a goal (Jekyll).[37] In such a context, Jekyll and Hyde maintain their original connotations as good in contrast to bad. Performance becomes indicative of personality in the sports context. While the Jekyll and Hyde connotations are indicators of performance, using the term projects a particular notion of a split personality onto the teams or players.

"Jekyll and Hyde" is not just a term to describe human beings, policies, or actions; it can also qualify forces of nature. *The New Zealand Herald* published the article "Jekyll and Hyde summer weather continues—scorcher forecast for Invercargill, rain and thunderstorms further north." In this piece, the reporter describes a "crazy topsy-turvy summer."[38] The article does not describe Jekyll weather but focuses on Hyde weather of high temperatures, heavy rain, and thunderstorms. The article claims that the inconsistency in weather over the course of the summer indicates a "Jekyll and Hyde" climate. Using a personality indicator to describe the weather further demonstrates the malleability of the term. It can be inserted into any context, and people will understand the extremes that it represents.

Since its inception, the qualification "Jekyll and Hyde" has informed an understanding of the world. "Jekyll and Hyde" has been reshaped to connote various forms of inconsistency. As a descriptor, "Jekyll and Hyde" signals caprice, instability, and unpredictability. It has gone far beyond a man who struggles with self-control, as it now finds a place in discussions of crime, politics, business, sports, and weather. The phrase is timeless and has the versatility to enter any discussion topic. Because it is recognizable and enticing, the term continues to be successfully applied in such varying contexts. "Jekyll and Hyde" carries historical significance, cultural appropriation, and scientific inquiry. Timeless in its range, expansive in its reach, and multifaceted in its meaning, "Jekyll and Hyde" is a lexiconical phenomenon.

NOTES

1. Steven Brocklehurst, "The Real Jekyll & Hyde? the Deacon Brodie Story," *BBC News,* Januar`0y, 29 2015, http://www.bbc.com/news/uk-scotland-31018496.
2. "Dr. Jekyll and Mr. Stevenson," *Legal Studies Forum* 29.2 (Apr. 2005): 760.
3. Brocklehurst, "The Real Jekyll & Hyde?"
4. "Dr. Jekyll and Mr. Stevenson," 760.
5. Robert Louis Stevenson, *The Strange Case of Dr. Jekyll and Mr. Hyde,* 2nd ed., ed. Martin A. Danahay (Ontario: Broadview Editions, 2005), Appendix C, 121.
6. *Ibid.,* 78–79.
7. *Ibid.,* 81.
8. *Ibid.,* 85.
9. Jennifer Jones, "The Face of Villainy on the Victorian Stage," *Theatre Notebook* 50.2 (1996), Rpt. in *Nineteenth-Century Literature Criticism 212,* ed. Kathy D. Darrow.
10. *Ibid.*
11. "White Chapel Startled by a Fourth Murder," *The New York Times,* September 9, 1888, http://www.casebook.org/press_reports/new_york_times/nyt880909.html.
12. "Anonymous Letter to City of London Police About Jack the Ripper," October 5, 1888, *London Metropolitan Archives,* https://www.bl.uk/collection-items/anonymous-letter-to-city-of-london-police-about-jack-the-ripper.

13. "Dramatic and Musical," *The Daily Telegraph*, October 12, 1888, http://www.casebook.org/press_reports/daily_telegraph/dt881012.html.

14. Stan Lee, writer, and Jack Kirby, pencils, "The Hulk," *The Incredible Hulk* 1, Marvel Comics, May 1962.

15. Adam Capitanio, "'The Jekyll and Hyde of the Atomic Age': *The Incredible Hulk* as the Ambiguous Embodiment of Nuclear Power," *The Journal of Popular Culture* 43.2 (2010): 252.

16. *Ibid.*, 259.

17. *Ibid.*, 265.

18. I analyze this in depth in "Hyde the Hero: Changing the Role of the Modern-Day Monster," *University of Toronto Quarterly* 87.1 (Winter 2018): 234–248.

19. *Family Matters*, "Dr. Urkel and Mr. Cool," 5.8, directed by John Tracy, written by Jim Geoghan, ABC, November 12, 1993.

20. Steven Morris, "Man Who Murdered Adopted Daughter Was 'Jekyll and Hyde Character,'" *The Guardian*, November 20, 2017, https://www.theguardian.com/uk-news/2017/nov/20/man-who-murdered-adopted-daughter-was-jekyll-and-hyde-character.

21. David Rosenberg, quoted in Lauren Keene, "'My Crimes Are Unforgivable,' Says West Sacramento Man Who Killed His Children," *Enterprise*, January 19, 2018, https://www.davisenterprise.com/local-news/my-crimes-are-unforgivable-says-west-sacramento-man-who-killed-children/.

22. Ellie Pilmoor, "Suspended Sentence for 'Jekyll and Hyde' Stalker," *The News*, February 3, 2018, https://www.portsmouth.co.uk/news/crime/suspended-sentence-for-jekyll-and-hyde-stalker-1-8363636.

23. *Ibid.*

24. Drew Altman, "The Republicans' Jekyll-and-Hyde Health Care Plan," *The New York Times*, June 22, 2017, https://www.nytimes.com/2017/06/22/opinion/senate-health-care-bill.html.

25. Thomas Wright, "Trump's Jekyll and Hyde Foreign Policy," *Politico Magazine*, March 13, 2017, https://www.politico.com/magazine/story/2017/03/trumps-jekyll-and-hyde-foreign-policy-214903.

26. Bruce Barnbaum, "President Jekyll, Mr. Hyde," *The Spokesman-Review*, January 31, 2018, http://www.spokesman.com/stories/2018/jan/31/president-jekyll-president-hyde/.

27. Ricardo Acuña, "A Tale of Jekyll and Hyde," *VUE Weekly*, December 6, 2017, http://www.vueweekly.com/a-tale-of-jekyll-and-hyde/.

28. John Rizzo, "Real Estate Issues Loom in a Jekyll and Hyde Economy," *Long Island Business News*, November 20, 2017, https://libn.com/2017/11/20/rizzo-real-estate-issues-loom-in-a-jekyll-and-hyde-economy/.

29. Kathy Mulvey, "ExxonMobil's Jekyll-and-Hyde Act: A Year in Holding Fossil Fuel Companies Accountable," *Union of Concerned Scientists* blog, January 24, 2018, https://blog.ucsusa.org/kathy-mulvey/exxonmobils-jekyll-and-hyde-act-a-year-in-holding-fossil-fuel-companies-accountable.

30. Joel Brockner, "Why Bosses Can Be Dr. Jekyll and Mr. Hyde," *Psychology Today*, February 1 2017, https://www.psychologytoday.com/us/blog/the-process-matters/201702/why-bosses-can-be-dr-jekyll-and-mr-hyde.

31. *Ibid.*

32. *Ibid.*

33. *Ibid.*

34. Don Day, "Bagel Joint with Split Personality Planned for Downtown," *Boise Dev*, January 22, 2018, https://boisedev.com/news/2018/1/22/bagel-joint-with-split-personality-planned-for-downtown.

35. Jamie Teather, "Roy Hodgson Frustrated by Crystal Palace's Jekyll and Hyde Show," *Evening Standard*, February 4, 2018, https://www.standard.co.uk/sport/football/crystal-palace-news-roy-hodgson-frustrated-by-jekyll-and-hyde-show-a3757621.html.

36. Adam Gretz, "Trying to Figure Out the Wild's Jekyll and Hyde Home and Road Act," *NBC Sports*, January 26, 2018, http://nhl.nbcsports.com/2018/01/26/trying-to-figure-out-the-wilds-jekyll-and-hyde-home-and-road-act/.

37. James Robinson, "Serge Gnabry Had a Jekyll and Hyde 15 Minutes Against Parent Club Bayern Munich," Dream Team, January 27, 2018, https://www.dreamteamfc.com/c/news-gossip/375128/serge-gnabry-bayern-munich-hoffenheim/.

38. Cherie Howie, "Jekyll and Hyde Summer Weather Continues—scorcher Forecast for Invercargill, Rain and Thunderstorms Further North," the New Zealand Herald, January 13, 2018, http://www.nzherald.co.nz/nz/news/article.cfm?c_id=1&objectid=11974129.

Bibliography

Acuña, Ricardo. "A Tale of Jekyll and Hyde." *VUE Weekly*, December 6, 2017. http://www.vueweekly.com/a-tale-of-jekyll-and-hyde/

Altman, Drew. "The Republicans' Jekyll-and-Hyde Health Care Plan." *The New York Times*, June 22, 2017. https://www.nytimes.com/2017/06/22/opinion/senate-health-care-bill.html.

"Anonymous Letter to City of London Police About Jack the Ripper" (October 5, 1888). *London Metropolitan Archives*. https://www.bl.uk/collection-items/anonymous-letter-to-city-of-london-police-about-jack-the-ripper.

Barnbaum, Bruce. "President Jekyll, Mr. Hyde." *The Spokesman-Review*, January 31, 2018. http://www.spokesman.com/stories/2018/jan/31/president-jekyll-president-hyde/.

Brocklehurst, Steven. "The Real Jekyll & Hyde? the Deacon Brodie Story." *BBC News*, January 29, 2015. http://www.bbc.com/news/uk-scotland-31018496.

Brockner, Joel. "Why Bosses Can Be Dr. Jekyll and Mr. Hyde." *Psychology Today*. February 1, 2017. https://www.psychologytoday.com/us/blog/the-process-matters/201702/why-bosses-can-be-dr-jekyll-and-mr-hyde.

Capitano, Adam. "'The Jekyll and Hyde of the Atomic Age': *The Incredible Hulk* as the Ambiguous Embodiment of Nuclear Power." *The Journal of Popular Culture* 43.2 (2010): 249–270.

Day, Don. "Bagel Joint with Split Personality Planned for Downtown." *Boise Dev*, January 22, 2018. https://boisedev.com/news/2018/1/22/bagel-joint-with-split-personality-planned-for-downtown.

Dr. Jekyll and Mr. Hyde. Directed by John S. Robertson. 1920. Bridgeport, CT: Synergy Entertainment, 2007. DVD.

Dr. Jekyll and Mr. Hyde. Directed by Rouben Mamoulian. 1931. Burbank, CA: Warner Archive Collection, 2018. DVD.

Dr. Jekyll and Mr. Hyde. Directed by Victor Fleming. 1941. Burbank, CA: Warner Archive Collection, 2018. DVD.

"Dr. Jekyll and Mr. Stevenson." *Legal Studies Forum* 29.2 (Apr. 2005): 759–763.

"Dramatic and Musical." *The Daily Telegraph*, October 12, 1888. http://www.casebook.org/press_reports/daily_telegraph/dt881012.html.

Family Matters. "Dr. Urkel and Mr. Cool." 5.8. Directed by John Tracy. Written by Jim Geoghan. ABC, November 12, 1993.

Gretz, Adam. "Trying to Figure Out the Wild's Jekyll and Hyde Home and Road Act." *NBC Sports*, January 26, 2018. http://nhl.nbcsports.com/2018/01/26/trying-to-figure-out-the-wilds-jekyll-and-hyde-home-and-road-act/.

Howie, Cherie. "Jekyll and Hyde Summer Weather Continues—scorcher Forecast for Invercargill, Rain and Thunderstorms Further North." *The New Zealand Herald*, January 13, 2018. http://www.nzherald.co.nz/nz/news/article.cfm?c_id=1&objectid=11974129.

Jones, Jennifer. "The Face of Villainy on the Victorian Stage." *Theatre Notebook* 50.2 (1996), pp. 95–108. Rpt. in *Nineteenth-Century Literature Criticism 212*. Edited by Kathy D. Darrow.

Lee, Stan, writer, and Jack Kirby, pencils. "The Hulk," *The Incredible Hulk* 1. Marvel Comics, May 1962.

McCrystal, Erica. "Hyde the Hero: Changing the Role of the Modern-Day Monster," *University of Toronto Quarterly* 87.1 (Winter 2018): 234–248.

Morris, Steven. "Man Who Murdered Adopted Daughter Was 'Jekyll and Hyde Character.'"

The Guardian, November 20, 2017. https://www.theguardian.com/uk-news/2017/nov/20/man-who-murdered-adopted-daughter-was-jekyll-and-hyde-character.

Mulvey, Kathy. "ExxonMobil's Jekyll-and-Hyde Act: A Year in Holding Fossil Fuel Companies Accountable." *Union of Concerned Scientists* blog, January 24, 2018. https://blog.ucsusa.org/kathy-mulvey/exxonmobils-jekyll-and-hyde-act-a-year-in-holding-fossil-fuel-companies-accountable.

The Nutty Professor. Directed by Jerry Lewis. 1963. Burbank, CA: Warner Home Video, 2004. DVD.

The Nutty Professor. Directed by Tom Shadyac. 1996. Universal City, CA: Universal Pictures Home Entertainment, 1998. DVD.

Pilmoor, Ellie. "Suspended Sentence for 'Jekyll and Hyde' Stalker." *The News*, February 3, 2018. https://www.portsmouth.co.uk/news/crime/suspended-sentence-for-jekyll-and-hyde-stalker-1-8363636.

Rizzo, John. "Real Estate Issues Loom in a Jekyll and Hyde Economy." *Long Island Business News*, November 20, 2017. https://libn.com/2017/11/20/rizzo-real-estate-issues-loom-in-a-jekyll-and-hyde-economy/.

Robinson, James. "Serge Gnabry Had a Jekyll and Hyde 15 Minutes Against Parent Club Bayern Munich." *Dream Team*, January 27, 2018. https://www.dreamteamfc.com/c/news-gossip/375128/serge-gnabry-bayern-munich-hoffenheim/.

Rosenberg, David, quoted in Lauren Keene. "'My Crimes Are Unforgivable,' Says West Sacramento Man Who Killed His Children." *Enterprise*. January 19, 2018. https://www.davisenterprise.com/local-news/my-crimes-are-unforgivable-says-west-sacramento-man-who-killed-children/.

Stevenson, Robert Louis. *The Strange Case of Dr. Jekyll and Mr. Hyde*. 2nd edition. Edited by Martin A. Danahay. Ontario: Broadview Editions, 2005.

"White Chapel Startled by a Fourth Murder." *The New York Times*, September 9, 1888. http://www.casebook.org/press_reports/new_york_times/nyt880909.html.

Teather, Jamie. "Roy Hodgson Frustrated by Crystal Palace's Jekyll and Hyde Show." *Evening Standard*, February 4, 2018. https://www.standard.co.uk/sport/football/crystal-palace-news-roy-hodgson-frustrated-by-jekyll-and-hyde-show-a3757621.html.

Wright, Thomas. "Trump's Jekyll and Hyde Foreign Policy." *Politico Magazine*, March 13, 2017. https://www.politico.com/magazine/story/2017/03/trumps-jekyll-and-hyde-foreign-policy-214903.

ScatterGories

Class Upheaval, Social Chaos and the Horrors
of Category Crisis in World War Z

J. ROCKY COLAVITO

[handwritten margin note: ? disapproval]

Categories, organization, and social classes: these all contribute to a sense of security in everyday consciousness. People self-identify via occupations; they measure their worth by monetary or class status; ideological affinity is denoted through political allegiances, and any number of labels, both positive and *pejorative* establish identities for in/outliers. These efforts fit individuals and groups into categories and represent the ways by which societies and their constituents seek to provide a sense of organization and cohesion, using markers of socioeconomics to identify classes and their places within the accompanying socioeconomic spectrum. But what happens when catastrophe intervenes in the day-to-day functions of society? And what happens to class identity when individuals are confronted with a *bifurcated* menace that not only threatens their social status, but also their individual conceptions of their own humanity? Max Brooks, in the genre defining *World War Z* (2006, hereafter referred to as *WWZ*), offers clear insights into the ways by which a zombie pandemic undermines, overturns, and redefines social class. Consequently, the text's horrific dimensions are open to new conceptualizations. Yes, the recounting of the machinations of the zombies in their attacks on the living and their resistance are decidedly terrifying, but, more so, it is the after effects on class identity that offer a secondary, and, perhaps, more pressing, level of scares to be found in the novel, scares that are best conceptualized via Jeffrey Jerome Cohen's third Monster Thesis, "The Monster Is a Harbinger of Category Crisis."[1]

In Cohen's view, a category crisis complicates the relative ease of binary opposition and creates a "demand [for] a radical rethinking of boundary and

[handwritten margin notes: "·/o into", "∂ branches"]

41

normality."[2] Though applied to monsters here, and certainly applicable to Brooks' zombies, the definition also ties nicely to the terror that arises from the destruction of traditional class and socioeconomic boundaries. Entrenchment in upper middle and above social classes inspires contentment (having a good job, a nice house, a happy spouse, diligent, bright children, health insurance, and so on). But say the job is lost for one of a hundred reasons; the path to a new job is fraught with challenges. The family downsizes, moves into a smaller place or back in with the parents or other family members, and experiences a socioeconomic shock. They become "othered," which is often enough to redefine someone as monstrous (or, at the least, something to be avoided).

What's described here is the category crisis that is something that anyone might face at some point; jobs may seem safe, but the threat of downsizing is present for many, and redefinition of social class and status is uncomfortably close (as a stock market correction, outsourcing of jobs, industry downturns, or corporate re-sizing). One may think the boundaries and binaries are stable, but they are not necessarily so. It just takes one correction to throw the microcosm and macrocosm into disarray.

A pandemic, such as the one that occurs in *WWZ*, not only brings with it the social upheaval, but also the intellectual upheaval given the assault on binaries between the living and the dead. Dealing with something that conflicts the boundaries between life and death requires a reassessment of how to view the formerly dead. Are they humans that were formerly cared about, or are they adversaries to be terminated, again? Moreover, questions arise about how the living interact among themselves. Does altruism or self-interest drive the human consciousness? The word "normality" in Cohen's definition takes on major significance here; pandemics disrupt, and ultimately redefine, the concept of normal. The risen dead in and of themselves are an abnormality, and as such require the living to act in abnormal fashions, maybe making themselves monstrous in the process. This abnormality supplants the formerly normal, thus creating a new normal based upon dealing with the living dead and their effects on the living. These effects can cause no end of change in people's personalities, attitudes, and outlooks, innocence is lost, the everyday becomes distorted and adversarial, and there's the possibility that people will become "paranoid, pusillanimous pricks in the face of encroaching monsters."[3] When final victory is declared, the survivors (bearing wounds from the abnormality) are then forced to define and develop a new standard of normal. These transformations embody the more subtle and more threatening, horror dimension of *WWZ*. Zombie attacks are bad enough, but the effects on the survivors are even more horrifying. The tagline for the original version of *The Texas Chainsaw Massacre* (1974, Tobe Hooper) said it best: "Who Will Survive, and What Will Be Left of Them?"[4] That question applies threefold in *WWZ* to the individual survivors themselves, to the remnants of the societies that have been sundered by the outbreak, and to the new societies that develop in the aftermath.

Zombies and Marxism: The Hegemonic Battle Royale

In *Marxism and Literature* (1978), Raymond Williams describes the intersections between the titular constructs, and his observation that "culture … embodies [not only] the issues but also the contradictions through which it has developed."[5] These issues and contradictions form the crux of Brooks' novel, and are given form by another concept that Williams supplies: the notion of "dominant, residual, and emergent [hegemonies]"[6] The emergent hegemony (conceived as both the threat of zombie dominance and the new, less human[e] ideologies) is most crucial for exploring the development of the category crises that frame *WWZ*, for it is within this tension between the dominant (i.e., former ways of life and social stratification pre-outbreak) and emergent hegemonies that creates both internal and external conflict, and the subsequent scares that accompany each crisis. What's more, the emergent hegemony corrupts the residual hegemony (i.e., the newly developing one suggested by the stories told by the survivors). Burdened by guilt, traumatized by what they've experienced (or done), and skittishly vigilant, the survivors seek to create something new from the ashes of their former existence. Brief glimpses of the pre-revolution hegemony flash within the survivors' stories, but the newly developing world order gets the most attention. Ensuing discussions in this essay pinpoint more explicitly the ways by which these three hegemonies frame individual stories and reinforce the notion of the category crises that amplify the scary dimensions of *WWZ*. But a few preliminary examples offer a foundation for the longer discussions.

In the new world order following the outbreak, "class differences are reversed as manufacturing skills become paramount; formerly privileged white collar workers are burdens on the new society."[7] One of the more obvious examples that Brooks uses to illuminate this class inversion is the reversal of fortune that befalls Grover Carlson, a formerly high ranking White House official who is now charged with collecting bovine "debris" for use as fuel. His story is a tidily ironic one, for he describes acts that metaphorically align with his current job of shoveling shit. He describes a governmental commitment to "a measured appropriate response, in direct relation to a realistic threat assessment."[8] When asked if the government ever really developed efforts to address the outbreak, he responds "all you can hope for is to make them manageable enough to allow people to get on with their lives …

in politics, you focus on the needs of your power base."[9] It is thinking like this that embodied the old ways of life pre-outbreak; the focus on catering to the needs of one group at the expense of another represent formerly dominant thinking. Though Carlson's fall to his present position is not shown, his downward path from White House chief of staff to wielding a shovel and a wheelbarrow in search of cattle leavings for fuel represents the class inversion more closely analyzed later. Carlson embodies the formerly empowered, who, in a crisis situation, have little to contribute outside of the experience in their former positions (not to ignore his clearly stated political self-interest). In the new social matrix, he must now shovel shit since that's all he can really contribute. The former bourgeoisie has become the proletariat. *middle class* Arthur Sinclair's story, which receives more attention in the following section of this essay, addresses this particular category crisis that defines the inversion of social power. → what reading is on

This inversion of power in terms of status, along with the "bankruptcy of the system that allows [exploitative] practices to flourish"[10] is also evidenced in the many stories recounted in *WWZ*. One example is the story related by Breckinridge Scott, an entrepreneurial opportunist with connections to the pharmaceutical industry, who takes advantage of the outbreaks to market Phalanx, a supposed wonder drug that protects people from the virus. It fails on this promise, but makes Scott lots of money, which allows him to lease an Antarctic research station, a means of protecting himself from both the outbreak and those who are probably after his hide for false promises. Uncontrite, he declares the users of Phalanx complicit, pointing out that all that was needed was "a little responsible research"[11] to determine the drug's limitations, and expressing the hope that, should he meet the angry mob at some point, "that they don't want a refund."[12] It's important to note here that Scott is cut off from the rest of the world, and while he is safe, he is also alone, and, for all purposes, can never go back lest he have to face the consequences. He has his money and his sanctuary, but that's all. Maybe that's what he wants, but what good does his money do him when it takes extended periods of time to get anything (and even obtaining anything might become an issue given the slow pace of resetting the world). His outlook appears grim; all he appears to have bought himself is time. He may still have material wealth, but he is in no position to use it. → teaching

Scott's story and its didactic nature are brought into sharper relief by T. Sean Collins's story, dealt with at greater length in section three of these discussions. Collins recounts perhaps the clearest example of class upheaval and rebellion, a case where the haves are assailed and overcome by the have nots. While sticking to the trope of inversion, the category crisis is sharpened by the realization that the living dead are not the only threat to security, and that even seemingly impregnable sanctuaries have weaknesses.

The last category crisis to be analyzed has its roots in one of Todd Wainio's stories; he mentions the reality that "Zack was [not] the only bad guy out there."[13] He details a "threat pyramid [comprising] ... Zack at the bottom, F-critters, Ferals [humans], Quislings, and LaMOEs [last man on earth]."[14] The "threat pyramid" illuminates a new social order with new types of categories all characterized as dangerous. The most interesting threat is the quislings ("the people that went nutballs and started acting like zombies"[15]), essentially turncoat humans who seek to live among the zombies by becoming them (similar to the Whisperers in *The Walking Dead*). Though the feral humans have compromised or stunted humanity, the quislings make a choice to become one with the enemy, thus suggesting further disruption to the categories of survivors. Wainio and Muhammad's stories are an inkling of the category crises in Jesika Hendricks's story, the focus of a subsequent section. Hendricks, part of a refugee caravan that fled north to the Canadian wilderness, details a microcosm of the category crisis that overtakes the group when resources run low; a crisis that, in no small way, reinforces the fundamental similarities between the living and the living dead.

Category crises based upon social upheaval and class inversion form a dominant trope in *WWZ*. The loss of status, community, and humanity all stem from the state of war and its aftermath, thus reinforcing the horrifying dimensions in the text, magnifying the senses of loss and othering brought about by the zombie war. The impact of the crises are variable, and ensuing discussions analyze how three individual stories illuminate different sorts of category crises and their effects upon the survivors. The effects support the notion that this war, like its predecessors, is still going on as civilization seeks to rebuild.

But I Have "an MFA in Conceptual Theater"! Class Reorganization in the Aftermath[16]

The Holmes-Rahe Stress Inventory identifies five (out of forty-three) stressors that are rooted in changes in employment or living conditions.[17] While not on the level of losing a loved one or domestic upheaval, these stressors define day-to-day fears that afflict the working public in an era of corporate downsizing, attacks on tenure, and workplace closures. Loss of income is only the starting point; the gradual slide down the socioeconomic ladder from white to blue collar (and even lower) wreak havoc on the individual psyche.

Arthur Sinclair, Jr., former "Director of the Department of Strategic Resources ... during the [zombie] war,"[18] provides valuable insight into the employment inversions that the zombie war necessitated, and the category crisis that, while not threatening to the reestablishment of civilization, does magnify the fears that come with any sort of threat to one's employment (and the identity that comes with a job) and living conditions.

"We needed carpenters, masons, machinists, gunsmiths," Sinclair informs the interviewer, but what he had to work with were primarily people in possession of soft skills "perfectly suited to the prewar world, but all totally inadequate for the present crisis."[19] When systemic queries reveal that the majority of the surviving workers possess few to no needed skills, these former "'executives' ... 'representatives' ... 'analysts' and 'consultant[s]' ... [got their] white collars dirty ... [as] unskilled labor: clearing rubble, harvesting crops, digging graves."[20] There's lots of category crises in play here: literal loss of a job (in that the job not only no longer exists but is obsolete in the new world), movement from the office to physical labor in the field, the slow acquisition of new skills that must take place in order to become a more viable contributor to the new world order, and, illuminated most pointedly in Sinclair's story, the ascension of the proletariat as the new bourgeoisie.

Sinclair recounts the experience of observing one of the many re-education classes designed to retrain the individuals with minimal skills to contribute elsewhere:

> The trainees had all held lofty positions in the entertainment industry ... before the war, entertainment had been the most valued export of the United States. Now they were being trained as custodians for a munitions plant ... one woman, a casting director, exploded. How dare they downgrade her like this! ... I found out later that ... [the instructor] used to be this woman's cleaning lady.[21]

In microcosm, Sinclair's anecdote illuminates how the category crises with respect to jobs, job status, and employment power relations created just one of many challenges to the development of a new civilization. Those with formerly marketable skills that carried with them higher class status, now occupy the social strata formerly held by the people that used to do the sorts of jobs the upper class didn't, or wouldn't, touch. It's one of those moments in the text that may give a reader pause, wondering what, if any, skills they possess that might be of use in a crisis situation (the everyday unease over job longevity is also part of the stress). Category crises tend to reveal the weaknesses in both individuals and societies; a natural disaster is often made more destructive because of the exposure of poor workmanship or inadequate preparation (Hurricane Katrina is a case in point). A zombie war, in this case, magnifies the shortfall in useful skills, and the need for retraining to acquire those skills. Essentially, rebuilding requires "founding ... a community ... that is no longer grounded on a concept of life or politics in the proper sense."[22] The new community requires a focus on what you can do/contribute, not what you are, based on the former class system.

Sinclair does indicate that the retraining does have its benefits:

> Yes, it was very hard for some, but a lot of them later admitted that they got more emotional satisfaction from their new jobs ... it gave the people the opportunity to see the fruits of their labor; it gave them a sense of individual pride to know that they were making a clear, concrete contribution to victory.[23]

The eventual attitude adjustment aside, Sinclair's story introduces the first of many category crises that operate within *WWZ*. The one discussed here functions at a more psychological level than some of the others to be analyzed. While the loss of social status associated with one's job is admittedly a strong stressor, it is not one that ultimately represents a clear and present danger to one's person (the loss of health benefits aside). As will be seen, the other category crises under consideration represent a far greater danger to the individual.

"If you got it, flaunt it": Proletarian Revolt on "A Long Island"

T. Sean Collins describes his skill set as "knowing how to kill someone while keeping others from being killed"[24] and this set of skills is enough to gain him employment as security for a

> client [who] liked to know people who were known by all. His plan was to provide safety for those who could raise his image during and after the war, playing Moses to the scared and famous ... actors, ... singers, ... rappers, ... pro athletes ... professional faces ... like the ones you see on talk shows or reality shows, ... [and] even that little rich, spoiled, tired-looking whore who was just famous for being a rich, spoiled, tired-looking whore.[25]

worker

The top of the class structure is clearly defined, but there is also a proletarian group:

working class

> What I didn't expect was all their "people." Every one of them, no matter who they were or what they did, had to have ... I don't know how many stylists and publicists and personal assistants ... the fat fuck who won that talent show ... must have had fourteen people around him![26]

The distinctions between the classes are thus illuminated, and they are exacerbated by the host's choice to webcast life in the compound ("a survivalist's wet dream"[27]); "he didn't just want to ride out the storm in comfort and luxury, he wanted everyone to know he'd done it; that was the whole celebrity angle, his way of ensuring high-profile exposure."[28] This desire sows the seeds for the inevitable class tension that is prelude to the full blown category crisis that occurs at the conclusion of Collins's story.

The webcast produces the attention the host desires, but not the sort of attention he had expected. The sanctuary is "attacked" by people seeking a safe place from the outbreak. The gates are blown, the house is breeched, and the proletarian revolt (or the uprising of the have nots against the haves) is in full swing. Collins recounts:

> here were also the peons that turned and joined the attackers. I saw this ... hair-dresser stab an actress in the mouth with a letter opener.... It was bedlam, exactly what you thought the end of the world was supposed to look like. Part of the house was burning, blood everywhere, bodies or bits of them spewed over all that expensive stuff.[29]

Collins's observation is on point; it is the end of the world where celebrity and social status count for something, and it's also the end of a world where traditional class boundaries keep the haves and the have-nots separated. By flaunting the life that the haves were clinging to when others were at risk, they expose themselves to attack and subsequent loss of the very safety that was sought. The attack illuminates another category crisis in a panic situation "we the living always turn out to be worse than the zombies ... we turn on each other and display a zombielike aggression against what should be community."[30] This isn't a victory for the have-nots, either. By blowing the gates and setting fire to the house, the sanctuary has been compromised. The haves and the have nots are now equal. Nobody wins, except those who get out.

Collins, as one of the survivors, provides the epilogue that brings home the point about the horrors brought on by this category crisis:

> We'd been paid to protect rich people from zombies, not against other not-so-rich people who just wanted a safe place to hide. You could hear them shouting as they charged in through the front door. Not "grab the booze" or "rape the bitches"; it was "put out the fire!" and "get the women and kids upstairs!"[31]

Beyond the obvious commentary on class struggles, the selfishness/clueless-ness of the rich, and the concerns over the poor taking their frustrations out on the rich, the most terrifying thing about the story is the fact that the sanc-tuary was lost, or, at least severely damaged. The revolution went nowhere and neither side is, really, any better off than they were.

Collins leaves the narrator with the following to ponder:

> Sometimes I ask myself, why didn't they all just shut the fuck up ... all of those pam-pered parasites. They had the means to stay outta harm's way, so why didn't they use it ... just stay where they were but stay the hell outta the public eye? ... maybe they couldn't ... maybe it's what made them who they were in the first place.[32]

The inability to stay out of the limelight is the root cause of this category crisis; in a crisis situation the flaunting of resources is just asking for someone to try and take them, thus reversing the status from haves to have nots. This contrast becomes all the more telling when Collins, in describing a newsfeed showing crowds attempting to take on the zombies themselves, are assisted by a sporting goods store manager who supplies the crowd with baseball bats.[33] It was a lesson that was lost in this case, and the result was an even greater loss for all concerned, except those that managed to get out.

When There's No More Room in Hell You Will Find It by Going North

So far the essay has examined the loss of social status and its identity and the immediate loss of possessions and status via "revolution." Both category crises evince the destabilization of socioeconomic strata, and depict the horrors associated with attacks upon, and eventual loss of, wealth and prestige. But there is another, more devastating, category crisis that Brooks illuminates in *WWZ*, one which destroys the binary between human and zombie. The quislings mentioned by Todd Wainio and Joe Muhammad are *traitor* one example; the story recounted by Jesika Hendricks is more personal and *collab-* brings home the notion of the category crisis as it affects both the individual *orates* and the group. *with enemy*

In the early days of the outbreak, Jesika Hendricks and her family opt to heed counsel and head north into the Canadian wilderness, despite the fact that her family, like many of those who join the Northern exodus, has little to no experience camping, let alone subsisting in the wilderness.[34] The trip up proves challenging; the family manages to avoid roving groups that carjack people who stop for hitchhikers. The one they do decide to take in is found to have been bitten, and she is ejected forcibly from the car. They eventually arrive at their destination, and, initially, all seems jolly:

> We had this great campsite on the shore of a lake, not too many people around, but just enough to make us feel "safe" … Everyone was really friendly … it was kind of like a party at first … we all sang around the campfires at night.[35]

But the sense of community doesn't last. Resources get depleted via dynamite fishing, over hunting, and the loss of trees used for firewood. The strain on the community becomes palpable. → *capable of being ruined*

> But after the first month, when the food started running out … people started getting mean … no more communal fires … no more cookouts or singing … you'd see lot of fights … two women wrestling over a fur coat tore it right down the middle … one guy [caught] another guy trying to steal some stuff out of his car and beat his head in with a tire iron.[36]

The loss of community, except in the face of occasional zombie incursions, suggests a category crisis similar to the one recounted by T. Sean Collins; the haves and have nots struggle over resources. This part of the story also represents the category crisis that accompanies the descent from civilization into savagery; the return of the "buried past"[37] where pillaging for resources was both normal and graded against. Both are depressing and scary, but neither is out of the ordinary or any scarier than any of the other category crises depicted. But, as the winter grows colder and the resources disappear, another category crisis comes to the fore.

Jesika takes ill, and with no resources available to her family, they make a choice that raises the category crises to higher levels than anywhere else depicted in the book. The smell of something cooking in a nearby RV is more than the starving Hendricks family can take:

> Mom said "it" was the only way … "it" wasn't "that bad" because the neighbors, not us, had been the ones to actually "do it" … Dad said we weren't going to stoop to that level…. Mom really laid into Dad [the exchange prompts an incidence of domestic violence] … [Dad] had this look I'd never seen before … he went back out toward the RV … he came back ten minutes later … with a big bucket of this steaming hot stew.[38]

Though not stated at the time, the chief component of this recipe becomes clearer later, as older, wiser Jesika leads the narrator to a pile of bones:

> [The Narrator] I kneel to examine the bone pile. They have all been broken, the marrow extracted.
> [Jesika] Winter really hit us in December … the camp got silent. No more fights, no more shooting. By Christmas Day there was plenty of food.
> [The Narrator] She holds up what looks like a miniature femur. It has been scraped clean by a knife.[39]

Desperate times call for desperate measures; the reassignment of the formerly white collared to menial jobs collecting crap, digging graves, or custodial work and the inevitable armed struggles for resources between the haves and the have nots are expected category crises. But Jesika Hendricks' story goes far beyond the social equalization seen in the story told by T. Sean Collins where all become unsafe as the sanctuary is compromised. Jesika, her family, and the few survivors at the lake, are rendered equal to their adversaries, the zombies via their acts of cannibalism. The category crisis here is the most powerful; the binary between living and dead is shattered as the humans turn to cannibalism in order to survive. Driven temporarily mad by starvation, the survivors turn to their only option. It isn't clearly stated that people at the lake killed their neighbors for food, but one has to wonder given that children were among those consumed.

A descent into seemingly equal social footing with the zombies represents the culmination of Brooks' use of the notion of category crisis as a means of elevating the horror in WWZ. In the struggle to maintain a shred of humanity, Jesika Hendricks reveals to us just how far people will go to maintain that status. Without realizing it at the time, these survivors became just what they were trying to avoid, signaling that the contagion doesn't always produce the living dead. In this particular case, it is the dead living, clinging by a thread to a fraying remnant of prior social status.

"The best epitaph to hope for": Category Crises Anew

Brooks uses *WWZ* to depict more than just the by now familiar tropes and storylines that accompany the myriad of zombie films and stories. The tropes validate the text and give it credibility to the die-hard fans of the genre who seek the new bottles that the old wine pressed by George A. Romero in *Night of the Living Dead* (1968) now fills. But Brooks also goes further, and in so doing, emulates Romero by imbuing *WWZ* with a stinging sense of social commentary reminiscent of Romero's seminal film. In *Night of the Living Dead*, the principal cast couldn't get along, fought over tactics, and ultimately lost their sanctuary to the horde of the living dead. It's a microcosmic category crisis colored by discord involving age, gender, and race, and it intersects with the macrocosmic category crisis in the conclusion of the film where the last survivor in the home is mistaken for a zombie and shot by a roving group of militiamen doing clean-up work. Brooks keeps the category crises focused on microcosms in *WWZ*, letting survivors reveal the inexorable breakdowns caused by category crises (T. Sean Collins, Jesika Hendricks) and the eventual larger scale category crises that arise in the aftermath when civilization needs to rebuild (Arthur Sinclair). The focus on these microcosmic crises allows the text to posit some observations about the genesis and effects of these crises, thus elevating the text to something beyond a war memoir. Brooks uses the survivor stories to illuminate the effects of small category crises in the face of global ones brought on by war. The interplay between the category crises in defining humanity, its depths, and the lengths to which people will go to maintain a former way of life is also brought into sharp relief. It is these macrocosmic comments, subtle though they may be, that provide the deepest horrors of *WWZ*. In one of the most visible validations of an observation from Walt Kelly's old comic strip, *Pogo*, Brooks shows that, during the zombie war and its attendant category crises, "We [will] meet the enemy. And he is us!"[40]

NOTES

1. Jeffrey Jerome Cohen, "Monster Culture (Seven Theses)," in *Monster Theory: Reading Culture*, ed. Jeffrey Jerome Cohen (Minneapolis: University of Minnesota Press, 1996), 6.
2. *Ibid.*
3. William Larkin, "Res Corporealis: Persons, Bodies, and Zombies," in *Zombies,*

Vampires, and Philosophy: New Life for the Undead, eds. Richard Greene and K. Silem Muhammad (Chicago: Open Court Publishing, 2010), 19.

4. "The Texas Chainsaw Massacre (poster)," *Amazon*, accessed October 21, 2018, https://www.amazon.com/Chainsaw-Massacre-Leatherface-Silhouette-Poster/dp/B015R2J5KG.

5. Raymond Williams, *Marxism and Literature* (New York: Oxford University Press, 1978), 12.

6. Williams, 121ff.

7. Aalya Ahmad, "Gray Is the New Black: Race, Class, and Zombies," in *Generation Zombie: Essays on the Living Dead in Modern Culture*, eds. Stephanie Boluk and Wylie Lentz (Jefferson, NC: McFarland, 2011), 136.

8. Max Brooks, *World War Z: An Oral History of the Zombie War* (New York: Broadway Books, 2006), 59.

9. *Ibid.*, 61.

10. Ahmad, 136.

11. Brooks, 58.

12. *Ibid.*, 59.

13. *Ibid.*, 317.

14. *Ibid.*, 320.

15. *Ibid.*, 155.

16. *Ibid.*, 140.

17. "Holmes-Rahe Stress Inventory," *American Institute of Stress*, accessed October 21, 2018, https://www.stress.org/.

18. Brooks, 137.

19. *Ibid.*, 138.

20. *Ibid.*, 138–39.

21. *Ibid.*, 141.

22. Seth Morton, "Zombie Politics," in *The Year's Work at the Zombie Research. Center*, eds. Edward Comentale and Aaron Jaffe (Bloomington: Indiana University Press, 2014), 338.

23. Brooks, 140–41.

24. *Ibid.*, 84.

25. *Ibid.*

26. *Ibid.*

27. *Ibid.*, 85.

28. *Ibid.*

29. *Ibid.*, 85–86.

30. Jeffrey Jerome Cohen, "Grey: A Zombie Ecology," in *Zombie Theory: A Reader*, ed. Sarah Juliet Lauro (Minneapolis: University of Minnesota Press, 2017), 388.

31. Brooks, 88.

32. *Ibid.*

33. *Ibid.*, 83.

34. *Ibid.*, 123.

35. *Ibid.*, 126–27.

36. *Ibid.*, 127.

37. Edward Comentale and Aaron Jaffe, "Introduction: The Zombie Research Center FAQ," in *The Year's Work at the Zombie Research Center*, eds. Edward Comentale and Aaron Jaffe (Bloomington: Indiana University Press, 2014), 2.

38. Brooks, 128–29.

39. *Ibid.*, 129.

40. Bush, Larry, "The Morphology of a Humorous Phrase: We Have Met the Enemy and He Is Us," *Humor in America*, accessed October 21, 2018, https://humorinamerica.wordpress.com/2014/05/19/the-morphology-of-a-humorous-phrase/.

BIBLIOGRAPHY

Ahmad, Aalya. "Gray Is the New Black: Race, Class, and Zombies," in *Generation Zombie: Essays on the Living Dead in Modern Culture*, edited by Stephanie Boluk and Wylie Lentz, 130–47. Jefferson, NC: McFarland, 2011.

American Film Institute. "NIGHT OF THE LIVING DEAD: Full Movie." *YouTube* video, 1:35:17. August 26, 2014. https://www.youtube.com/watch?v=vZy6P72Uu3Y.

Brooks, Max. *World War Z: An Oral History of the Zombie War.* New York: Broadway Books, 2006.

Bush, Larry. "The Morphology of a Humorous Phrase: We Have Met the Enemy and He Is Us.'" *Humor in America.* Accessed October 21, 2018. https://humorinamerica.wordpress. com/2014/05/19/the-morphology-of-a-humorous-phrase/.

Cohen, Jeffrey Jerome. "Grey: A Zombie Ecology," in *Zombie Theory: A Reader*, edited by Sarah Juliet Lauro, 381–94. Minneapolis: University of Minnesota Press, 2017.

_____. "Monster Culture (Seven Theses)," in *Monster Theory: Reading Culture*, edited by Jeffrey Jerome Cohen, 3–25. Minneapolis: University of Minnesota Press, 1996.

Comentale, Edward, and Aaron Jaffe. "Introduction: The Zombie Research Center FAQ," in *The Year's Work at the Zombie Research Center*, edited by Edward Comentale and Aaron Jaffe, 1–58. Bloomington: Indiana University Press, 2014.

"Holmes-Rahe Stress Inventory." *American Institute of Stress.* Last accessed October 21, 2018. https://www.stress.org/.

Larkin, William. "Res Corporealis: Persons, Bodies, and Zombies," in *Zombies, Vampires, and Philosophy: New Life for the Undead*, edited by Richard Greene and K. Silem Muhammad, 15–27. Chicago: Open Court Publishing, 2010.

Morton, Seth. "Zombie Politics," in *The Year's Work at the Zombie Research Center*, edited by Edward Comentale and Aaron Jaffe, 315–40. Bloomington: Indiana University Press, 2014.

"The Texas Chainsaw Massacre (poster)." *Amazon.* Accessed October 21, 2018. https://www. amazon.com/Chainsaw-Massacre-Leatherface-Silhouette-Poster/dp/B015R2J5KG.

Williams, Raymond. *Marxism and Literature.* New York: Oxford University Press, 1978.

Spotlighting
Horror Writers

Marjorie Bowen
and the Third Fury

JOHN C. TIBBETTS

My life was not set in pleasant places.
In the jostle of the hundreds I always stood alone.
I saw the devil look through many laughing faces
And often felt his likeness rising in my own.
—Marjorie Bowen[1]

In Marjorie Bowen's novel, *The Haunted Vintage* (1921) a Christian monastery and vineyard in Bavaria are overrun by resurgent pagan gods. Legend held that long ago evil spirits had rushed in, took possession, and debauched all the monks. As the novel concludes, they "reveled every harvest and held their orgies in the wine cellars and chapels."[2] It's a fine pagan frenzy, the scene replete with

all the crude wildness, the black melancholy, the morbid glooms, the religious terrors, of Gothic fancy. All the fierce passions, the untamed imagination, of the North were in these uncouth fairy tales, which, darkened by superstition, saddened by fanaticism, sullied by ignorance and cruelty, yet showed here and there glimpses of a yet older world, joyous, human, lovely, the age of the Pagan gods before monk and nun, ghost and demon, robber knight and goblin, came to dwell on the banks of the Rhine.[3]

All is unbound. And then, suddenly, the pagan Harvest is finished. The grapes pressed, the wine finished, the perfumes distilled, the unholy vintagers return to the surrounding woods. Left behind are two mortal men who meet very different fates. The Duke of Nassau follows the seductive Gertruda, a nixie in human form, into the forest, where, later, his body is found, "but not alive, and scarcely in human shape."[4] Shaken free of his "poor bones and flesh," he now wanders "in some region of which it was best not to think."[5] Meanwhile, Lally Duchene, the Duke's friend and former commandant of the fallen Eberbach Monastery, fears a similar fate. "I am lost now," he confesses to his beloved, the fair Paulina. "I must go with them; there is no hope. I think they make a sacrifice in the woods."[6] But Pauline puts her arms around him and "the touch of her warm humanity gave him a certain strength; and he breathed more freely; the air seemed less oppressive."[7] They return to the world, "loving each other at last in a kind and human fashion."[8] Damnation and salvation, evil and grace, death and life—they all prevail, neither triumphant, neither defeated, but ongoing, together, everlasting.

The Haunted Vintage is only one of the more than 152 novels, story collections, social/historical commentaries, and autobiographical essays written by the British writer, Marjorie Bowen (1885–1952). While The Haunted Vintage, along with many other works, notably, The Man with the Scales (1954), plunges headlong into the realms of myth and fantasy, other novels mark out very different territories. For example, The Circle in the Water (1939), The Poisoners (1936), and The Abode of Love (1944) are sober historical period dramatizations about, respectively, intrigues in the France of Louis XIV, witchcraft in the Scotland of the 17th-century Covenanters, and religious cults in the England of the mid–19th century. The Crime of Laura Sarelle (1942), The Devil Snar'd (1932), and "Five Winds" (1927) are tales of ghostly possession. Stinging Nettles (1923), Moss Rose (1934), and Airing in a Closed Carriage (1943) examine the status of women in a contemporary repressive society.

Regrettably, the bulk of these novels do not enjoy today the celebrity and prestige of Bowen's weird short stories, which still find their way into anthologies and studies of the weird tale. Contrasted with the intensity and compression of the short stories, the novels, while sharing their themes and subjects, are more leisurely, detailed, and complex in character and incident. Inasmuch as they enjoyed a measure of public and critical acclaim in her day, their obscurity now is unwarranted and deserves special consideration on their own. They constitute an oeuvre whose sheer variety of subjects and narrative complexities baffle, dismay, challenge and delight. Reading them is no mere lazy afternoon's entertainment. They demand attention and concentration. The rewards are immense. Selected for examination are several works most characteristic of the range of her achievement.

To begin with, one might reasonably expect that a body of work of such abundance and variety could not possibly be the work of a single writer. Indeed, those 152 books are published under the names "Joseph Shearing," "George Preedy," "Robert Paye," "John Winch," "Margaret Campbell," and even "Marjorie Bowen." They all belong to one woman, whose impressive birth name was Margaret Gabrielle Vere Campbell, born in 1885 on Hayling

Island, Hampshire. Her autobiography, *The Debate Continues* (1939), rather compounds this name game. It was published under the name Margaret Campbell but subtitled as "Being the Autobiography of Marjorie Bowen"! This is intriguing, to say the least because "I have used many names for business purposes," Bowen declared, rather disingenuously, "but they were none of them of my own choosing and seemed rather to be fastened on me like a series of masks."[9] She adds, mysteriously, "I did not greatly care for any of them, nor does my other name—legally mine—appear to belong to me."[10]

It is best to group all these personae under the sobriquet by which she is best known, "Marjorie Bowen,"[11] which is the name that she published her first novel, *The Viper of Milan* (1906), at the age of 16. This roaring melodrama of Renaissance violence and intrigue drew raves from the *New York Times* and so impressed Mark Twain and Rebecca West that they sought interviews with her.[12] It so dazzled the young Graham Greene that, as he recalled later, "One could not read her without believing that to write was to live and to enjoy, and before one had discovered one's mistake it was too late…. Anyway, she had given me my pattern—religion might later explain it to me in other terms, but the pattern was already there—perfect evil walking the world where perfect good can never walk again."[13]

More recently, several of her staunchest admirers have espoused her case. Noted scholar and anthologist, Edward Wagenknecht, has described her as "a literary phenomenon" with a "dazzling talent," whose work recalls, by turns, Virginia Woolf, E.T.A. Hoffmann, and Franz Kafka: "Many writers have surpassed her in this area or that, but who else ever did so many different things so well? … And she had few equals and no superiors as a creator of atmosphere."[14] Moreover, the acclaimed author of fantasy and the supernatural, Jessica Amanda Salmonson, has argued:

> I declare her supernatural romances not merely among the best ever composed, but more than that, they deliver evidence that even at our lowest and meanest, there is something of merit and beauty in the transience and suffering of human existence.[15]

And in his recent assessment of weird fiction by women, including Elizabeth Gaskell, Vernon Lee, and Edith Wharton, Pulitzer-Prize winning critic Michael Dirda declares Bowen the finest British woman writer of the uncanny of the last century.[16]

A Female Gothic

Any consideration of Bowen must consider her place in the tradition of what has come to be known as the "Female Gothic." Bowen is following in the literary footfalls of Ann Radcliffe, Mary Shelley, the Brontës, George Eliot,

Charlotte Perkins Gilman, Edith Wharton, and other women who, since the late 18th century, have demonstrated a profound insight into the darker aspects of the human experience, particularly the tangled mysteries of female identity. Ellen Moers famously described the Female Gothic as a construction wherein "woman is examined with a woman's eye, woman as girl, as sister, as mother, as self."[17] More precisely, Moers continues, it is a genre to which women "give *visual* form to the fear of self"[18] and impart a feminist perspective on patriarchal societies that thrive on the marginalization and outright repression of women. This has produced nothing less, declares Patricia Murphy in *The New Woman Gothic* (2016), than a recent reinvigoration of Gothic studies in general.[19] Bowen's novels and stories—particularly *Stinging Nettles, Moss Rose, The Golden Violet* (1941), *For Her to See* (1947), *Airing in a Closed Carriage*—are, underneath their intense and near-hallucinatory surfaces, devastating indictments of the stifling bonds of society and gender that impede women's struggle against male authority of Victorian and late Victorian England—the limitations of education, the lack of professional advancement, and prohibitions on sexual freedom. Bowen deploys Gothic tropes to illuminate her portraits of women in their plight as passive victims or, alternately, as empowered characters forging their own destiny, as either maligned victims or monstrous aggressors. In the famous dialectic pursued by Sandra M. Gilbert and Susan Gubar in *The Madwoman in the Attic* (1984), the stories may be grouped roughly into the categories of the "Angel in the House" and the "Madwoman in the Attic."[20]

Of these titles, *Stinging Nettles* is especially interesting, in that the action transpires during the immediate post–World War I years in London, when protests and debates about feminism, the double standard, and suffrage were in the air. The protagonist, Lucie Uden, already unhappy with her conventional marriage and prepared to embark on a decidedly unconventional liaison, regards the commotion with a disdainful eye toward "the men really hating the women because they were so unwomanly, the women really despising the men who were giving in to them, all the broad outlines of sex difference lost, obscured, denied, yet every one, in one way or another secretly centred round sex."[21] Inasmuch as *Stinging Nettles* is demonstrably a self-portrait, it may be regarded as suggestive of Bowen's own attitudes toward the subject.

The Third Fury

Indeed, Marjorie Bowen is a mysterious woman. How and why did this modest, self-effacing, and outwardly conventional wife and mother of three children, who survived a wretched, lonely childhood, lacked a formal education, lived through two world wars, endured two troubled marriages, and was perpetually burdened as the principal supporter of house and home, manage such a prodigious output, one informed, moreover, by such dark and sinister impulses? On one level, the answer is simple enough: Assailed by more than her share of misfortunes, she wrote out of necessity: "I found myself harnessed to a career of hard work, and I had to earn all I possibly could, to chase every odd five-pound note in order to keep with expenses."[22] On the other hand, she obeyed the more imaginative dictates of the born storyteller: "I had an inexhaustible fund of invention, a fluent and easy style, a certain gift for colour and drama, and such a passionate interest in certain periods of history that I was bound, in reproducing them, to give them a certain life."[23]

There is a third motivation: Bowen's penchant for the dark and infernal. As Jessica Amanda Salmonson, observes: "As fast as the Mirthless Cosmic Jester poured misery into her, she made ink of bile to fill pages with dark visions, calamitous adventure, and cynical romances—tales populated by innocents and villains alike ill-fated—delightsome unpleasantries to mesmerize her faithful public."[24] Bowen herself declared, "I write to escape from the world in which I lived. And I found that, by writing of dark and gloomy subjects, I, in a way, rid my mind of them."[25] At the same time, she confesses to a profound *empathy* for these subjects. Through one of her characters, she voices her own credo: "As an artist, human material must interest me. I might have to draw a murderer or his victim. I must assimilate their characters."[26]

This dark empathy, by her own admission, owes much to her muse, the Third Fury. "I might term myself the Messenger of Tisiphone, the Third Fury," declares a character in the novel, *For Her to See*, "who was the avenger of blood."[27] The vengeful goddess Tisiphone was the third of the *Erinyes*, the Greek Furies of mythology. Tisiphone exists, as Camille Paglia has explained in her book, *Sexual Personnae* (1991), "under the chtonian cloud."[28] Tisiphone administers to her male victims a fatal poison extracted from the froth of the mouth of Cerberus. It is immediately apparent, when delving into Bowen's novels, how prevalent these poisonous agencies are. These include Madame de Montespan and Catherine Montvoisin in the court of Louis XIV in *The Poisoners*; and Angelica Cowley, Olivia Sacret, and May Beale in *The Golden Violet, For Her to See*, and *Airing in a Closed Carriage*, respectively. There is even a nonfiction study, *The Lady and the Arsenic* (1937), which is about the notorious Madame Lafarge. Most spectacularly, *Blanche Fury* (1939) adapts into late 19th-century settings John Webster's gruesome 17th-century Jacobean revenge tragedy, *The White Devil* (1612), itself a veritable farrago of poisons and poisoners. Thus, Bowen, while happily not a poisoner herself, but perhaps under a chtonian cloud of her own at times, may be regarded as an agent of the Third Fury, bowing in obedience to her and her sisters, Alecto and Megaera, while administering savage justice to her characters.[29]

These female characters, variations on Gilbert and Gubar's "mad women" and "angels,"[30] include vengeful women aplenty in the "realistic" narratives about blackmailers, the aforementioned *For Her to See* and *Forget-Me-Not* (1942); preternaturally seductive creatures in *Julia Roseingrave* (1933) and *The Veil'd Delight* (1933); outright supernatural creatures in *Haunted Vintage* and *"Five Winds"*; self-sacrificing wives in *I Dwelt in High Places* (1933) and *Stinging Nettles*; and passive victims of female oppression in the aforementioned *Airing in a Closed Carriage*. Many of them, like the deliciously villainous governess Lucille Clery, in one of Bowen's best novels, *Forget-Me-Not*, declare that a repressive patriarchy and limited opportunities have forced her into a life of crime: "Good God! Have I not been trained to be an adventuress? If there is no place for me in society, must I not make one?"[31] As a result, she admits, "I have had nothing out of life, nothing at all, my duty to myself is to get all I can."[32]

Some Gothic Tropes

Her mastery of Gothic tropes, such as ghosts and haunted houses, is everywhere in abundance. *"Five Winds,"* *The Devil Snar'd*, and *Blanche Fury* present fine old mansions inhabited for generations by the evil doings of ill-starred women. In the first, Denis Burgoyne, the latest in his family line, has inherited the mansion known as "Five Winds":

> a home full of sinister echoes, a house to people the long loneliness of the dales with phantoms. But Burgoyne belonged there; he knew that when he reached "Five Winds" he would at last be at home.[33]

In *The Devil Snar'd* Medlar's Farm, despite recent exorcisms, is "the worst haunted house in the North of England,"[34] the site of a century-old murder that threatens to claim as victims the newly arrived Grace and Philip Fielding:

> Even scientific researches admitted [it is a] commonplace that awful and violent deeds left behind them a hideous force which haunted the scene of their unnatural actions, and which could seize on to a receptive person exposed to its influence.[35]

Blanche Fury's Clere Hall, with its "oddly gloomy air hard to account for,"[36] is a mansion that for generations resists the intrusion of those interlopers who would illicitly claim old Adam Fury's estate. When one such interloper, the murderess, Blanche Fury, claims the house, she ends up living in isolation and becomes a "living" ghost:

Her flesh seemed to have withered and shrunk so that the bony structure of her head showed in an unpleasant fashion. Her clothes hung loosely on a figure that once been plum and trim.[37]

In regard to ghosts, some seem to be, on the one hand, psychological manifestations in the tradition of Nathaniel Hawthorne, Henry James, and Edith Wharton. How apt are the words of Zenobia in Hawthorne's *The House of the Seven Gables* (1851), "It's not exactly a ghost-story, but something so nearly like it that you shall hardly tell the difference."[38] As the character Grace Fielding declares in *The Devil Snar'd*, "It's the devil in ourselves we've got to snare."[39] On the other hand, some are frankly nastily external manifestations of all manner of spooks and goblins, in the more traditional sense of M.R. James.

Bowen also incorporates the spirits derived from folklore that haunt so many of her stories, like these apparitions in the Scottish glens in *Lindley Waters* (1942):

In the early morning, when the light strikes athwart the glen and the eagle hovers in the silver mist, one may see perhaps wraiths crossing lonely fords, one may behold the spirit of the water kelpie waiting with his flowing white mane to catch the unwary traveler … hobgoblins lurk in the granaries of the lonely farmhouses, and it is possible when passing through some lonely ravine to behold on a distant slope phantom armies.[40]<

Bowen is always careful to tip-toe along the boundaries dividing the factual from the fanciful, from sincere belief and delusion, from the quick and the dead. "Nothing is more attractive than a good ghost story," Bowen declares in the introduction to *Kecksies* (1976): "Some have a foundation of truth, inasmuch as they are based on some ancient tradition that the author chanced to hear or to read," while other ghost stories "are inventions, expressions of the desire to relate the terrible, the monstrous, or the incredible."[41] She admits she "never made any nice investigations into the difference between objective and subjective vision, between hallucination and spectre, between the delusions of delirium and the projections of an over-excited imagination."[42] However, she detests certain ghosts from the Ann Radcliffe tradition which prove to be shams and waxworks. Near to these phantoms in contempt, "is the gliding lady, who floats, always with tapping of high heels and rustling of silk, through so many well-worn old legends of so many well-worn old houses."[43]

There are Faustian Pacts aplenty in these infernal pages. *The Abode of Love* reveals the fate of the prophet, Stephen Finett, a self-appointed Divine mouthpiece who preaches the Second Coming of Christ and, as a result of his failures, barely escapes crucifixion at the hands of his disgruntled congregation. *I Dwelt in High Places* is a historical novel about the idealistic man of science, John Dee, Queen Elizabeth's astrologer, and his assistant, the darkly charismatic magician, Edward Kelly, and the consequences of their descent into occult experiments to obtain "god-like powers of wisdom, of healing, and to learn secrets hitherto unguessed at by man."[44] Both men are cast down in their presumptions, or were they merely delusions? Most spectacularly, *Black Magic* (1909) is a gender-bending story set in 13th-century Italy about two practitioners of the Satanic arts whose machinations topple the papal seat in Rome and bring the world to the brink of an apocalypse. The presumptive Pope, the apocryphal "Pope Joan," declares: "Though the world I rule rot about me, though ghouls and fiends make my Imperial train—I will join hands with Antichrist and see if there be a God or no!"[45]

Haunted Histories

It is clear by now that regardless of their variety and tone, most of Bowen's novels are set against the contexts of history, from medieval times to the present day, from papal Rome to contemporary London. One is reminded that in her lifetime she was lauded as one of the greatest historical romancers of her time. "Her historical judgments are usually sound," writes Pamela Cleaver in her overview, "and her historical backgrounds are full of well-researched detail and period clothes."[46] Bowen herself charmingly takes stock of her historical agendas in her preface to *Shadows of Yesterday* (1916):

> If one could look back—beyond the dust, beyond the years to the time when all these dead things were fresh—when the originals of those portraits moved and worked and laughed, when beer was really brewed in those jugs and tea drunk from those cups, when those cards were dashed on to the playing table, when that sword graced some gallant's thigh, that paste necklace some woman's neck.... If one could look back to those times, might not one find curious stories, sad stories, and gay stories attached to these old worthless objects?—as staring at ashes one may recall the flames.[47]

In her preface to *The Circle in the Water*, a tale of witchcraft in 17th-century Scotland, Bowen describes her method: "The present tale is told in the first person, as this method seems best suited to the wild subject, bringing the reader close as it does to the matter and allowing those strange events to be related by an eye-witness...."[48]

At the same time, Bowen is preoccupied with historical crime cases about murderers, some of which involve women.[49] Although Truman Capote dubbed his *In Cold Blood* (1966) a "non-fiction novel," Bowen seems to have been, along with William Roughead, one of the first to make a career in researching and writing about them.[50] In *Airing in a Closed Carriage*, for example, Amy Beale is tried, convicted, and sentenced to hang for the murder of her husband. It is based on a London trial in 1889, from whose transcripts Bowen liberally quotes. In her introduction, Bowen rhetorically asks why write about true-life subjects:

The answer can only lie largely in the perversity of human nature—we desire to attempt the impossible. We hear from our earliest childhood of a certain subject or a certain character until we become fascinated, perhaps obsessed. Although reason tells us that everything is known and everything has been said on this matter, yet we long to rearrange these familiar materials according to our own sense of design or of decoration, to make our own deductions from bare facts, to re-tell, by the light of our own experience, these experiences with which everyone is familiar. We think that perhaps there is something which has not yet been said and that we can say it. In brief, we wish to paint our own pictures of the familiar scene, to give these legendary creatures faces of our own fashioning, to draw our own design on their robes.[51]

She concludes that her views of the question of May's guilt—a matter of controversy at the time—are her own interpretation, albeit they "seemed the only possible explanation of these events."[52]

More Haunted Women

In conclusion, Bowen's place within the ranks of other British women roughly contemporary with her, May Sinclair (1865–1946), Daphne du Maurier (1907–1989), and Vernon Lee [Violet Paget] (1857–1935), should be considered. All of them, writes critic Michael Dirda, share with Bowen a predilection for themes and tropes of historical settings, ghostly possessions, neurotic women, and supernatural sex.[53] In particular, du Maurier's *My Cousin Rachel* (1951) and *Jamaica Inn* (1936) are both 19th-century tales set on the Cornish coast; and are fraught with smuggling, violence, and illicit love. More to the point are her several collections of short stories of a distinctively weird and unsettling nature, including *The Apple Tree* (1952), with its title story, a cruel study in neurotic obsession; and *Don't Look Now* (1971), whose title story is a tangle of psychics, precognition, and violent death amidst the maze of the Venetian canals. Perhaps the most interesting and with whom the closest comparison can be made, is Vernon Lee. Like Bowen, she set many of her stories in 17th- and 18th-century Italy. "Amour Dure" and "Dionea" (1890), for example, blend ghostly possession, medieval magic, and mythological devices in their colorfully wrought prose.

Finally, Marjorie Bowen assesses her worth and her position within the great Female Gothic narrative, in the concluding pages of her memoir, *The Debate Continues*. This unvarnished account of her years up to 1939 surely belongs with the best memoirs of any writer, past or present. Looking back on her youth and her position as a female writer working in a man's world, she declared, with characteristic bluntness:

I seemed to have no common ground with anyone whom I met because I was in myself composed of so many contradictions. I was a girl and earning a good income; I was a girl and I liked serious things; I was a woman and in the place of a man as breadwinner; I had intellectual aspirations and a longing to sit at the feet of the learned and the wise.[54]

Further, referring to herself in the third person, she added, "She cultivated her mind as far as her powers enabled her.... Rationalism attracted and convinced her mind, but the heart has reasons that the mind knows not of, and she delighted in the mystics."[55]

Today, we relish these contradictions, the hard, dry, unsentimental detachment with which she regards nightmares and horrors, and her heartfelt admission that she relishes, in the words of the 17th-century clergyman-poet, George Herbert, the "music at midnight"—which she interprets "as the courage to find beauty in dark places."[56]

And so we leave Marjorie Bowen—only for the moment—as we turn again to her great novel of witchcraft in 17th-century Scotland, *The Circle in the Water*. When the ageing protagonist, Thomas Maitland, sadly reviews the failures of his life, he asks his companion—none other than William, Prince of Orange—if there was any real meaning, any consolation he can take from it all. He offers only this curt response: "I have no time to think of it. I do my task as I see it set before me."[57]

And *that* can serve as the testament of the woman known as "Marjorie Bowen."

Notes

1. Unpublished poem by Marjorie Bowen, Yale Papers, Box 25, Folder 182.
2. Marjorie Bowen, *The Haunted Vintage* (London: Odhams Press, 1921), 227.
3. *Ibid.*, 59–60.
4. *Ibid.*, 320.
5. *Ibid.*
6. *Ibid.*, 318.
7. *Ibid.*
8. *Ibid.*, 320.
9. Marjorie Bowen, *The Debate Continues: Being the Autobiography of Marjorie Bowen* (London: William Heinemann, 1939), 41.
10. *Ibid.*
11. "Bowen" was her maternal great-grandfather's name, and "Marjorie" is a diminutive of Margaret.
12. In "A Precocious Author," the *New York Times* critic observed, "It would seem to such a reviewer simply incredible that a mere child could succeed ... in transferring to the pages of a novel the spirit, the scenes, and the people of a long-past ago, and infusing them with the breath of life and reality" (17 November 1906, BR751, ProQuest Historical Newspapers). The two letters by Mark Twain are dated 25 March 1907 and 27 May 1907. He issues an invitation when he is next in England: "I think you will have to do as the American girls do: waive youth, sex, and the other conventions and call on me." the letter from Arthur Conan Doyle is dated 3 July 1916 and is in response to a later book, *Shadows of Yesterday*: "May I say how really splendid I think your new book.... I don't like women's work as a rule, on account of a certain lack of substance, but here the detail, the atmosphere and the dramatic effect are all equally good." (Bowen Papers, Beinecke Library, Box 35, Folder 23).
13. Graham Greene, *The Lost Childhood* (New York: Viking Press, 1962), 17.

14. Edward Wagenknecht, *Seven Masters of Supernatural Fiction* (Westport, CT: Greenwood Press, 1991), 180.

15. Jessica Amanda Salmonson, "The Supernatural Romances of Marjorie Bowen," in *Twilight and Other Supernatural Romances,* ed. Jessica Amanda Salmonson (Ashcroft, BC: Ash-Gate Press, 1998), xix.

16. Michael Dirda, "Ghostly Women," *The Weekly Standard*, March 6, 2017, 41.

17. Ellen Moers, quoted in Donna Heiland, *Gothic & Gender: An Introduction* (London: Blackwell, 2004), 57–58.

18. *Ibid.,* 58.

19. Patricia Murphy, *The New Woman Gothic: Reconfiguration of Distress* (Columbia: University of Missouri Press, 2016), 1–30.

20. Sandra M. Gilbert and Susan Gubar, *The Madwoman in the Attic* (New Haven, CT: Yale University Press, 1984), 3–44. Virginia Woolf declared that before women can write, they must "kill" the "Angel in the House" (Gilbert and Gubar), 17.

21. Marjorie Bowen, *Stinging Nettles: A Modern Story* (London: Ward, Lock & Co., Ltd, 1923), 80.

22. Bowen, *The Debate Continues*, 95.

23. *Ibid.,* 92.

24. Jessica Amanda Salmonson, "Rose Petals, Drops of Blood: The Life of Marjorie Bowen, Mistress of the Macabre," accessed December 13, 2018, https://web.archive.org/web/20130628075333/http://www.violetbooks.com:80/bowen.html.

25. Bowen, *Debate*, 84–85.

26. Bowen, *For Her to See*, 91.

27. *Ibid.,* 219.

28. Camille Paglia, *Sexual Personae* (New York: Vintage Books, 1991), 5.

29. "A writer needs her poisons," wrote Philip Roth appositely, "and the antidote is often a book" (quoted in "Roth Agonistes," by Nathaniel Rich, in *NYRB*, March 2018, 38).

30. Gilbert and Gubar, *The Madwoman in the Attic*, 3–44.

31. Marjorie Bowen, *Forget-Me-Not* (London: Endeavor Press, 2015), 56.

32. *Ibid.,* 82.

33. Marjorie Bowen, *"Five Winds"* (London: Hodder & Stoughton, 1927), 32.

34. Marjorie Bowen, *The Devil Snar'd* (London: Ernest Benn, 1932), 52.

35. *Ibid.*

36. Marjorie Bowen, *Blanche Fury* (New York: 1965), 222.

37. *Ibid.*

38. Nathaniel Hawthorne, *The House of Seven Gables* in *The Complete Novels and Selected Tales of Nathaniel Hawthorne,* ed. Norman Pearson (New York: Modern Library, 1937), 502.

39. Bowen, *The Devil Snar'd*, 154.

40. Marjorie Bowen, *Lindley Waters* (London: Hodder and Stoughton, 1942), 47.

41. Marjorie Bowen, *Kecksies* (Sauk City, WI: Arkham House, 1976), ix.

42. *Ibid.,* x–xiii.

43. These notes by Bowen were not published until a quarter century after her death.

44. Marjorie Bowen, *I Dwelt in High Places* (London: Collins, 1933), 25.

45. Marjorie Bowen, *Black Magic* (London: Sphere Books, 1974), 273.

46. Pamela Cleaver, "Marjorie Bowen," in *Twentieth-Century Romance and Historical Writers,* ed. Lesley Henderson (Chicago: St. James Press, 1990), 68.

47. Marjorie Bowen, preface to *Shadows of Yesterday: Stories from an Old Cataloque* (London: Smith Elder & Co., 1916), 5.

48. Marjorie Bowen, *The Circle in the Water* (London: Hutchinson & Co., 1939), 8.

49. See an admirable treatment of the subject in Mary S. Hartman's *Victorian Murderesses* (New York: Schocken Books, 1977).

50. For a survey of the writings of William Roughead, see Roughead, *Classic Crimes: A Selection from the Works of William Roughead* (New York Review of Books, 2000). The Introduction of this edition is by Luc Sante.

51. Marjorie Bowen, *Airing in a Closed Carriage* (New York: Harper & Brothers, 1943), v.

52. *Ibid.*, v.
53. Dirda, "Ghostly Women," 38–41.
54. Bowen, *The Debate Continues*, 110.
55. *Ibid.*, 293.
56. George Herbert (1593–1631) was a seventeenth-century metaphysical poet whose poems were published only shortly after his death. Perhaps Bowen felt a kinship with Herbert in that the poet forsook a career at court for a more "commonplace" life as a cleric in a country church. His was an ordinary human ambivalence with regard to faith. It's unclear to me at this writing where Marjorie Bowen found this quotation. One source that could have been available to her was the *Dictionary of Burning Words by Brilliant Writers* (1895), edited by Josiah Hotchkiss Gilbert, where the quote appears on page 20. The quote seems to have been originally from a letter or essay rather than from one of his poems. as for the quotation itself, it can be found on the internet in a review by Mark Jarman of John Drury's biography of Herbert, *Music at Midnight* (2014). Jarman's critique is titled "Writing for God: The Life and Work of George Herbert":
   The story is that one night on his way to a gathering of musicians like himself [George Herbert] stopped to assist a man who was exasperated with his horse, who had fallen under its load. Herbert, after providing the man with help in getting the horse loaded again and giving him some money to refresh himself and his animal—a typical gesture of his—proceeded to his rehearsal. Herbert, who was known for the care he took with his clothing and his cleanliness and neatness of dress, arrived soiled and in disarray. Asked about the reason, he shrugged it off and explained what had transpired and said that helping the man as he had—and advising him against beating his horse—would provide a solace for his own conscience that would be "music at Midnight" in the future." See https://hudsonreview.com/2014/10/writing-for-god-the-life-and-work-of-george-herbert/#.WyrpoqdKiUk, 298.
57. Bowen, *The Circle in the Water*, 170.

BIBLIOGRAPHY

Bowen, Marjorie. *Abode of Love*. London: Hutchinson & Co., 1944 [as Joseph Shearing].
_____. *Airing in a Closed Carriage*. New York: Harper & Brothers, 1943 [as Joseph Shearing].
_____. *The Bishop of Hell*. London: Bodley Head, 1949.
_____. *Black Magic*. London: Sphere Books, 1974.
_____. *Blanche Fury*. New York: 1965.
_____. *The Circle in the Water*. London: Hutchinson & Co., 1939.
_____. *The Crime of Laura Sarelle*. New York: Berkeley, 1965 [as Joseph Shearing].
_____. *The Debate Continues: Being the Autobiography of Marjorie Bowen*. London: William Heinemann, 1939 [as Margaret Campbell].
_____. *The Devil Snar'd*. London: Ernest Benn, 1932 [as George Preedy].
_____. *"Five Winds."* London: Hodder & Stoughton, 1927.
_____. *For Her to See*. London: Hutchinson & Co., n.d., 1947 [as Joseph Shearing].
_____. *Forget-Me-Not* (1942). London: Endeavour Press, 2015 [as Joseph Shearing].
_____. *The Golden Violet*. New York: Readers Club, 1941 [as Joseph Shearing].
_____. *The Haunted Vintage*. London: Odhams Press, 1921.
_____. *I Dwelt in High Places*. London: Collins, 1933.
_____. *Julia Roseingrave*. in *Twilight and Other Supernatural Romances*, edited by Jessica Amanda Salmonson, 191–255. Ashcroft, BC: Ash-Tree Press, 1998.
_____. *Kecksies*. Sauk City, WI: Arkham House, 1976.
_____. *Lindley Waters*. London: Hodder and Stoughton, 1942 [as George Preedy].
_____. *Man with the Scales*. London: Hutchinson, 1954.
_____. *"Margaret Campbell,"* in *Myself When Young*, edited by Margot Oxford, 41–64. London: Frederick Muller, 1938.
_____. *Moss Rose*. New York: Berkeley, 1934 [as Joseph Shearing].
_____. *The Poisoners*. New York: Endeavour Press, 2017.
_____. *Shadows of Yesterday: Stories from an Old Catalogue*. London: Smith Elder, 1916.
_____. *Stinging Nettles: A Modern Story*. London: Ward, Lock, 1923.

_____. *Twilight and Other Supernatural Romances*, edited by Jessica Amanda Salmonson. Ashcroft, BC: Ash-Tree Press, 1998.

_____. *The Veil'd Delight.* London: Odhams Press, 1933.

_____. *The Viper of Milan.* London: Endeavour Press, 2015.

Cleaver, Pamela. "Marjorie Bowen," in *Romance and Historical Writers*, Edited by Lornie Leet-Hodge, 65–68. Chicago: St. James Press, 1990.

Dirda, Michael. "Ghostly Women." *The Weekly Standard*, March 6, 2017, 38–41.

du Maurier, Daphne. "The Apple Tree," in *The Apple Tree.* London: Victor Gollancz. 1952.

_____. "Don't Look Now," in *Don't Look Now.* New York: Doubleday, 1971.

_____. *Jamaica Inn.* London: Victor Gollancz, 1936.

_____. *My Cousin Rachel.* London: Victor Gollancz, 1951.

_____. Unpublished poem. Yale Papers, Box 25, Folder 182.

Gilbert, Sandra M., and Susan Gubar. *The Madwoman in the Attic.* New Haven and London: Yale University Press, 1984.

Greene, Graham. *The Lost Childhood and Other Essays.* New York: Viking Press, 1951.

Hawthorne, Nathaniel. *The Complete Novels and Selected Tales of Nathaniel Hawthorne.* Edited by Norman Pearson. New York: Modern Library, 1937.

Heiland, Donna. *Gothic & Gender: An Introduction.* London: Blackwell, 2004.

Lee, Vernon. "Amor Dure," in *Hauntings.* Ashcroft, BC: Ash-Gate Press, 1998.

_____. "Dionea," in *Hauntings.* Ashcroft, BC: Ash-Gate Press, 1998.

Murphy, Patricia. *The New Woman Gothic: Reconfigurations of Distress.* Columbia: University of Missouri Press, 2016.

Salmonson, Jessica Amanda. Introduction to *Twilight and Other Supernatural Romances*, xix–xl. Edited by Jessica Amanda Salmonson. Ashcroft, BC: Ash-Gate Press, 1998.

_____. *Rose Petals, Drops of Blood*, addendum to Salmonson's Introduction to *Twilight and Other Supernatural Romances*. See https://web.archive.org/web/20130628075333/http://www.violetbooks.com:80/bowen.html.

Wagenknecht, Edward. *Seven Masters of Supernatural Fiction.* Westport, CT: Greenwood, 1991.

"When the cage came up there was something crouched a-top of it"

The Haunted Tales of L.T.C. Rolt

Danny Rhodes

Lionel Thomas Caswell Rolt's (1910–1974) collection of ghost stories, *Sleep No More* was published in 1948 by Constable. At the time of publication Michael Sadleir hailed Rolt as the successor to Montague Rhodes (M.R.) James.[1] This essay will present the argument that Rolt's short collection marks an important way-point in the evolution of the ghost story. It will introduce the ghost story and examine what James thinks makes an effective ghostly tale before going on to explore how Rolt builds off James' observations and techniques in the creation of his own work. In doing so, it aims to demonstrate how the unique characteristics of Rolt's tales, particularly his richly detailed presentation of post-industrial England and his relationship with the natural world, make them more than simply Jamesian imitations. In his most effective works Rolt carries the form towards untrodden places and provides an end-point for the Victorian and Edwardian ghostly tale, forging the way for the urban stories that preponderate the horror genre today.

The Ghost Story

In his essay "The Passing of the Ghost Story," Rolt laments how a "venerable branch of the storyteller's art seems to have fallen into neglect."[2] There was a time, Rolt mourns, when "no Christmas annual or Christmas number of a magazine was considered complete without a ghost story."[3]

Many literary critics argue a "golden age of the ghost story"[4] existed between the decline of the Gothic novel in the 1830s and the start of the First World War. Julia Briggs makes the point that "the most characteristic form taken by the Gothic from, perhaps, 1830 to 1930 is the ghost story."[5] Improvements in technology and education during the Victorian era "resulted in a higher general rate of literacy"[6] and as a result "many journals and magazines were launched to meet the demands of a new reading public,"[7] with ghost stories high on the list of desired reading. "As time went on," quotes Susan Owens, "a younger generation of story-writers wrested ghosts from their time-honoured haunts and made them more immediate and topical by placing them in modern, urban settings."[8] Over half a century later, Rolt would do the same, utilizing and adapting the ghost story to tackle "a world full of sinister possibilities."[9]

Reflecting on the end of the 19th century, Owens points out how "underneath the apparent confidence of the times was a sense of unease and a mood of introspection … the sheer scale and momentum of house building and industrialization in the late Georgian and Victorian era had rapidly and irreversibly changed the character of Britain."[10] The populace looked to the landscape as a means of preserving a sense of national identity. "When the National Trust was founded in 1895," observes Owens, "the country was re-imagined as a repository of ancient history and legend."[11] No writer was better suited to serve the reading public a concoction of ghost stories and ancient history than James.

James harkens back to the Victorian era in his fiction, but he also warns against the over-zealous plundering of the present. He respects the past and understands something of the layers that keep things buried within it. Many of his tales offer stark and terrifying examples of what might happen to an individual who chooses to sweep these layers away. Rolt's tales acknowledge the past, and the literary traditions in which they are rooted, while also embedding themselves firmly in their own contemporary surroundings.

James is widely acknowledged as the master of the ghost story. Rolt respected his works and re-visited them with precise regularity. Typical features of a Jamesian tale include the employment of a familiar setting, a gradual building of tension, malevolent spirits, vehicles of retribution and the careful application of reticence.

The preface to *More Ghost Stories of an Antiquary* (1911) contains initial insight into James' approach, "the setting should be fairly familiar and the majority of the characters and their talk such as you may meet or hear any day."[12] Modern settings are preferred by James so that "the ordinary reader can judge of its naturalness for himself."[13] This technique of allowing the reader to "identify himself with the patient"[14] is one of Rolt's greatest strengths as a story-teller. Throughout his tales, Rolt's rich *mise-en-scène* and attention to detail firmly ensnares the reader in a world that is contemporary and recognizable.

In the introduction to *Ghosts and Marvels* (1924) James stresses the importance of a gradual building of horror, beginning with the reader being "introduced to the actors in a placid way" before allowing "into this calm environment … the ominous thing … unobtrusively at first, and then more insistently, until it holds the stage."[15] The ghost should be "malevolent or odious"[16] and he develops this idea further, a pre-requisite being the notion that a ghost story must actually do its job of "inspiring a pleasing terror in the reader."[17] Rolt employs these same techniques, introducing his characters and locations with deft patience and restraint, gradually building layer upon layer of atmosphere and, ultimately, terror.

Should the premise of a story involve some link to a distant past, James offers techniques for bridging such a gap: "many common objects may be made the vehicles of retribution, and where retribution is not called for, of malice."[18] Rolt calls this technique the "Aladdin's Lamp method,"[19] explaining how James' antiquarians, in their search for greater knowledge, invariably uncover a relic from a bygone age and "pay a high price for their curiosity."[20]

James also stressed how "it is not amiss sometimes to leave a loophole for a natural explanation; but, I would say, let the loophole be so narrow as not to be quite practicable."[21] James understood the power of the imagination to infiltrate the dark places where the story may not tread. It is in these places of uncertainty where true horror lies.

By "Some Remarks on Ghost Stories," James was critically engaged in identifying unworkable traits in modern writings within the genre. He particularly stressed the importance of reticence and the problematic employment of blatancy, "Reticence conduces to effect, blatancy ruins it."[22]

James was not a fan of overly explained stories and reiterates this point with specific criticism of the writings of Ann Radcliffe, celebrating her ghosts but bemoaning how her ghosts are "with exasperating timidity … all explained away."[23]

By the time James wrote his article "Ghosts—Treat Them Gently!" for the *Evening News* in 1931, he had covered most of his key points elsewhere. Still, there was room for some further embellishments: "We need not, we should not," he states, "use all the colours in the box."[24] Interestingly, Rolt felt that James was guilty of employing too few colors. "To change the metaphor," he writes, "the basic ingredients are seldom varied, and all the skill lies in the way they are mixed and seasoned."[25]

In the early part of the 20th century many writers attempted to imitate the style of James, with mixed success. James' quietly observed tales with their perfect concoction of foreboding atmosphere and detailed milieu, their richly observed "odious" spirits and terrifying endings have withstood the test of time while other tales have vanished into history alongside the ghosts that inhabited them. The strongest of Rolt's ghostly tales share many of James' most admirable traits and are similarly endurable.

Rolt not only accepted James' techniques, he also applied a unique approach to the genre to carry the Jamesian ghost story out of the early 1900s and into the mid–20th century. In Rolt's hands the distant and largely inaccessible academic world inhabited by James is transformed into one that is terrifyingly familiar. Rolt's protagonists are miners, foundry workers, signal operatives and country ramblers. These are the places and people Rolt knew and his ability to describe and capture them lends authenticity to his tales. Sometimes his protagonists are the victims of their own curiosity. Rolt's malevolent antagonists meanwhile are disturbed supernatural entities, entombed prisoners or tragic lovers.

To summarize thus far, this essay has identified the following suggestions from James himself about what makes a ghost story work: lack of melodrama and an emphasis on reticence; deliberately malevolent and odious spirits; an easily understood tale; familiar settings; a gentle introduction leading to a nicely managed crescendo; a loophole for a natural explanation; a slight haze of distance; objects as vehicles of retribution; horror.

Rolt not only accepted James's suggested techniques for his storytelling, and often utilized the same, but also applied a unique approach to the genre to modernize the ghost story into the mid–20th century. Rolt's fiction casts the traditional ghost story of the Victorian and Edwardian age into a form that enables, in some small way, the creation of the more familiar horror that contemporary readers recognize today.

The Ghost Stories of M.R. James and L.T.C. Rolt—Some Shared Approaches and Techniques

This section will highlight some examples of how Rolt borrowed and built upon James' approaches and techniques. It will specifically explore Rolt's employment of detailed milieu, landscape, setting and the natural world, work and industry and the technique of proximity, powerlessness and forced voyeurism.

Detailed Milieu

The greatest strength to Rolt's storytelling is his focus on detail. Rolt's meticulous approach echoes the Jamesian technique of embedding a tale in a "familiar setting."[26] His work is firmly grounded in time and place. Strong factual information, or fictional information presented as fact, is combined with imaginative elements to firmly embed the story in the reader's consciousness.

Susan Hill's introduction to Rolt's *Sleep No More* includes the following observation, "The point is in the juxtaposition between this ordinary, apparently 'real' place ... and that which is bizarre, strange, frightening, otherworldly and unaccountable."[27] As Hill explains, Rolt "is best of all in the setting of scenes and the conjuring up of atmosphere. He adds detail slowly and patiently."[28]

In "New Corner" for example, Rolt grounds the story in motor-racing language, "Talk was of blowers and blower pressures, of gear ratios, suspension and braking systems and of twin rear wheels versus single."[29] He captures specific sights and sounds of race-day, "he gave one sharp flick of the wrist and the engine broke into its characteristic deep-throated roar, little puffs of black smoke spurting vertically upward from sixteen short pipes."[30] Rolt's knowledge of the world of motor-racing, the sights, sounds and smells of race day, all add to the story's authenticity. The writer was involved in the formation of the Vintage Sports Car Club in 1934 and a founder of the Prescott Hill Climb on which the story "New Corner" is based.

In "The Garside Fell Disaster" Rolt's authentic first-person narrator, Alf Boothroyd, presents a working-class voice from a family of railwaymen, "Bert our youngest went east to Grantham. He hadn't been there long before he was faring on one of Patrick Stirling's eight-foot singles ... finished up driver on Ivatt's Atlantics while Harry and Fred were working Jumbos and Precursors out of Crewe."[31] Note once again, the detailed employment of railway terminology. It layers the story with authenticity.

Rolt is adept at incorporating working class dialect into his fiction and he does so far more assuredly than James. In "The Mine," the old man narrating the tale uses colloquial expression, dialect and regional variation, "never got much forrader," "seemed to get on their nerves like," "for it be a queer lonely place."[32] The inclusion of "like" at the end of the middle of these three example sentences demonstrates Rolt's appreciation of the subtleties of regional dialect. Rolt knows his working-class characters. He drops authoritative knowledge of their ways, mannerisms and colloquialisms into his stories. They read realistically. The old man in the tale refers to himself as once being a "nipper"; he describes himself also as "proud as Punch"; and the brass on his engine is kept in "Bristol fashion" which "shone like my mother's kettle."[33] He knows his mining terms too. Rolt provides meticulous factual information concerning the technical aspects of mining and the means of moving the coal: "In the old days when my father were a young man there was a horse-tram road—Ginny Rails we call 'em—between the mines and Cliedden Wharf" [...] "Shroppie Cut by Fen Moss."[34] One can imagine being able to locate the location of this story specifically. "You can still see the engine-house plain as can be on top of the hill, while the old chimney be a landmark ten mile away on a clear day,"[35] remarks the old man.

In "Hawley Bank Foundry" Rolt's industrial detail echoes the antiquarian features in James' stories as "builders, bricklayers, painters, glaziers and labourers; steel trusses and joists; corrugated sheeting, bricks, sand, bags of cement, gravel ... scaffolding, planks ... small engines driving hoists and concrete-mixers"[36] are utilized as the foundry is brought back into service.

In "Bosworth Summit Pound" Rolt even makes time for what is clearly a direct nod in the direction of James. Rolt's narrator alludes to antiquaries who "collect" village churches. "When they stand in the nave to admire the remarkable fourteenth-century rood-screen or the delicate tracery of the clerestory windows," the narrator observes, "they do not realize that the waters of the Great Central Canal lie directly beneath their feet."[37] Rolt points unswervingly at industrial heritage and makes the case for its importance and recognition in history. The detailed contextual background in all of his tales, a Jamesian technique, gives them extra weight and authority. When the terror arrives, it makes itself present in a world that the reader has already accepted as genuine and recognizable, thus heightening its effect.

Landscape, Setting and the Natural World

While setting and location add to James's tales, the tales are less reliant upon landscape. James does pay particular attention to landscape in one of his earliest stories, "Lost Hearts" but this is, by and large, an uncharacteristic approach. His stories do take place in recognizable settings and they are always atmospheric, but it is unusual for James to concentrate large sections of his stories on descriptions of the physical landscape, Parkins' walk along the beach at Burnstow in "Oh, Whistle and I'll Come to You" being a further example, the opening description of Seaburgh in "A Warning to the Curious" another.

However, atmospheric descriptions of landscape are crucial components in Rolt's stories. Rich and evocative descriptions enable the reader to inhabit the locations in which Rolt's horror takes place. The locations become real places populated by real folk. They may be fictional stories, but they often read like accounts of factual events. This section focuses on three specific stories that are firmly rooted in geographical authenticity.

In "The Mine" Rolt begins with the specific setting of Wenlock Edge, the Shropshire Marches and Long Mynd, imagining the village of Cliedden. Rolt's setting is intimidating. The November wind is "a boisterous, buffeting wind"; the rain is "hurled" and "rattles like flung gravel" against the window-panes of the pub from which the story's telling will take place; and the limestone escarpment of Wenlock Edge is described as a "mane," conjuring images of wild creatures.[38] The main character of the story, Joe Beecher, becomes increasingly unsettled, "scared of the dark and hush"[39] and aware of the "darkness being angry."[40] The dark is personified. It takes on a physical form, despite its intangibility.

Similar techniques can be seen in the opening of "Bosworth Summit Pound." The initial set-up is classic ghost story territory, the lock-keepers in their "lonely cottages," the "infrequent boatmen," the "narrow, tortuous course" and "little-used" section of canal that is the setting for the story.[41] Rolt employs a haunting and unsettling place name and location in that of "Cold Bosworth," based on the village of Husband's Bosworth in Leicestershire and the Bosworth Tunnel that runs alongside it, though not, as suggested, under it.

On arriving at the entrance to Bosworth Tunnel, Fawcett, the protagonist, finds it "singularly unpleasant," a "narrow cavern of crumbling brickwork as cold and dark as a vault" containing an "evil-smelling mist."[42] Rolt foreshadows the horror that will come later. The reader can feel the dankness of the tunnel and hear the hollow echo of each water droplet as it falls into the canal.

Rolt's "The Garside Fell Disaster" begins with a precise geographical location, albeit an imaginary one, "Garside on the Carlisle line south of Highbeck junction."[43] Local place names are hybrids of almost familiar locations, e.g., Ennerthwaite and Frithdale. The reader is placed in a "real" setting that does not exist and Rolt then stresses its remoteness. "Garside Box takes its name from Garside Fell same as the tunnel. There's no station there, for there isn't a house in sight, let alone a village."[44]

It is the isolated location that gives the story its strength. "I doubt you'd find a more lonesome spot than Garside, or one so mortal cold in winter," informs the protagonist, Boothroyd, "Not a soul for company and all so quiet," he complains.[45] The irony that "Hundreds and hundreds of folks must have passed me by every day, and yet there I was on my own"[46] is not lost on him. He is not only powerless in the wake of what is coming, but also invisible.

As the weather turns and the signal box becomes increasingly lonely the mist takes on a personality. "They're queer things are those mountain mists. Sometimes all day I'd see one hanging on the moor, perhaps only a hundred yards away, but never seeming to come no nearer."[47] Boothroyd is completely and utterly alone in a vast and empty landscape and rendered blind by mountain mist. When the inevitable horror unleashes itself, the protagonist has nowhere to turn but inwards on himself.

Rolt's appreciation of the natural world and his close observance of it, the seamless amalgamation of real and imagined places, give his stories an extra layer of depth.

Rolt's widest diversion from the style of James comes in his stories set amongst the Black Mountains of Wales. In these tales Rolt seems more aligned to Arthur Machen and Algernon Blackwood. Here, Rolt leans towards the poetry of W.B. Yeats and his upbringing on the border of England and Wales where the Black Mountains were an enticing and foreboding backdrop.

Rolt explores his relationship with the natural world and its potential for harboring supernatural evil in his story "Cwm Garon." The longest tale in his collection opens gently enough, employing James' technique of beginning in a placid way. At the beginning of "Cwm Garon" the reader is presented with images of "hills stippled with April cloud shadows, of neat farms buried in the white mist of fruit orchards, and of rich meadows dotted with sheep or the red cattle of Herefordshire."[48] There are "black-gaitered farmers and their plump, basket-laden wives."[49] There is the "lilt of Border speech."[50]

Rolt's protagonist, Carfax, sets off in the direction of the inn at Llangaron Abbey, but as he walks the landscape becomes increasingly disorientating and Carfax finds himself isolated in a "premature dusk."[51] Inclement weather threatens, and the protagonist suffers "a feeling of utter isolation, intensifying the loneliness."[52]

It is as if the landscape has a personality, a dark element which Carfax cannot fully comprehend. Myth and legend become palpable as he contemplates "the creatures which were believed to haunt the mountain mists, and he felt he knew the terror that might come with this loneliness as terror comes with darkness to the child."[53]

Eventually, Carfax locates the ruined abbey and its adjoining inn where he meets a mysterious fellow guest, Professor Elphinstone. Carfax looks out of window at the "dark brooding"[54] mountain. "Here, truly, heaven seemed nearer earth…" he contemplates, to which Elphinstone adds, "And hell, too, maybe…"[55]

The next day, an idyllic pastoral scene of a shepherd and his flock greets his vision. He drops into the adjoining valley, which is friendlier. But returning to Cwm Garon he notices how the "silence seemed to well up from the valley like water from a spring" and the "feeling of loneliness and of strange oppression"[56] returns. He suffers a feeling of "unwelcome intrusion"[57] and hostility. Elphinstone, believes that "some evil force" dominates Cwm Garon, a "dark power."[58]

Carfax wakes just before midnight to witness Elphinstone leaving the building. He spots "lights, moving and dancing along the slopes of the mountain."[59] It is the first of May. When Carfax reaches the crags of Black Daren he finds the body of Elphinstone lying there.

Cwm Garon becomes "repulsive"[60] to Carfax but after several weeks in London he is lured back. On a black and starless night he notices moving lights within the church and "a considerable company of men and women …

naked ... lacquered ... short in stature."[61] Carfax spots "a horned figure seated upon some kind of throne—a man clothed in skins and wearing a horned head-dress."[62] The figures "writhe" and are "obedient to the measure of some inaudible rhythm."[63] The valley yawns like "the mouth of hell."[64] There is "soundless desolation," "darkness blacker than any midnight" and Carfax realizes that "there stalked through the valley something intangible, unearthly, monstrous and very terrible."[65] Carfax flees in the direction of Black Daren but "two squat figures" follow him "lithely," "moving in swift silence over the screes."[66]

Rolt was influenced by the writings of Francis Kilvert, curate at Clyro between 1865 and 1872, a Radnorshire village just across the Wye from Hay. Rolt's family moved to Hay in 1914. The surrounding countryside had a profound effect upon him. As he explains in *Landscape with Machines (1971)*, "its beauty and wildness was capable of inducing in me a strange feeling of intense exaltation ... part awed reverence and part terror."[67] Because Rolt studied the mystical writings of Silurist Henry Vaughan and his contemporary Thomas Traherne and realized "with shock and wonderment"[68] that they had been similarly influenced by the same landscape. Rolt also read works by Machen and recognized that Machen, born at Caerleon, "had experienced (the region's) darker side."[69]

Through Kilvert's diaries Rolt discovered a "single terse and otherwise inexplicable sentence" that he would come to repeat in two stories, "An angel satyr walks these hills."[70] Is this the monstrous and terrible thing that Carfax encounters in "Cwm Garon"? In *Landscape with Machines* Rolt recalls a childhood family outing. The family traversed the flank of Pen y Beacon, where a "breath-taking view unfold(ed)"[71] but then they moved into the Gospel Pass or the Pass of the Evangelists. "I found myself translated into a landscape much smaller in scale but in my eyes far more fascinating because it appeared so lonely, so secret and so strange."[72] This was the Vale of Ewyas and the lost hamlet of Capel-y-ffyn. Rolt explains, "I will only say that if ever it is vouchsafed to man to see visions, then it would be in such a place as this valley whose very air seemed to a child to be numinous and charged with magic."[73]

Rolt learned to love the natural world during his childhood. But he also faced a dilemma when it came to marrying his love of the natural world with his fascination for machinery and engineering. It was during his first journey aboard the canal boat Cressy (on which he was to live and of which he was to write about in his bestselling book *Narrow Boat* [1944]) from Ellesmere to the Trent and Mersey canal, that the "consuming interest in engineering and my feeling for the natural world ... had begun disturbingly to conflict with each other ... suddenly reconciled."[74] Rolt describes the scene with the same care and attention to visual detail and landscape as he does in his fiction,

The long level pound of canal that we first traversed passes through a country strangely remote and of a mysterious beauty ... across Whixall Moss, a great expanse of peat bog ... morning dawned dry but cold and still with an overcast sky of a uniform pearly grey ... black interlacement of bare branches silhouetted against this colourless sky, of a thin white mist lying waist high over the dark waters ... silent landscape of a dream and through it Cressy glided smoothly and quietly ... she did not intrude upon the landscape; she became part of it like the canal itself.[75]

Rolt was learning that "however beautiful a landscape may be aesthetically, without the sustenance of continuing life it becomes starved, dead and forlor."[76] He would explore this amalgamation of the natural world and the world of men and machinery in his stories.

Work and Industry

The story that best illustrates Rolt's relationship with the world of men and machinery, and therefore his contribution to a new type of industrial ghost story, is "Hawley Bank Foundry." Hawley Bank Ironworks was once a pioneering and "prosperous" business with a "good reputation for sound work" albeit one "old-fashioned in its methods."[77] In the story, the introduction of a stranger, or outsider, to this settled environment, Druce, and his relationship with the old "traditional country squire"[78] type owner, Josiah Darley who later disappears in mysterious circumstances, leads to Druce inheriting the old man's wealth. Under Druce, "time-honoured methods and routines" of working are "swept away."[79] This leads to the gradual decline of the iron-works, the antagonizing of a once happy workforce, extraordinary minor misfortunes, and a fatal accident that kills three men, until Druce himself is found hanging in the same shop.

Rolt loved the skilled craftsman he worked with in the years after he left school, particularly his time at Pitchill on the fringe of the Vale of Evesham, and he recognized too, the hurt and damage when works were closed, experiencing such an event himself when the Kerr Stuart Works in Stoke were shut down in 1930. This, in marked contrast to the voluntary visits Rolt used to make to the works simply to observe them in action, "I found this fierce and violent drama of the steelworks at night so hypnotically fascinating that I visited it repeatedly ... it excited me, yet at the same time it filled me with a strange sense of apocalyptic foreboding."[80]

Rolt utilizes that sense of foreboding to dramatic effect in "Hawley Bank Foundry," setting the story in the Ironbridge gorge which he often visited on summer evenings during the war, wandering amongst the crumbling ruins of the old works. "The whole area seemed to me to be haunted,"[81] he writes. And in the story, it is.

The first sign of something odd at Hawley Bank is the feeling of being watched. The scene mirrors James' "A Warning to the Curious" where Paxton first discovers the location of the crown of East Anglia and threatens to disturb its rest. "It began when I was first prospecting," tells Paxton, "There was always somebody—a man—standing by one of the firs.... I always saw him with the tail of my eye on the left or the right, and he was never there when I looked straight for him."[82]

Arthur Clegg is alarmed enough by a series of strange events leading him to visit the foundry at night where he experiences a "sensation of discreet but purposeful surveillance."[83] He feels a "clammy, tentative touch upon his face ... something of indeterminate shape and of dirty white colour disappearing into the sand" convincing him that "some power of malevolent and hostile purpose was fast gathering strength in the ironworks, pressing close about the place like the encircling woods."[84]

One local, old Charlie Penrice, maintains that both the ghosts of Druce and Durley haunt the foundry, "Druce with a bit of rope round his neck, and old Josh hopping after him like a spider."[85]

Further tragedy awaits Hawley Bank. As the molten metal is poured into the molding-floor a "deadly hail" shoots high into the air, catching the "wretched skimmer" who stumbles "screaming like a woman, his clothes reduced to smoking rags"[86] towards the door. One of the pourers trips and his fate is sealed. There is the "sickly smell of burnt flesh" and in the "translucent" metal the remaining men see a corpse "burned beyond hope of recognition" and also "in the last stages of decomposition."[87]

In the final paragraph of "Hawley Bank Foundry," nature reclaims the site once more. The ghosts fall silent. The lost benevolence and respect for craftsmanship and the workforce of the original Darley's who were "proud and jealous of the family tradition" with its "respected but old fashioned ... methods"[88] may never be replaced.

Rolt's characters, Will Hughes suggests, are "a modern, artisan equivalent of the travelling antiquarians and academics favoured by M.R. James."[89] "Not surprisingly," argues Hughes, "British culture in the immediately post-war period wavered between nostalgia for a stable, comfortable past and the fearful perception of an uncertain future."[90] Rolt's stories befit the post-war period in the same fashion that James' stories were apt for the new century.

Proximity, Powerlessness and Forced Voyeurism

In some of their tales, both Rolt and James share the technique of delivering horror from a distance, that is, to describe horrific scenes to the reader from a place by which the horror itself cannot be affected by those who witness it. The most effective example of this technique occurs in James' "Wailing

Well." A morality tale written by James for an audience of cub scouts somehow takes the form of a voyeuristic horror show. From a distance, the cub scout Wilfred Pipsqueak witnesses "something in ragged black—with whitish patches breaking out of it … waving thin arms"[91] and then sees one of his fellow scouts, Stanley Judkins approaching it. "Hideous black figures"[92] rise out of the bushes and crawl towards Judkins. There is something hungry about the creatures. The male moves "painfully."[93] The female waves her arms in "exultation" then quickens her pace while "nodding gleefully."[94] The three of them drag Judkins into the trees and there is nothing Pipsqueak can do about it.

Sometimes, the crucial moments of a story take place "off stage" altogether. In Rolt's "The Mine" Joe Beecher is chased out of the lift and is last seen "running for dear life over the waste mound and along the hill-side"[95] in an attempt to flee a pursuer none of the witnesses can see. Later one of the men claims to have witnessed something making after Joe "as quick and quiet as a cat after a sparrow. This thing made never a sound though it went fast enough and was catching up on him, so that when he got to the edge of the wood it looked as if it was reaching out for him with its arms."[96]

Rolt employs a similar technique in his story "New Corner." Once the drivers pull on their goggles and gloves, they are alone. Rolt detaches the reader from any visual representation of the scene, focusing on sound instead. As the drivers disappear up the hill there is only the sound of the engine negotiating the track. As each car ascends the hill in the direction of the new corner, the reader is left to listen alongside Nelson, the nervous course director, for the telltale signs of a good run or the horrific silence that signals an accident.

When the German driver Von Eberstraum begins his run that will ultimately see him meet his fate on New Corner, all Nelson can do is wait for the sound of the time-keeper's message on his headphones signaling Von Eberstraum's finish time. When no message comes, Nelson, already suffering from a sleepless, nightmare filled evening, is filled with anxiety. His nightmare becomes reality and the new corner is to blame.

In "The Garside Fell Disaster," the protagonist, Boothroyd doesn't even witness the rail accident at the story's culmination. He only witnesses the aftermath from afar when he sees "the tunnel shafts … flaming away like ruddy beacons."[97] Later, he learns of the details of the disaster from his work mate Perce Shaw who he finds with his hair all singed, his face as white as a wall. "My God!" says Perce, "You can't do nothing" and he repeats this "over and over again."[98]

The technique of situating the narrator or protagonist a distance from the action forces them, and the reader, to become a powerless voyeur. With no means to affect the outcome of the horror taking place, the effect of the horror is magnified. The protagonist is helpless, a mere spectator to somebody else's misfortune. And so is the reader.

L.T.C. Rolt—A Final Word

Rolt only wrote one collection. He is remembered for his nonfiction, for his founding of the Inland Waterways Association and the Talynn Railway Preservation Society. A canal bridge on the Oxford canal bears his name, as does a blue plaque at Tooley's boatyard in Banbury. While his ghost stories have occasionally been anthologized, it is only recently that his slim collection has begun to garner recognition.

This essay argues that Rolt's *Sleep No More* marks an important intersection in the development of the ghost story. Rolt learned from studying the genre, just as James did before him. The essay demonstrates how Rolt's work is ingrained with some of James' most recognizable and effective techniques but also how Rolt developed his own slant on the ghost story, replacing James' cloistered and academic milieu with a more working-class theme, and encompassing his appreciation and awe of the natural world into his tales. Kai Roberts suggests that Rolt "possessed an authentic vision."[99] Mark Andersen points out that Rolt's tales are "more than borderline derivative,"[100] while Christopher Roden highlights his "individual style," "sense of realism" and the "freshness of actuality to his writings about rural and industrial Britain."[101]

Rolt's short stories deserve to be recognized for contributing to the transition of the ghost story from its traditional Gothic roots into the working-class, urban and industrial environments that are familiar in the genre today.

NOTES

1. L.T.C. Rolt, *Landscape Trilogy: The Autobiography of L.T.C. Rolt* (Gloucestershire, UK: History Press, 2005), 124.
2. L.T.C. Rolt, "The Passing of the Ghost Story," in *Sleep No More* (Ashcroft, Canada: Ash-Tree Press, 2012) Kindle edition, paragraph 3.
3. *Ibid.*
4. Jack Sullivan, "Golden Age of the Ghost Story," in *The Penguin Encyclopedia of Horror and the Supernatural* (New York: Viking Press, 1986), 174–6.
5. Julia Briggs, "The Ghost Story," in *A New Companion to the Gothic*, ed. David Punter (Chichester, UK: John Wiley & Sons), 177.
6. Susan Owens, *The Ghost–A Cultural History* (London: Tate Publishing, 2017), 189.
7. *Ibid.*
8. *Ibid.*
9. Rolt, "The Passing of the Ghost Story," paragraph 18.
10. Owens, *The Ghost–A Cultural History*, 220.
11. *Ibid.*, 221.
12. M.R. James, *Collected Ghost Stories*, ed. Darryl Jones (Oxford, UK: Oxford University Press, 2013), 406.
13. *Ibid.*, 408.
14. *Ibid.*

15. *Ibid.*, 407.
16. *Ibid.*, 406.
17. *Ibid.*, 411.
18. *Ibid.*, 410.
19. Rolt, "The Passing of the Ghost Story," paragraph 11.
20. *Ibid.*
21. James, *Collected Ghost Stories,* 407.
22. *Ibid.*, 414.
23. *Ibid.*, 411.
24. *Ibid.*, 417.
25. Rolt, "The Passing of the Ghost Story," paragraph 13.
26. James, *Collected Ghost Stories,* 406.
27. L.T.C. Rolt, *Sleep No More* (Gloucestershire, UK: History Press, 2010), ix.
28. *Ibid.*, x.
29. *Ibid.*, 27.
30. *Ibid.*, 31.
31. *Ibid.*, 59.
32. *Ibid.*, 1.
33. *Ibid.*, 2.
34. *Ibid.*, 1.
35. *Ibid.*, 3.
36. *Ibid.*, 90.
37. *Ibid.*, 15.
38. *Ibid.*, 1.
39. *Ibid.*, 2.
40. *Ibid.*, 3.
41. *Ibid.*, 15.
42. *Ibid.*, 17.
43. *Ibid.*, 59.
44. *Ibid.*
45. *Ibid.*, 60.
46. *Ibid.*
47. *Ibid.*, 61.
48. *Ibid.*, 33.
49. *Ibid.*
50. *Ibid.*
51. *Ibid.*, 35.
52. *Ibid.*
53. *Ibid.*
54. *Ibid.*, 38.
55. *Ibid.*
56. *Ibid.*, 41.
57. *Ibid.*, 42.
58. *Ibid.*, 44.
59. *Ibid.*, 45.
60. *Ibid.*, 47.
61. *Ibid.*, 48.
62. *Ibid.*, 48.
63. *Ibid.*
64. *Ibid.*
65. *Ibid.*
66. *Ibid.*, 49.
67. Rolt, *Landscape Trilogy: The Autobiography of L.T.C. Rolt,* 11.
68. *Ibid.*
69. *Ibid.*, 12.
70. *Ibid.*

71. *Ibid.*, 20.
72. *Ibid.*
73. *Ibid.*, 21.
74. *Ibid.*, 113.
75. *Ibid.*
76. *Ibid.*, 155.
77. Rolt, *Sleep No More*, 85.
78. *Ibid.*
79. *Ibid.*, 86.
80. Rolt, *Landscape Trilogy: The Autobiography of L.T.C. Rolt*, 88.
81. *Ibid.*, 43.
82. James, *Collected Ghost Stories*, 350.
83. Rolt, *Sleep No More*, 93.
84. *Ibid.*, 94.
85. *Ibid.*, 95.
86. *Ibid.*, 98.
87. *Ibid.*
88. *Ibid.*, 85.
89. Will Hughes, "'A God-forsaken hole': War Work, Labour Migration, and the Industrial Gothic of L.T.C. Rolt," paper presented at the Gothic Migrations: The 12th Biennial Conference of the International Gothic Association, Vancouver, Canada, July 28–August 1, 2015.
90. *Ibid.*
91. James, *Collected Ghost Stories*, 388.
92. *Ibid.*, 389.
93. *Ibid.*
94. *Ibid.*
95. Rolt, *Sleep No More*, 4.
96. *Ibid.*, 5.
97. *Ibid.*, 64.
98. *Ibid.*
99. Kai Roberts, "An Appreciation of the Weird Fiction of L.T.C. Rolt," last accessed February 23, 2019, https://kairoberts.wordpress.com/2010/01/13/the-weird-fiction-of-l-t-c-rolt-an-appreciation/.
100. Mark Andersen, "Sleep No More: Railway, Canal & Other Stories of the Supernatural by L.T.C. Rolt, the History Press," last modified April 23, 2011,http://panreview.blogspot.co.uk/2011/04/sleep-no-more-railway-canal-other.html.
101. Christopher Roden, Introduction to *Sleep No More* by L.T.C. Rolt (Ashcroft, Canada: Ash-Tree Press, 2012) Kindle edition, paragraph 2.

BIBLIOGRAPHY

Andersen, Mark. "Sleep No More: Railway, Canal & Other Stories of the Supernatural by L.T.C. Rolt, the History Press." Last modified April 23, 2011, http://panreview.blogspot.co.uk/2011/04/sleep-no-more-railway-canal-other.html.
Blackwood, Algernon. *Pan's Garden*. Eureka, CA: Stark House Press, 2007.
Briggs, Julia. "The Ghost Story." In *A New Companion to the Gothic*, edited by David Punter. Chichester, UK: John Wiley & Sons, 2012.
Hughes, Will. "'A God-forsaken Hole': War Work, Labour Migration, and the Industrial Gothic of L.T.C. Rolt." Paper presented at the Gothic Migrations: The 12th Biennial Conference of the International Gothic Association, Vancouver, Canada, July 28–August 1, 2015.
James, M.R. *Collected Ghost Stories*. Edited by Darryl Jones. Oxford, UK: Oxford University Press, 2013.
_____. *Morning Post*, October 9, 1923.

Machen, Arthur. *The White People and Other Weird Stories*. London, UK: Penguin Modern Classics, 2012.

Owens, Susan. *The Ghost—A Cultural History*. London, UK: Tate Publishing, 2017.

Roberts, Kai. "An Appreciation of the Weird Fiction of L.T.C. Rolt." Last accessed February 23, 2019, https://kairoberts.wordpress.com/2010/01/13/the-weird-fiction-of-l-t-c-rolt-an-appreciation/.

Roden, Christopher. Introduction *to Sleep No More* by L.T.C. Rolt. Ashcroft, Canada: Ash-Tree Press, 2012. Kindle Edition.

Rolt, L.T.C. *Landscape Trilogy: The Autobiography of L.T.C. Rolt*. Gloucestershire, UK: History Press, 2005.

_____. *Narrow Boat*. Gloucestershire, UK: History Press, 2014.

_____. "The Passing of the Ghost Story," in *Sleep No More*. Ashcroft, Canada: Ash-Tree Press, 2012. Kindle Edition.

_____. *Sleep No More*. Gloucestershire, UK: History Press, 2010.

Sullivan, Jack. *Elegant Nightmares: The English Ghost Story from Le Fanu to Blackwood*. Athens: Ohio University Press, 1980.

_____. "Golden Age of the Ghost Story," in *The Penguin Encyclopedia of Horror and the Supernatural*. New York: Viking Press, 1986.

Richard Laymon's Rhetorical Style

Minimalism, Suspense and Negative Space

GAVIN F. HURLEY

American writer Richard Laymon's horror fiction has been a mainstay in the horror community. Horror writers and readers applaud his 40-plus novels published between the late 1970s and 2001. For example, *Science Fiction Chronicle* named *Flesh* (1987) the "Best Horror Novel of the Year" in 1988; *Flesh* and *Funland* (1989) were nominated for a Bram Stoker Award in 1989 and 1991[1]; and he won the Bram Stoker award for *The Traveling Vampire Show* in 2001. Laymon's influence on horror writing resulted in the creation of the Richard Laymon President's Award given out during the Horror Writers Association's annual StokerCon and presented to a volunteer who serves the HWA with above-and-beyond commitment.[2]

Despite his legacy, Richard Laymon is not a household name. He is not as familiar as Stephen King, Dean Koontz, or Anne Rice. Rather, he has established a strong cult following of dedicated fans. Laymon is fairly well-known in the United Kingdom; however, in America he did not receive a warm reception after American agents and publishers mismanaged his book *The Woods Are Dark* (1981) early in his career.[3] After recovering his writing career and gaining momentum in the United Kingdom in the late 1980s, Laymon was able to embrace his vocation as a fulltime writer and received respectable book contracts.[4]

His signature seductive writing style was a natural element in his success. Laymon's books offer unique expressions of horror fiction. Much of this uniqueness can be traced to *what* he writes about, but also *how* he writes it. Laymon's style is fresh, crisp, and suspenseful, but also sincere, honest, and conversational. His characters often find themselves in outlandish situations:

sometimes violent, sometimes sexual. Despite the potential awkwardness for readers, Laymon manages to keep the fiction readable. His prose is remarkably rhetorical as it escorts readers through potentially uncomfortable material while commanding their attention.

This essay traces two dimensions of Laymon's signature writing style—minimalism and negative space—and their cooperative overlapping rhetorical functions. Laymon's style will be broadly analyzed through the "at"/"through" lens: a distinction forwarded by rhetorician Richard Lanham. First, Laymon's style will be analyzed "at": that is, how he crafts a uniquely, persuasive and readable experience by means of rhetorical style itself. Second, Laymon's style will be analyzed "through": that is, how his rhetoric works as a vehicle of content toward his unique brand of horror fiction. Finally, the essay will conclude by spotlighting some playful postmodern mechanisms of Laymon's work and the complimentary roles that minimalism and negative space serve, both "at" and "through," toward an effective rhetoric of horror experience: one that can be celebrated by both readers and writers of horror fiction.

Laymon's Minimalism

To put it plainly, rhetorical style "clothes" the communicative message. Style is often advantageously threaded, to help audiences connect with the text, adhere to the message, and be persuaded to continue to engage with a text. Style is deliberate. According to rhetorician Paul Butler style involves "the deployment of rhetorical resources, in written discourse, to create and express meaning ... [that] involves the use of written language features as habitual patterns, rhetorical options, and conscious choices at the sentence and word level."[5] Therefore, to study style is to study linguistic forms, patterns, and structures, how they help the text function, and how they cooperate with a text's purpose.[6]

According to contemporary rhetorician Lanham, style can be examined "at" or "through." Reading "at" the style concerns its stylistic surface and rhetorical strategy; reading "through" the style looks toward the truths that the style communicates.[7] In other words, to read "at" the style is to recognize the textual page as a world in itself; to read "through" the style is to look toward how the reality is being represented.[8] In the case of fiction, reading "through" a text looks toward fictional content as its reality. The operations of the textual surface can result in a bi-stable cooperation between the two dimensions,[9] one that can coalesce within postmodern dimensions of the fiction.

To more fully understand the postmodern elements of Laymon's style, his minimalism should first be explained, specifically using ancient rhetorical underpinnings. Early philosophers and rhetoricians, especially Aristotle, praised clarity as a chief virtue of style.[10] This stylistic emphasis was defined as "plain style." According to Cicero, the ancient Roman rhetorician, plain style was commonly meant to instruct.[11] Plain style can be defined as easily digestible, conversational prose; although in the 21st century, such clear, plain style can be associated with technical and science writing as well. In short, plain style looks to communicate clearly and unobtrusively without relying on artistic ornamentation. Accordingly, plain style contrasts "grand style" or eloquent style. Grand style, with various rhetorical devices such as embellishment, metaphor, allegory, and irony, is primarily used to move an audience into action. Consequently, contexts of grand style often greatly contrast plain style. A grander style is frequently practiced in motivational speaking or powerful political speeches. Grand style is commonly more effective in shaping belief, igniting emotions, or motivating audiences, and can craft memorable communication experiences.

Laymon writes fiction, not technical writing or persuasive speeches. However, the spectrum between plain and grand styles can still apply in the arena of fiction. First, Laymon's clear writing avoids the trappings of overly grand style. In other words, he avoids emulating more literary horror writing traditions such as European Gothic horror of the 19th century that depend on long sentences and lengthy descriptions. Instead, Laymon opts for minimalistic style: short sentences, short paragraphs, hard stops with periods, and prominent use of conjunctions. As a result, Laymon's style resembles the minimalistic style of American author Ernest Hemingway as well as later American authors who are influenced by Hemingway such as Bret Easton Ellis or Denis Johnson. Laymon was surely influenced by Hemingway. In Laymon's autobiographical guidebook to writing, *A Writer's Tale* (1998), he offers a list of his favorite books, non-horror writers, and favorite short stories/novellas. In these lists, Laymon names Hemingway as one of his favorite authors[12]; he names *For Whom the Bell Tolls* (1940), *Old Man and the Sea* (1951), and *A Moveable Feast* (1964) as three of his favorite books[13]; and he names four of Hemingway's works on his top twenty-eight "favorite short stories/novellas" list.[14] Additionally, to inspire readers before the cover page of *A Writer's Tale*, Laymon supplies a brief paragraph written by Hemingway about the craft of writing.[15]

Hemingway's influence clearly pervades Laymon's style. Like Hemingway, Laymon uses minimalism in an artistic, albeit rhetorical, manner. Minimalism does not have to completely align with technical prose or conversational plain style. When purposed toward persuasive operations, minimalistic writing can be rhetorically and literarily powerful. It can offer a mitigated balance: clearly prosaic and basic, but also stylized like verse. Laymon implements this mitigated technique. Using minimalism, Laymon moderates his style toward persuasive ends: a goal that ancient rhetoricians, such as Aristotle and Quintilian, praise as an effective means to "delight" audiences.[16] As endorsed by Aristotle and Quintilian,[17] Laymon does not overwhelm his audience with eloquence, but rather, through minimalism, he tempers his ornamentation and embellishment. Appropriately, Laymon establishes a stylistic middle ground by using minimalism in a rhetorical capacity. Rather than threading ornate lengthy phrases, he uses fewer words and more common words. Rather than constructing large blocks of text, he spaces the text across and down the page. Overall, Laymon's writing offers a "mixed style": plain language that is stylized by rich cadence. As a result, the writing is clear, fluid, and seductive. For example, from Laymon's 1997 book *After Midnight*:

> At the top of the driveway, I turned left. There was no traffic in sight, so I kept the headlights off and drove along the two-lane country road by moonlight. With the windows wide open, the night air rushed in. It felt wonderful, blowing against me. And it smelled so fine, too. Sweet and moist and woodsy.
>
> I almost turned on the radio. It would've been great to be tooling along in the darkness with a summertime song in my ears. But I was on a stealth mission. I kept the radio off, so the only sounds came from the car's engine and the hiss of its tires on the pavement and the wind rushing by.
>
> It was lovely, even without a song.
>
> It made me want to go out every night—but not with a dismembered body in the trunk.[18]

In this passage, Laymon uses plain vocabulary and shorter words. He stylizes the plain style with sensory descriptions and vivid poetic phrasings such as "summertime song" and "hiss of its tires." Moreover, the variety of sentence lengths, placement of punctuation, use of conjunctions, and short paragraph units all contribute to its poetic rhythm. These traits allow the plain style to be artistically and rhetorically purposed. It entices a reader to engage, and to continue to engage, with the text. Conversely, Laymon's style avoids being overly flowery or grand. Rather, Laymon strikes an effective middle ground between plain and grand styles that is comfortably moderate. Overall, such a rhetorically purposed minimalism begins to explain how Laymon's writing style is so effective at hooking readers and persuading readers to continue to read his fiction.

Negative Space and Horror Fiction

Negative space offers another crucial rhetorical element of Laymon's style, one that is bound to the minimalistic approach. Specifically, Laymon's minimalism, more than Hemingway's minimalism, utilizes negative space (that is, "white space," "blank space," or "absence") to orchestrate a rhetorical read and an affect-charged experience. In short, negative space offers wordless vacancies in between paragraphs via indentations and in between the sentences via punctuation. Rhetorical use of negative space is the audience-driven utilization of such vacancies. By means of shorter sentences and more frequent paragraph breaks, minimalistic style provides more white space on the page. As a result, minimalistic writing includes more frequent and longer pauses in the reading experience. When reading short sentences and paragraphs, the reader must stop and start more often. Moreover, the reader must more frequently scan over blank space on the page. This experience allows more chances for a reader to "breathe." Therefore, when combined with conversational vocabulary and accessible content, Laymon's style offers an inclusive reading experience. Laymon's style can easily appeal to a range of reading levels and literature experiences. A wide range of audiences has a chance to fully engage with Laymon's writing.

How do readers read "through" the negative space toward the horror fiction itself? These operations can be seen as working dialectically. Negative space (or lack of action) contrasts the positive space (or busy action) as a means to establish a synthesis or a balanced aesthetic experience. Negative space and positive space emphasize one another. The dialectic between negative space and positive space becomes specifically useful when crafting affective, suspenseful horror.

John Carpenter's classic 1978 film *Halloween* can illustrate such dialectic. Carpenter admits that it is a movie that ultimately has nothing going on.[19] The downtime in the film is substantial compared to the amount of action in the film. For example, about 70 minutes into the film, Laurie Strode (Jamie Lee Curtis) walks from one house to another across the street in real time. Producer Debra Hill calls the slow scene the "longest walk in Hollywood" since it takes over two minutes of the film.[20] This scene provides a cinematic example of how negative space can highlight the positive space. After the walk, Laurie finds the dead bodies of her friends and then she is pursued by Michael Myers (Nick Castle). The lengthy period of no action along with the repetitive rhythm of the minimalistic score allows the scene to "build up the maximum dread" according to Carpenter.[21] Much of that anxious affect depends upon the suspension between the negative non-action and the final actions themselves.

Unlike film directors, Laymon cannot lead audiences through stretches of time on a screen; instead, he leads readers through reading experiences whereby time unfolds on the page. Negative space becomes instrumental in orchestrating such experience. Negative space between sentences and space between the paragraphs elongate the reading experience. Seconds tick by as readers read through and over the negative space on the page. Blank space pushes the action further down the page, suspending the anticipation to "build up the maximum dread." Such anticipation, when combined with suspenseful plot points, can rhetorically hook and maintain readers within the fictional world. Laymon is so effective at combining minimalism and negative space that he can electrify even the most minor scenes with anticipation and suspense. An example can be found in *The Traveling Vampire Show* where several children sneak a bite to eat from the kitchen:

> We turned away from the refrigerator, I eased the door shut, and we headed across the kitchen. Rusty took a cheese slicer out of a drawer. At a clear place on the counter, he set down the Velveeta and peeled back its shiny silver wrapper. With the taut wire of the slicer, he cut off an inch-thick slab.
> He handed it back to me. As I sank my teeth into it, he started to cut off another slab.
> One of the doors behind us *swooshed* open.
> We both jumped.
> Through the swinging door stepped Bitsy.
> The actual name of Rusty's fourteen-year old sister was Elizabeth. Her nickname used to be Bitsy. [...][22]

In this relatively trivial scene, Laymon suspends minor actions, and in doing so, incorporates suspense and a jump-scare into the read. He paces out the scene by including precise details about the characters' basic actions, but he conveys these details in short sentences and one-sentence paragraphs. The content itself is not particularly suspenseful; rather, the way it is written makes it suspenseful. The stop-and-start reading experience along with the blank space on the page builds anticipation that can excite readers.

Minimalism, Negative Space and Postmodernity

Unlike literary postmodernist dark fiction such as Ellis' *American Psycho* (1991) or Mark Danielewski's *House of Leaves* (2000), Laymon does not write novels that play with simulations, fluidities, multi-genre formats, or the avant-garde. Therefore, Laymon's books may not be officially categorized as "postmodernist fiction." However, Laymon's novels exhibit some postmodernist properties. Specifically, the minimalism and negative space work with the content of Laymon novels to highlight some of the postmodern playfulness at work in his horror fiction.

The postmodern use of negative space can differ from the aforementioned dialectical use of negative space. Unlike dialectical use of negative space, postmodern use of silence, absence, and negativity does not necessarily illustrate positivity; rather it can serve a deconstructing aim, subverting the dominant ontology found in traditional fictional texts. Overlapping (not replacing) the dialectical functioning, this subversion subtly implemented through the style of Laymon's writing can signal an effective playfulness that is not evident in more rigid, customary horror fiction.

Subversion of Traditional Text

As already alluded to the aforementioned *Halloween* analogy, Laymon's negative space combined with the minimalistic language can resemble cinematic techniques that build suspense. Yet despite *The Stake* (1990) being optioned at least three times whereby several "Hollywood types" wrote screen adaptations of it,[23] only one novel was ever adapted for the screen: *In the Dark* (1994), a low-budget, independent release via the now defunct Gemineye Productions.[24] Notwithstanding the lack of film versions of his novels, readers of Laymon's fiction sometimes compare the reading experience to watching a "B horror movie."[25] These evaluations offer a generative comparison. After all, a Laymon novel is just that: a novel. However, readers of Laymon's work observe, whether consciously or unconsciously, that his fiction reads like film. Although Laymon's pulp-horror content helps formulate to these readers' impressions, Laymon's writing style contributes to this broader impression that Laymon's texts resemble cinema. Upon a closer look, Laymon's fiction writing resembles screenplay writing by which readers experience dialogue, setting, and plot points as if it were film. Minimalism and negative space are key characteristics of screenwriting as both elements of style lend themselves to quick pacing of action. Similarly, much like scripts, Laymon's characters' internal/external dialogue drives the movement of the plot. Moreover, his descriptions of setting and objects are crisp. Much like stage directions, his descriptions of action are also sharp. For example, from *Night in the Lonesome October* (2001):

> The kitchen had a door to the back yard, so we used it. After the darkness inside the house, the night seemed very bright. We stood on the elevated deck just outside the door and looked all around.
> No sign of the man who had chased us.
> No sign of anyone else, either.
> We descended a few stairs into the yard, then went around the side of the house.
> At the front corner, we stopped in the shadows and stood motionless for a long time.
> No one was in sight.
> "I guess the coast is clear," I said.
> "Looks that way."[26]

As already suggested, such streamlined prose can beneficially provide an inclusive and quick-moving reading experience. However, through the lens of postmodernity, screenplay-like novels offer readers cinematic experiences that disrupt representations of reality within the written text. In other words, reading a text that reads like script more fully distances the text from the real. According to postmodern theorist Brian McHale, strategies of incorporating film techniques and references into fiction destabilizes the novel as a representation of reality because the novel represents a movie that represents reality.[27] The "real" becomes the "reel" which is housed within a novel. Ultimately, these levels of separation from reality allow the novel to move more closely toward its own ontology.

Negative space itself also destabilizes the traditional material text itself; again, such an approach orients the fiction toward its own ontological world more distant from the real. According to McHale, traditional large blocks of texts with expected occasional indentations offer a sign of prose, whereas short paragraphs that liberally use blank spacing offer a sign of "verse."[28] Its unmarked fluidity allows the fictional world to interrupt traditional conventions of prose fiction as well as the typical scaffolding of novels in general.[29] Additionally, blank space can lead to a more fluid read that may resemble the ease of a passive cinematic experience rather than require the active labor of a textual reading experience.

As another perspective, postmodern theorists also suggest that the blank space on the page can foreground the presence and materiality of the book itself. It can allow the material book to "show through the fiction."[30] The explicit materiality complicates traditional ontological demarcations, and consequently, destabilizes conventional metaphysics. The negative textual space subverts the traditional literary reading experience by introducing "ontological hesitation" or schizophrenic fluctuation between the fictional world the real world object itself.[31]

Anxiety and Emptiness

The postmodern traits of the Laymon's style can rhetorically cooperate with the content of his fiction. Laymon coaxes readers to continue reading because his meandering characters ultimately explore the unknown. Laymon's characters are relatable: ordinarily unremarkable, but likable. They are commonly young people, often ranging from twenty to thirty years old, with everyday problems: relationship issues, searching for a mate, craving intimacy, and generally yearning for a meaningful existence. Interestingly, his characters are not specifically driven by any pervading ideology or constitution. Apart from a handful of novels (such as *Cuts* [1999] and *Come Out Tonight* [1999]), Laymon's main characters are not particularly nihilistic or criminally motivated. Many of the characters maintain a code of morals, but they do not overtly adhere to romantically or financially stable lives. Specifically, his characters are often childless, not married, and working at part-time jobs;

moreover, characters do not generally have family or religious commitments. In short, these liberated individuals navigate their worlds through the constant act of decision-making that remains generally untainted by characters' jobs, families, or institutional ideologies. In his fiction, Laymon meticulously illustrates these characters' decisions: large and small. Such choices do not always operate on a macro-level; they can be micro-level choices that trigger a chain of events toward large-scale consequences. Regardless of the size of the decisions, all choices can carry anxiety with them. The conscious hesitation and rational self-deliberation found in characters' decision-making processes can lead to anxious tensions that are absorbed by readers. Therefore, an author who chooses to closely emphasize characters' decision-making processes, as Laymon does, heightens the anxiety that pervades the fiction as a whole. Laymon uses choice-fueled subjective anxiety to spark the primary effect of his suspenseful horror.

Laymon's novel *Body Rides* (1996) provides an example of the evocation of anxiety through his main character's decisions. On the first page of *Body Rides*, readers are introduced to Neal via internal dialogue as he is driving through Los Angeles toward a video rental store at night. It is a decision that he turns over again and again in his mind. Neal knows that driving in L.A. is a dangerous option but Laymon traces the character's initial self-deliberation. By revealing Neal's thoughts, readers begin to understand how he justifies his actions. In Laymon's words:

> He was only twenty-eight years old, too young to become a hermit. For safety's sake, he might make a few concessions—but he wouldn't surrender and stay home for the rest of his life.
> You take precautions and you go anyway.
> Even if it's just to return the video rentals.[32]

This passage innocently describes Neal's decision-making process, one that is particularly filled with anxiety because he may be plunging himself into unnecessary danger by driving around Los Angles at night. A page later, Neal explains another underlying reason for risking his life for videotapes: he would lose respect from his girlfriend if he waited until morning to visit the video rental store.[33] This reason offers additional motivation but also anxiety. After evaluating his options, Neal finally chooses to pursue the late night drive to the store. Later describing the seedy section of Los Angeles through a third-person omniscient point of view, readers are then presented with Neal's routine driving decision on his way to the store. Each sentence is split into an individual paragraph:

> His car bumped over the train tracks.
> Time for another decision.
> Make a left onto the back road or go straight ahead to Venice Boulevard?[34]

This short passage is deceptively simple. When combined with the previous seemingly mundane decisions made by Neal, Laymon builds anxiety and suspense. This method is a signature strategy that Laymon implements throughout many of his novels. He paces out everyday micro-level decisions over the course of the novel that eventual build toward more substantial, macro-level life-or-death decisions. In the first pages of *Body Rides*, readers understand Neal as a man torn by everyday decisions: leaving the house at night, videotape rental, and which roads to drive on. Laymon builds suspense into these everyday decisions by weaving levels of anxiety into the story. The rhetorical style of characters' self-deliberation, that is, simple language, short sentences, and single sentence/single sentence fragment paragraphs, reflects that anxiety.

However, readers soon discover that Neal's micro-level decisions (and Laymon's style) add up to more macro-level, terrifying decisions. While driving in L.A., Neal hears a shrieking woman who is in danger. Neal has to decide whether to act on this information and how to investigate the source of the screams. His decision escalates from there. Eventually, Neal finds the woman, Elise, tied to a tree being tortured by a man with pliers. Then, Neal has to decide whether he should try to save her. Laymon, using his signature minimalism and short sentences, packs this escalating decision-making all within the first short chapter of *Body Rides*.

The first pages of *Body Rides* exemplify a typical Laymon novel's sequencing: characters' mundane choices at the beginning of the novel snowball into a multifaceted odyssey of anxious suspense. Laymon's style, the minimalism and negative space, cooperates with his characters' hesitation to act. The space on the page and the space between paragraphs simulates this anticipation between attitudes, ideas, lines of reasoning, and—ultimately—actions. Through a cooperation of Laymon's content and style, readers are transported to an anxious headspace. When Laymon paces out the character's internal dialogue and actions by using sentence and paragraph breaks, the moments of hesitation lengthen. Consequently, the emphasis on characters' subjective decision-making is amplified, and as a result, the affective anxiety becomes more palpable.

A character's disenfranchisement, apathy, or frustration with their current stagnant situation is a central ingredient in Laymon's work. However, Laymon's main characters charm readers with their everyday realism. For example, in *Body Rides*, Neal is a poor high school substitute teacher who writes screenplays of crime stories,[35] in *Night in the Lonesome October*, Ed is a college student who is initially struck with "desire, rage, and sorrow" after his girlfriend breaks up with him[36]; other characters like Alice from *After Midnight* and Jane from *In the Dark* seem bored with the monotony of their lives. Such emptiness becomes the exigence that motivates the main character to *want to* feel around in the dark and make decisions toward unknown destinations. Rhetorically, by means of the minimalism and negative space, the reader can develop similar attitudes since they are placed in similar headspace as these characters. Within the fictional space on the page, they similarly journey through unknown terrain with the character. This mysterious exploration can act as motivation for the reader; it can urge them to continue reading the fiction. Like many of Laymon's characters that are empty, bored, or disenfranchised, the stylistic surface of the prose mirrors the emptiness. Similar to characters that look to fill their emptiness by moving toward adventure into the unknown, readers also embark on these journeys. The reader yearns to fill in the textual emptiness on the page by reading more narrative content. The uncomfortable silences on the page can bait the reader toward seeking more action.

Nakedness

Laymon's minimalism and negative space allow a reader to "grope around in the dark" much like Laymon's main characters. However, Laymon's minimalistic use of space also *shows* such emptiness on the material page itself. Returning to Richard Lanham's terminology, readers do not only read "through" the style, readers can also read "at" the style. In other words, the style, and reader's experience of the style, can speak a message in itself. Some postmodern thinkers, such as Georges Bataille and proto-postmodern thinkers such as Friedrich Nietzsche, shape labyrinths with their rhetorical style to communicate the fluid play of fragmentation and deconstructed meaning. However, Laymon does not shape labyrinths with his style; instead, his style communicates vulnerability through "nakedness." Specifically, Laymon novels are often infamous for the sustained emphasis of characters' lust, nudity, and sexuality. Frankly, since readers are sexual creatures, the promise of human nakedness can charge the narrative with primitive excitement and erotic appeal. However, characters' nudity can more rhetorically cooperate with the nakedness of Laymon's style itself.

Nudity and sexuality often pervades the horror genre; however, Laymon's stylized fiction demonstrates a rhetorical function of nakedness similar to that found in the 1960s and 1970s horror tradition. Carpenter's *Halloween* can again provide an illustration of this tradition. In particular, the nudity in Carpenter's *Halloween* functions similarly to Alfred Hitchcock's inferred nudity found during the famous the shower scene in *Psycho* (1960): both directors use nudity as a device that communicates vulnerability to heighten audience anxiety. This approach should not be a surprise considering *Halloween* is partially inspired by Hitchcockian suspense. According to Debra Hill's 1995 commentary of *Halloween*, the characters' nudity offers two functions in the narrative. First, it serves a practical role: to justify characters moving through rooms and around the grounds of the setting.[37] For instance, in *Halloween*, the character of Annie (Nancy Kyes) drips butter on her clothes while babysitting, so she has to remove her shirt and pants and wash them; Annie then becomes justified in roaming about the house and grounds. Consequently, such character movement offers reasonable occasions to build suspense and scares: more places for Michael Myers to appear. Secondly, Hill explains that nudity also increases the vulnerability of the characters, serving a similar function to Hitchcock's *Psycho*'s shower scene.[38] Michael Myers kills his sister when she is combing her hair in the nude; Lynda (P.J. Soles) is killed when she is naked; Annie is killed in her underwear. Therefore, nudity in *Halloween* was not primarily implemented to increase the sexual appeal or the taboo intrigue of the film, but instead, it purposefully heightens the vulnerability of characters, and thus, intensifies the anxiety of audience members—a different affective purpose than a crude appeal to the libido.

Much like Carpenter's iconic minimalist (or naked) score that pulsates throughout *Halloween*, Laymon's silence-heavy stylistic cadence acts as the "score" of his novels. His style hums along as a background soundscape, kindling character and audience vulnerability. When reading "through" his naked style, it can reflect both the literal and figurative nakedness of the characters—which, in sum, bolsters an effect of anxiety and urgency in the reader as they are placed in the headspace of such vulnerable characters. Simultaneously, reading "at" Laymon's style on the page reveals another level of nakedness and vulnerability. Minimalism is plain style, unclothed by garments of eloquence. The silences communicated by the negative space become moments of vulnerability, barren of linguistic content. Therefore, with so much blank space on Laymon's pages, reading "at" his style can require readers to move from space to space rather than word to word. Readers become suspended within the emptiness. Ultimately, readers can feel naked much like the vulnerable characters in Laymon's stories.

Conclusion

In his 2017 book *Why Horror Seduces*, Mathias Clasen explains that "play behavior" can insulate readers from being completely repulsed by horror. Play behavior allows horror to be an entertaining experience rather than an off-putting experience.[39] Laymon invites readers into such play behavior with his conversational style and rhetorical use of negative space. However, his style should not be merely reduced to pulp fiction "parlor tricks"; rather, they should be celebrated as balanced rhetorical mechanisms within his contemporary horror fiction. Such balance seduces readers with his captivating style while simultaneously unsettling them with anxious content. Naturally, this content has a tendency to appall his readers.[40] Dean Koontz clarifies this in his introduction of Laymon's *In the Dark*. Koontz mentions that readers either love the shock and horror of Laymon's stories, or dislike the experience.[41] To this point, Koontz reports Laymon simply smiling and saying, "What am I writing for if not to *affect* readers?"[42] Ultimately, Laymon focuses on engaging his readers. However, this focus is sometimes misinterpreted. Sometimes critics oversimplify Laymon's work as mere splatter-punk fiction solely meant to overwhelm readers with shock-appeal. Clearly, Laymon does not write highbrow literature. However, Laymon also does not write hackneyed horror interspersed with simple shock appeals. Rather, as shown by analyzing the stylistics of minimalism and negative space, Laymon writes rhetorically complex, affective fiction. Laymon delivers gritty horror fiction experiences that can delight readers through a playful stylistic charm.

Overall, Laymon's attention on the horror fiction *experience* is what makes him a contemporary master of horror. Laymon can package disturbing content (expected of the horror genre) within play behavior on the page. Laymon does not undercut the grittiness of the content by relying on cheap humor or sappy romance. Rather, the work of Richard Laymon demonstrates how authentic stylistic writing choices can seduce a readership into reading bristling content—and it can generatively reveal some of the rich rhetorical intricacies of horror fiction writing and reading.

NOTES

1. Christopher Fulbright, "Richard Laymon," *Realms of Night*, last modified October 30, 2016, http://realmsofnight.com/2016/10/30/richard-laymon/.
2. "2017 Richard Laymon President's Award Winner—Greg Chapman," *StokerCon 2018*, last modified February 16, 2018, http://stokercon2018.org/2018/02/2017-richard-laymon-presidents-award-winner-greg-chapman/.
3. Richard Laymon, *A Writer's Tale* (Land O' Lakes, FL: Deadline Press, 1998), Ebook, 264–266.
4. Fulbright, "Richard Laymon."
5. Paul Butler, *Out of Style: Reanimating Stylistic Study in Composition and Rhetoric* (Logan, UT: Utah State University Press, 2008), 3.
6. Paul Simpson, *Stylistics* (New York: Routledge, 2008), 2.
7. Richard Lanham, *The Electronic Word: Democracy, Technology, and the Arts* (Chicago: University of Chicago Press, 1993), 63.
8. *Ibid.*, 5.
9. *Ibid.*
10. Butler, *Out of Style*, 34.
11. *Ibid.*, 39.
12. Laymon. *A Writer's Tale*, 131.
13. *Ibid.*, 114.
14. *Ibid.*, 166.
15. *Ibid.*, 9.
16. Butler, *Out of Style*, 41.
17. *Ibid.*, 41.
18. Richard Laymon, *After Midnight* (New York: Leisure Books, 2006), 57–58.

19. John Carpenter, "Audio Commentary," *Halloween*, directed by John Carp Troy, MI: Anchor Bay, 2007), DVD.
20. Debra Hill, "Audio Commentary," *Halloween*, directed by John Carpenter (1978; Troy, MI: Anchor Bay, 2007), DVD.
21. Carpenter, "Audio Commentary."
22. Richard Laymon, *The Travelling Vampire Show* (New York: Leisure Books, 2001), 111.
23. Laymon. *A Writer's Tale*, 324.
24. Brian Keene, "Brothers and Arms: An Interview with Dwayne and Clifton Holmes," *Richard Laymon Kills!*, last modified December 2000, http://rlk.stevegerlach.com/rlitdmov. htm#1.
25. "Books: Richard Laymon," *Amazon*, accessed November 21, 2018, https://www. amazon.com/s/ref=nb_sb_noss?url=search-alias%3Dstripbooks&field-keywords=richard+ laymon&rh=n%3A283155%2Ck%3Arichard+laymon.
26. Richard Laymon, *Night in the Lonesome October* (New York: Leisure Books, 2001), 204.
27. Brian McHale, *Postmodernist Fiction* (London: Routledge, 1991), 129.
28. *Ibid.*, 181.
29. *Ibid.*
30. *Ibid.*
31. *Ibid.*, 184.
32. Richard Laymon, *Body Rides* (New York: Leisure Books, 2004), 1.
33. *Ibid.*, 2.
34. *Ibid.*, 3.
35. *Ibid.*, 32.
36. Laymon, *Night in the Lonesome October*, 10.
37. Hill, "Audio Commentary."
38. *Ibid.*
39. Mathias Clasen, *Why Horror Seduces* (London: Oxford University Press, 2017), Kindle, 58–59.
40. Dean Koontz, introduction to *In the Dark*, by Richard Laymon (New York: Leisure Books, 2001), xii.
41. *Ibid.*
42. *Ibid.*

BIBLIOGRAPHY

"Books: Richard Laymon." *Amazon*. Accessed November 21, 2018. https://www.amazon.com/s/ref=nb_sb_noss?url=search-alias%3Dstripbooks&field-keywords=richard+laymon&rh=n%3A283155%2Ck%3Arichard+laymon.
Butler, Paul. *Out of Style: Reanimating Stylistic Study in Composition and Rhetoric*. Logan: Utah State University Press, 2008.
Clasen, Mathias. *Why Horror Seduces*. London: Oxford University Press, 2017. Kindle.
Fulbright, Christopher. "Richard Laymon." *Realms of Night*. Last modified October 30, 2016. http://realmsofnight.com/2016/10/30/richard-laymon/.
Halloween. Directed by John Carpenter. 1978. Troy, MI: Anchor Bay, 2007. DVD.
Keene, Brian. "Brothers and Arms: An Interview with Dwayne and Clifton Holmes." *Richard Laymon Kills!* Last modified December 2000. http://rlk.stevegerlach.com/rlitdmov. htm#1.
Koontz, Dean. Introduction to *In the Dark*, xi–xiii. by Richard Laymon. New York: Leisure Books, 2001.
Lanham, Richard A. *The Electronic Word: Democracy, Technology, and the Arts*. Chicago: University of Chicago Press, 1993.
Laymon, Richard. *After Midnight*. 1997. Reprint, NY: Leisure Books, 2006.
_____. *Body Rides*. 1996. Reprint, NY: Leisure Books, 2004.
_____. *In the Dark*. 1994. Reprint, NY: Leisure Books, 2001.

_____. *Night in the Lonesome October*. New York: Leisure Books, 2001.

_____. *The Travelling Vampire Show*. 2000. Reprint, NY: Leisure Books, 2001.

_____. *A Writer's Tale*. Land O' Lakes, FL: Deadline Press, 1998. Ebook.

McHale, Brian. *Postmodernist Fiction*. London, UK: Routledge, 1991.

Simpson, Paul. *Stylistics*. New York: Routledge, 2008.

"2017 Richard Laymon President's Award Winner—Greg Chapman." *StokerCon 2018*. Last modified February 16, 2018. http://stokercon2018.org/2018/02/2017-richard-laymon-presidents-award-winner-greg-chapman/.

Four Quadrants of Success

The Metalinguistics of Author Protagonists in the Fiction of Stephen King

James Arthur Anderson

Stephen King, the acknowledged king of horror, uses authors as characters and protagonists in much of his fiction. It is almost the rule of thumb in writing to write about what you know, so authors as protagonists are nothing new in fiction; however, King has taken the device to new levels. While his fictional authors make for interesting characters, they also perform a metalinguistic function as they speak about writing in what Roland Barthes terms a "metalinguistic code"[1] where writing calls attention to itself, as, for example, when a poet writes a poem about writing poems.

As both a bestselling and critically acclaimed author who has also written his own writing manual where he advises authors to "write what you know … especially work,"[2] King knows something about what it takes to be successful as a writer. A close look at King's author-characters reveals the traits necessary to find success as a writer and the traits that might destroy an otherwise successful writer. Literary achievement, of course, can be defined in different ways. One measure, commercial success, is the number of books that sell; making the *New York Times* bestseller list is definitely an objective determination of this. The other is critical success: favorable critical reviews, studies of a book by academics, and awards, such as the Pulitzer Prize or the National Book Award, certainly qualify. King's author-characters vary greatly in terms of their success: some, like Scott Landon in *Lisey's Story* (2006) who is a National Book Award recipient, enjoys praise from the critics, and fame and financial success from the masses. Others, like Wesley Smith, from "Ur" (2009), have achieved neither, since Smith is unpublished in every version of the multiverse, according to his pink Kindle.

This essay will examine varying degrees of success of King's author-characters by placing them into one of four quadrants based upon their sales and/or their critical reputation. These authors can then be classified according to their achievements in each area. Next, this essay will examine the talents, traits, and backgrounds of these fictional authors to show what, in King's mind at least, has been responsible for their success or failure and how they exemplify their creator's vision of success.

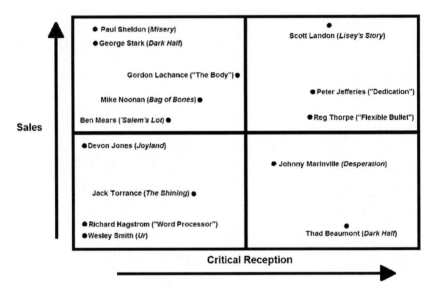

Figure 1. The four quadrants of success.

In this diagram, commercial success can be approximately measured on the vertical axis in terms of the number of sales that the protagonist has enjoyed, while critical success can be measured along the horizontal axis. This creates four quadrants of success: the "wannabe," the "bestseller," the "critics' choice," and the "unicorn," that mythical writer who enjoys both commercial and critical success.

The Wannabe

The lower left quadrant contains the author who has achieved neither critical recognition nor commercial success. The most unsuccessful protagonist of this group, Smith, from the novella "Ur," is a college English instructor who, "like all instructors of English... thought he had a novel in him somewhere and would write it someday."[3] Unfortunately, not only does he never write the book, but after receiving a Kindle that contains all of the books ever written in both this world and all of the worlds of King's multiverse, Smith discovers that he will never be published in this universe or in any other. Perhaps Smith never writes his book because of this discovery, but it is apparent that his chances of becoming an author were slim even before he received the Kindle with its bad news. When he reminds Don Allman that he is going to be a novelist, his colleague responds: "Yes! And President Obama is going to tab me as the new Poet Laureate!"[4]

The wannabe quadrant also includes Richard Hagstrom, the protagonist of the short story "The Word Processor of the Gods." Hagstrom, at least, had written and published one novel that "had not been lucrative, and the critics had been quick to point out that it wasn't very wonderful either."[5] He is even mocked by his wife, who asks him "Why don't you go write a Nobel Prize winning short story or something?"[6]

Devon Jones, the narrator from *Joyland* (2013), is a pragmatic writer that makes a living at his craft but has no illusions about becoming a bestselling novelist or a critical success. Although he had dreams of becoming a fiction writer whose books were "well reviewed,"[7] he settled for a position as a writer and editor for trade journals. "I never produced the books I dreamed of, those well-reviewed almost bestsellers, but I do make a good living as a writer.... I am now working at *Commercial Flight*, a periodical you've probably never heard of."[8] This puts him higher on the pay scale than Smith or Hagstrom, but he has no status with the critics.

Finally, there is Jack Torrance, the well-known character from *The Shining* (1977), who has had some modest critical success, and may be on his way to moving into the critics' choice quadrant. He is "a slowly blooming American writer" who had published two dozen short stories, one in *Esquire*, and was "well qualified to teach that great mystery, creative writing"[9] at a well-respected prep school. At this point, he has potential to be successful, but does not reach his potential. Although he is working on a play and has a novel "incubating in some mental back room,"[10] he struggles from writer's block and is unable to finish his play or begin his novel. After losing his teaching job, he takes on the stewardship of the Overlook Hotel, hoping it will give him the time and space he needs to complete his play. "If I can't finish that goddam play snowed in all winter, I'll never finish it,"[11] he says. Though Torrance has published fiction, he is a wannabe writer because he stalls, never does finish the work, and never makes it to the next level.

The Bestseller

The top left quadrant describes the bestseller, the author who is financially successful, sells lots of books and enjoys popular success, but who does not garner praise with the critics. For much of his career, King himself has been classified in this category, and, although his reputation has improved in academic circles, many critics still consider him nothing more than a popular writer. Noted critic Harold Bloom, in fact, has accused him of "dumbing down our cultural life."[12] Ben Mears, Mike Noonan, Paul Sheldon, Gordon Lachance, and Thad Beaumont's alter-ego, George Stark, are all in the bestseller quadrant. These fictional authors are professional in their work ethic and write to please a specific audience.

Mears, the protagonist of 'Salem's Lot (1975), writes popular novels that appeal to average readers but are not well reviewed. "I read a review of this in the Portland paper," Mrs. Norton says, "It wasn't very good."[13] Mears himself admits that "most of the critics clobbered Conway's Daughter. That's critics for you. Plot was out, masturbation in."[14] Three of his books are in the public library, and most of the residents of the town are familiar with his work. Mrs. Coogan at the drug store considers his new book "pretty racy,"[15] and Susan Norton thinks Air Dance is "an awfully good book."[16] Mears is a full-time writer and is able to make a living as a novelist, a rare feat in contemporary America. He comes to 'Salem's Lot to write a new book and he actually works on it until the vampire crisis occurs.

Noonan, the protagonist from Bag of Bones (1998), is another successful popular novelist who makes his living by writing popular fiction until he suffers from writer's block. After his wife's death he published old books that he had previously written and stored away until he runs out of material. "I was what midlist fiction used to be in the forties: critically ignored, genre oriented... but well compensated."[17] He claims he was "V.C. Andrews with a prick for ten years,"[18] and his creative writing teacher "damned [his first book] with faint praise, seeing its commercial qualities as a kind of heresy."[19] Noonan loves what he does, however, and is not ashamed of what he writes[20]: "some outlet for the baser instincts had to be provided and someone had to do that sort of thing."[21]

Sheldon, the protagonist from Misery (1987), also writes popular novels and is financially successful at it; however, he wishes to achieve critical success as well. Unfortunately, his Misery novels aren't well-liked by the critics and only appeal to a less literary audience: "hundreds of thousands of... people across the country—ninety percent of them women—who could barely wait for each new five-hundred-page episode."[22] Sheldon is a commercial success, having published eight novels, including four Misery books "that had been his main source of income for the last eight years."[23] Sheldon "wrote two kinds of books, good ones and bestsellers,"[24] and though his financial success depends on the bestsellers, he takes great pride in his work and wants to write serious fiction. It is this conflict with his desire to write good books and more Misery books that represents his battle between the author and his audience. Despite his desire for acceptance by the critics, however, Sheldon is firmly entrenched in the bestseller category, a label that Annie Wilkes is determined that he will retain when she burns the manuscript of *Fast Cars*, the book that Sheldon considers a candidate for the National Book Award that he so covets.

Lachance, the young man in "The Body" (1998), grows up to be "the bestselling novelist who is more apt to have his paperback contracts reviewed than his books."[25] Tess Thorne, the author/protagonist of *Big Driver* (2010), is also included in the lower part of the bestseller quadrant because she has risen above wannabes and is able to make a modest living writing fiction, even if she is not on the bestseller list. She has a devoted fan base of female authors who buy every book that she publishes.

George Stark, the pseudonym of Thad Beaumont in *The Dark Half* (1989), is another example of the bestseller. Under the alter ego that comes to life, "Thad had written one huge best-seller and three extremely successful follow-up novels."[26] Writing as Stark, he didn't have to worry about his critical reception and "could write any damn thing I pleased without *The New York Times Book Review* looking over my shoulder the whole time I wrote it."[27] As a university professor and National Book Award nominee, Beaumont had an image to uphold, and writing crime novels would tarnish that image. Therefore, he invented the George Stark persona to do the dirty work and earn the handsome royalty checks.

The Critics' Choice

By contrast, Thad Beaumont, the other half of *The Dark Half*, is an example of the critics' choice, the lower right square of the quadrant. "Thad Beaumont was a well-regarded writer whose first novel, *The Sudden Dancers*, had been nominated for the National Book Award in 1972,"[28] and he had only published one other novel under his own name. Unfortunately for Beaumont, writers who are embraced by the critics seem to lack financial or popular success. His award nomination "swung some weight with the literary critics, but the breathless celebrity-watchers of America didn't care a dime about Thad Beaumont."[29] The irony of the critics' choice is made clear when Thad recalls winning a certificate for a short story he'd written when he was just 11 years old. His father, not impressed by literary skill, grunts "if it was so good why didn't they give him some money?"[30]

Johnny Marinville, the author-character from *Desperation* (1996), is also a member of the critics' choice quadrant. While he does achieve some financial success, it is really because he has become a celebrity rather than because his books are so popular. He "had once been on the cover of *People* and *Time* and *Premiere* (when he'd married the actress with all the emeralds), and the *New York Times* (when he won the National Book Award)."[31] He "had been spoken of in connection with the Nobel Prize for Literature,"[32] and was once called "the only living American writer of Steinbeck's stature."[33] Unfortunately, Marinville's once illustrious career was ruined by drugs, alcohol, and scandal, and even though he'd managed to kick those bad habits, his "literary reputation had gone slipping through his fingers."[34] Once the darling of the critics, he appears more in the tabloids than in the literary journals. While Marinville might have had a reputation as a great writer, his work hadn't been embraced by the public. Cynthia admits that she had heard of him but never read anything by him: "I just read for pleasure."[35] Even Steve admits to having read one of his stories but didn't really understand it.

The Unicorn

The unicorn, a rarity among contemporary writers, is the author who has achieved both critical and commercial success and is represented by the top right section of the quadrant. This is the place where all writers dream of being, but since the age of Ernest Hemingway, John Steinbeck and F. Scott Fitzgerald, few have claimed this position. However, three of King's author protagonists may be considered unicorns because they have not only received admiration from the critics, but have popular appeal as well.

The short story, "The Ballad of the Flexible Bullet," contains two author-characters, both young writers on the way to becoming unicorns. The unnamed "celebrated young writer" who listens to the editor's story about the Fornits has published his first book, a novel that was "well-reviewed and had sold lots of copies."[36] This unnamed character reminds the editor of Reg Thorpe, "a young man about this young man's age and about as successful."[37] Thorpe's first novel had "great reviews, lovely sales in hardcover and paperback, Literary Guild, everything."[38] Not only was the book well received by the critics, it was a commercial success as well. "That fall, everybody had read it, or was reading it, or was on the library waiting list, or checking the drugstore racks for the paperback."[39] This author did have the best of both worlds during his short but eventful life.

Peter Jefferies, the "famous writer" in the short story "Dedication," also enjoys critical and commercial success. Martha, the maid who cleans his hotel room (and, "fathered" a son by him with the help of a sorcerer-woman), knows that he is a favorite of the critics but is much more interested in why he sells so many books. "I wanted to know what the critics saw in him, but I was more interested in what ordinary folks like me saw in him—the people who made his books best-sellers as soon as they came out."[40]

Landon, from *Lisey's Story*, is the most successful of all of King's author characters. A unicorn in every sense, he has been killed before the story begins, and so we learn about him through Lisey, his widow. Praised by the critics, Landon has won both the Pulitzer Prize and the National Book Award. Furthermore, after his death, the scholars were fighting over his unfinished manuscripts and where his papers would be housed. Joseph Woodbury, one of the scholars, had published "God knew how many scholarly articles"[41] about Landon's work. Landon has also been a commercial success, mostly based on one novel, *Empty Devils*, "the horrible, scary book that had put Scott Landon on the bestseller list for the first time and made them rich."[42] Interestingly enough, *Empty Devils* was also the only book that the critics hated.[43]

King's author-characters can be categorized by their commercial and critical success. Through the use of these characters, King is metalinguistically showing what he believes to be the qualities of a successful writer, and what it takes to achieve both commercial and critical success. There can be no doubt that King, who has sold hundreds of millions of books in his lifetime, is a popular, commercial success, a "brand-name" for horror fiction. As more academic studies are written about King's work, and he continues to win accolades and awards (not to mention be published in some of the most prestigious magazines, such as *The New Yorker*), it is apparent that he is also beginning to achieve respectability among scholars and critics. Therefore, it makes sense that King's ideas of what makes authors successful deserve some attention. Based upon the author-characters in his fiction, he shares a number of elements that determine a writer's success with the scholars and the general public.

First, in order for writers to be successful, they do need a certain amount of skill and talent. Smith, for example, seems to have no talent in any of the 10.4 million alternate realities and is "an unpublished loser in all of them."[44] His wannabe status is the result of a number of reasons, but if he had even some talent he surely would have published something in at least one of the worlds. Although Hagstrom does seem to have some talent, it is not enough to bring him either critical or financial success. On the other hand, writers like Landon and Jefferies almost seem to be born with a talent for writing. In Jefferies, this talent is passed down to his "natural son," the child of Martha. Lachance, the protagonist of "The Body," displays a talent for writing at young age, an innate talent, rather than a skill he has learned. The truly great writers, says King, are "geniuses, divine accidents, gifted in a way which is beyond our ability to understand, let alone attain....they are nothing but fortunate freaks, the intellectual version of runway models."[45]

Dedication to the craft and a strong work ethic is another essential quality that King sees in writers and that helps to determine the placement of his author characters in the success quadrant: "If you don't want to work your ass off, you have no business trying to write well."[46] In King's fiction, writers who don't work hard are much less successful than those who do. Smith claims that he will write a book someday, but he never does. Torrance, who had promise, goes to the Overlook Hotel so he will have the time and energy to write, but his work ethic breaks down and he spends his time researching the hotel instead of writing his play. His career had consisted of only writing short stories and he lacks the ambition to write a novel: "he was not ready to stumble into the swamp of another three-year undertaking."[47] Mears, who is "mildly successful"[48] does display a strong work ethic and puts time into his writing every day until the vampire crisis intervenes. Until he suffers from writer's block, Noonan publishes a book each year, and writes other books that he puts away in storage, to publish them later when he cannot write. Perhaps Stark publishes more books than Beaumont because he has a stronger work ethic. "Writing had always been hard work for [Thad].... It had come a lot easier for George."[49] Sheldon exhibits a strong work ethic, even when forced to write a story he hates. Landon, probably the most successful of King's characters, "had been prolific right up until the day he died. On the road or at home, Scott Landon *wrote*."[50]

A writer's audience also plays a major factor in his or her success. This is most apparent with Sheldon, whose audience is composed of 90 percent women.[51] Tess makes a modest living writing women's fiction about the "Willow Grove Knitting Society." Likewise, Jones has learned to write specific articles for trade journals. He is not a bestselling author, and doesn't write fiction, but he is able to earn his living catering to this audience. None of these writers are accepted by the critics, but as King has said, "critics and scholars have always been suspicious of popular success."[52]

By contrast, Marinville and Beaumont are writing for the critics, but don't appeal to the public. Marinville's work is considered pretentious. When Sheldon does write a book that he feels is worthy of critical praise, Annie, his "Number One Fan," critiques it as being "hard to follow. It keeps jumping back and forth in time."[53] Yet some author-characters such as Landon and Jefferies have managed to bridge the gap and appeal to both the critics and the public. Martha calls Jeffries' books "beautiful" but also entertaining—he "could write so you didn't never want to close the book."[54] King says, "the story should always be boss."[55]

Another element of a writer's success or failure lies in the use of drugs or alcohol. King himself admits to having a drug and alcohol problem, but learned that "the idea that creative endeavor and mind-altering substances are entwined is one of the great pop-intellectual myths of our time."[56] King's fictional authors demonstrate that substance abuse can destroy a career, as it did to Torrance and Marinville, whose "literary reputation had gone slipping through his fingers"[57] because of his "insatiable appetite for booze, drugs, and younger women."[58] Once King had completely recovered from his substance abuse problems in 1989, his works became more favorable with the critics. He published short works in the *New Yorker* in 1990 and 1994, was selected for a lifetime achievement award by the National Book Foundation in 2003, and was named guest editor of *The Best American Short Stories 2007*. Furthermore, his books have remained on the bestseller list since.

The final elements, and perhaps the most important ones for a writer to possess, are creativity, a sense of wonder, and a love for the craft. "Work has always been my drug of choice,"[59] Noonan says, just as King has said: "writing is an addiction for me."[60] Sheldon speaks of "the pride in your work, the worth of the work itself."[61] King has said, "books are portable magic,"[62] and therefore, writers have almost magical powers. Once Noonan is cured of writer's block, he calls writing "that old magic, so strange and wonderful."[63] The power to write has redemptive qualities; it saves Sheldon's life in *Misery*, while the inability to write destroys Torrance in *The Shining*. It also keeps Landon sane. Lisey says that "he had referred to his job of writing stories as a kind of madness,"[64] but the writing was one of the things that "tied him to the earth and saved him from the long boy."[65] Landon exemplifies creativity, and a child-like imagination as his sense of wonder allows him to tap into an alternate reality where he can take words from the "word pool" and stories from the "story pool."[66]

Most of King's author-characters have some basis in King's own life. Lachance represents a young King who wrote stories to entertain his classmates, and who matured into a professional writer. King admits that Torrance represents the time when he was suffering from alcohol abuse,[67] and says that *Misery* "was the best metaphor for drugs and alcohol that my tired, overstressed mind could come up with."[68] Noonan shares King's addiction to writing. Landon serves as a personification of King after he overcame his substance abuse problems and in many ways King has achieved the ideal success, praise of both the critics and the masses, that his fictional character achieved. Perhaps Landon says it best: "if you were lucky, if you were brave, if you persevered—it brought you treasure."[69] The best treasure for a writer, though, might not be either financial or critical recognition, but in discovering the truth. King says that "fiction is the truth inside the lie"[70] and that "the job of fiction is to find the truth inside the story's web of lies."[71] And King is able to use his fiction and his author-characters to find truth. Gordie finds it when he discovers the dead boy's body: "the hand of the drowned boy... told us the truth of the whole matter."[72]

To conclude, although King's fiction targets an audience of average, everyday readers, which has elicited harsh reviews from many academics (many of whom refuse to even read his work), the bottom line is that King does find truth in even the most improbable tales of fantasy and horror. In *The Shining*, for example, he shows the destructive powers of drugs and alcohol; in "The Word Processor of the Gods," *Lisey's Story*, and "The Body," he shows the redemptive powers of words and creativity. King writes about what he knows, and in doing so, uses author-characters to find the truth within the lie, not just the truth about writing, but truth about life itself.

NOTES

1. Roland Barthes, "Textual Analysis of Poe's 'Valdemar,'" in *Untying the Text*, ed. Robert Young (Boston: Routledge, 1981), 139.
2. Stephen King, *On Writing* (New York: Scribner, Paperback edition, 2010), 158, 160.
3. Stephen King, "Ur," in *The Bazaar of Bad Dreams* (New York: Scribner, 2015), 211.
4. *Ibid.*, 209.
5. Stephen King, "The Word Processor of the Gods," in *Skeleton Crew* (New York: Putnam, 1985), 309.
6. *Ibid.*, 323.
7. Stephen King, *Joyland* (London: Titan Books, 2013), 45.
8. *Ibid.*, 49.
9. Stephen King, *The Shining*, in *Three Novels* (New York: Random House, 2011), 684.
10. King., *The Shining*, 685.
11. *Ibid.*, 689.
12. Harold Bloom, "Dumbing Down American Readers," *The Boston Globe*, September 24, 2003.
13. Stephen King, *'Salem's Lot*, in *Three Novels* (New York: Random House, 2011), 222.
14. *Ibid.*, 210.
15. *Ibid.*
16. *Ibid.*, 209.
17. Stephen King, *Bag of Bones* (New York: Scribner, 1998), 20.
18. *Ibid.*, 19.
19. *Ibid.*, 18.
20. *Ibid.*, 19.
21. *Ibid.*, 20.
22. Stephen King, *Misery* (New York: Signet, 1988), 27.
23. *Ibid.*, 2.
24. *Ibid.*, 7.
25. Stephen King, "The Body," in *Different Seasons* (New York: Signet, Movie Tie-in Edition, 1998), 327.
26. Stephen King, *The Dark Half* (New York: Viking, 1989), 19.
27. *Ibid.*, 22–23.
28. *Ibid.*, 19.
29. *Ibid.*
30. *Ibid.*, 4.
31. Stephen King, *Desperation* (New York: Viking, 1996), 66.
32. *Ibid.*
33. *Ibid.*, 67.
34. *Ibid.*, 69.
35. *Ibid.*, 129.
36. Stephen King, "The Ballad of the Flexible Bullet," in *Skeleton Crew* (New York: Putnam, 1985), 443.
37. *Ibid.*, 444.
38. *Ibid.*

39. *Ibid.*, 446.
40. Stephen King, "Dedication" in *Nightmares & Dreamscapes* (New York: Scribner trade paperback, 2017), 278.
41. *Ibid.*
42. Stephen King, *Lisey's Story* (New York: Scribner, 2006), 178.
43. *Ibid.*, 48.
44. King, "Ur," 30.
45. King, *On Writing*, 142.
46. *Ibid.*, 144.
47. King, *The Shining*, 754.
48. King, *'Salem's Lot*, 191.
49. King, *The Dark Half*, 16.
50. King, *Lisey's Story*, 75.
51. King, *Misery*, 27.
52. King, *On Writing*, 190.
53. King, *Misery*, 21.
54. King, "Dedication," 279.
55. King, *On Writing*, 190.
56. *Ibid.*, 98.
57. King, *Desperation*, 69.
58. *Ibid.*, 68.
59. King, *Bag of Bones*, 381.
60. Stephen King, quoted in Lisa Rogak, *The Haunted Heart: The Life and Times of Stephen King* (New York: St. Martins, 2009), 2.
61. King, *Misery*, 29.
62. King, *On Writing*, 104.
63. King, *Bag of Bones*, 381.
64. King, *Lisey's Story*, 271.
65. *Ibid.*, 350.
66. *Ibid.*, 97.
67. King, *On Writing*, 95.
68. *Ibid.*, 97.
69. King, *Lisey's Story*, 418.
70. Stephen King, *Danse Macabre* (New York: Everest House, 1981), 375.
71. King, *On Writing*, 159.
72. King, "The Body," 406.

Bibliography

Barthes, Roland. "Textual Analysis of Poe's 'Valdemar.'" in *Untying the Text*, edited by Robert Young. Boston: Routledge, 1981.
Bloom, Harold. "Dumbing Down American Readers." *The Boston Globe*, September 24, 2003.
King, Stephen. *Bag of Bones*. New York: Scribner's, 1998.
_____. "The Ballad of the Flexible Bullet," in *Skeleton Crew*. New York: Putnam, 1985.
_____. " Big Driver," in *Full Dark, No Stars*. New York: Scribner's, 2010.
_____. "The Body," in *Different Seasons*. New York: Signet, Movie Tie-in Edition, 1998.
_____. *The Dark Half*. New York: Viking, 1989.
_____. *Danse Macabre*. New York: Everest House, 1981.
_____. "Dedication," in *Nightmares & Dreamscapes*. New York: Scribner trade paperback, 2017.
_____. *Desperation*. New York: Viking, 1996.
_____. *Joyland*. London, Titan Books, 2013.
_____. *Lisey's Story*. New York: Scribner's, 2006.
_____. *Misery*. New York: Signet, 1988.
_____. *On Writing*. New York: Scribner's, Paperback edition, 2010.

_____. 'Salem's Lot, in *Three Novels*. New York: Random House, 2011.

_____. *The Shining*, in *Three Novels*. New York: Random House, 2011.

_____. "Ur," in *The Bazaar of Bad Dreams*. New York: Scribner's, 2015.

_____. "The Word Processor of the Gods," in *Skeleton Crew*. New York: Putnam, 1985.

Rogak, Lisa. *Haunted Heart: The Life and Times of Stephen King*. New York: St. Martin, 2008.

Exploring Literary Theory in Horror

"The symptoms of possession"

Gender, Power and Trauma in Late 20th Century Horror Novels

Bridget E. Keown

Horror fiction, as Robert McCammon noted, is a kind of "guided nightmare," permitting readers to explore and question the most taboo, threatening, and unsettling aspects of their culture.[1] When seen in this light, the horror genre offers insight not only into the internal, psychological methods of *how* to scare an audience, but it also provides an ideal vantage point from which to explore the tensions and anxieties within a given culture at a given time, and to understand *why* a particular monster is reviled within a given context. This essay studies how fictional accounts of demon possession explore real fears and assumptions regarding the women, specifically pubescent women, in modern Western culture. From her emotional volatility and her potential irrationality, to the threat she poses to men's bodily safety and appetites, the pubescent female is portrayed as uniquely dangerous to patriarchal structures, and via the demon she hosts (whether willingly or unwillingly), to civilization itself. However, the fear of the possessed women in these novels obscures the very real, lived experience of trauma in each of these characters' lives by portraying their outbursts as a result of their possession, rather than as a reaction to and a condemnation of the world they inhabit and the systems that seek to prevent their autonomy. This essay considers the lived experiences and treatment of the young women featured in three modern novels of demonic possession and exorcism: *The Case Against Satan*, by Ray Russell (1963), *The Exorcist* by William Peter Blatty (1971), and *A Head Full of Ghosts* by Paul Tremblay (2015). In so doing, it seeks to understand how anxieties regarding women's minds and bodies have been exploited and controlled within these novels, as well as how the twin systems of patriarchal oppression, science and religion, are employed to silence the lived experience of its female subject, even as the text acknowledges the realities of such trauma in their lives. This analysis opens up a discussion of how women's bodies and minds are pathologized, specifically when their turbulent or rebellious behaviors challenge traditional masculine structures of authority. In so doing, by employing a feminist analysis that seeks to recover the experiences of the female characters at the center of male-dominated narratives, one can understand the ways in which female trauma and rebellion are interpreted as horrific and subsequently silenced by masculine authority figures as a symbolic return to patriarchal order.

Women who behaved outside specific norms, often defined both literally and spatially within the domestic sphere, were labeled as both "mad'" and "possessed," and their symptoms ascribed to a natural instability, rather than to the effects of the reality they were forced to inhabit. As a product of such culture, the Western horror novel has both re-affirmed and challenged this construction of women as inherently unstable, primitive, and emotional. The exorcism novel not only deploys these images, but also offers a "remedy" in the form of psychological and religious control and containment. Thus, the novels in question all feature a similar basic premise: a pubescent young woman, whose home life differs significantly from the stereotype of a happy nuclear family, suffers the sudden onset of strange and disturbing behavior that threatens both her and those around her, specifically, the authority of the men in her general vicinity. In *The Case Against Satan,* Susan Garth lives with her widower father who is forced to be both breadwinner and caretaker. In *The Exorcist,* Regan is also the child of a single parent, though in this case, her mother is the embodiment of the modern "working woman." Chris, Regan's mother, is a divorced actress who spends most of her time away from home, consorting with distinctly non-paternal men. In *A Head Full of Ghosts,* John Barrett loses his job during the Great Recession of 2008. Unable to afford his older daughter Marjorie's medical bills when her symptoms begin to manifest, John convinces his wife to allow a reality show to penetrate the privacy of their home and take the money they offer. In each of these novels, order is restored through the application of patriarchal power, embodied by a psychologist or psychiatrist, and a priest, the embodiment of perhaps the oldest form of patriarchal control. Both *The Case Against Satan* and *The Exorcist* feature a pair of priests, one of whom is suffering a personal crisis of faith. That faith is redeemed through the re-emphasis of masculine power over both the body of the young woman and the demon within her. In both cases, their work is successful because it returns the adolescent woman in question to an obedient, childlike state. While *The Case Against Satan* is deeply ambiguous in its allegations of possession, allowing a considerable amount of doubt as to whether paranormal or domestic trauma is at the root of young Susan's condition, *The Exorcist*, published eight years later, leaves little to the imagination. The possession of Regan by the demon Pazuzu is described in visceral, almost fetish-like detail, and her exorcism is performed in bombastic and sensationalistic prose. *A Head Full of Ghosts* takes a postmodern and highly self-conscious approach to its themes, providing a host of unreliable narrators to keep readers off-balance, even as it employs a host of patriarchal authority figures to judge whether Marjorie's symptoms are the result of a psychological breakdown or a demonic entity. As a result, even though the end result is entirely different in Tremblay's novel, it remains true to form in presenting us with an unknowable female character whose knowledge of the world, and of the systems of control, seems otherworldly.

Although medical knowledge and religious faith are traditionally posited as diametrically opposed systems of knowledge and understanding, when both are understood as systems of patriarchal authority, the two fields work admirably hand-in-hand. The history of both Western psychology and American Christianity were specifically premised on the superiority of men and control over women's bodies, minds, and behavior. A feminist critique of the history of psychiatry offers insight into the ways in which women's minds have been misunderstood, misrepresented, and mistrusted throughout the 20th century as a result of male medical authority, an analysis which can also be extended to understanding gendered control within the church. The rise in prominence of the medical profession in the late Victorian period led, first, to a rise in the authority of the "medical man" in society, as well as a wide diversification of medical specialties. The brain itself soon became a subject of study, considered to be much like any other organ in the body, operating independently from the rest of the body. Thus, "madness" was a disease of the brain that could be cured by medical expertise and intervention.

Like other scientists of the age, psychiatrists focused on sexual differences as a way of classifying and understanding the actions of the brain, emphasizing women's inherent inscrutability and inferiority in comparison to men. It was at the moment of puberty that the two sexes began to differ. As the *New York Journal of Gynaecology and Obstetrics* explained, "The two sexes start in life upon lines which run parallel until puberty is reached. Then there is divergence upon each side ... upon the male side much more marked than upon the female."[2] Menstruation, it was believed, diverted blood from the brain, while pregnancy and the concerns of motherhood leeched vital energy from the nervous system, rendering women physically incapable of the brilliance of men, and rendering their embodied experience utterly alien and unknowable to men. Women's difference and inferiority began with, and was embodied by, the act of menstruation that enabled the bearing of children. Such scientific "observations" were invoked to justify women's subordinate social positions, especially as women's economic, political, and social power was evolving and expanding, challenging the authority of men. When women did speak against their limited social roles, their inability to access educational opportunities and degrees offered to men, or the sexual freedoms granted to a man, they were deemed psychologically "abnormal." The medicalization of deviance reinforced men's biological and professional superiority and also invoked their scientific and medical authority to diagnose, treat, and even institutionalize those who were considered abnormal and mentally unhealthy.[3]

The evolution of Western, specifically American, Christianity was spurred by the fear of the destabilization of society following the First World War, when women's employment, education, and political horizons expanded, seemingly at a cost to men. As Betty DeBerg explained, "Women's nature and sphere of activity became the battleground on which men fought for their own identity as men."[4] Conservative Christian groups rebelled against the image of the increasingly liberated, economically mobile, and politically active "New Woman," who challenged what were believed to be the "natural" and preordained dominance of men over women in society, as well as within the family.[5] As A.D. Starkey explains, men were given a privileged role in society by virtue of their allegedly superior mind putting them "closer to the divine in a gendered hierarchy. On the other hand, women were associated with the body and matter, based on the reproductive capacity, which were less valued and further removed from the divine."[6] Even as the Western feminist movement made inroads into the religious hierarchy, and the pastoral constitution of Vatican II led to an increase in women's participation in the Catholic Church, the fundamental belief in women's inherent subservience and "otherness" ensured that they continued to be viewed as subordinate to men. Women's attempts to challenge this authority were often interpreted as sinful and a thing to be feared, as it flew in the face of preordained order.

The intertwined systems of masculine authority of science and religion are explicitly deployed in novels of female possession to restore patriarchal order. When Mr. Garth journeys to the rectory to ask his local priest about his daughter's potential possession in *The Case Against Satan*, one of the first issues Father Gregory brings up is the potential of taking Susan, the aforementioned possessed young lady, to a psychiatrist rather than to a priest. He thinks about a fellow priest he knows, who is a practicing psychiatrist, and asks, "What's the difference, Mr. Garth, between the psychiatrist's office and the confessional box?"[7] Father Damien Karras is himself the embodiment of the medical-religious patriarchal partnership, being both a lecturer in psychiatry and an ordained priest, who is employed throughout the novel as an authority in both fields. In attempting to get to the root of Marjorie Barrett's condition in *A Head Full of Ghosts*, Father Wanderly brings a psychiatrist named Dr. Navidson to the Barrett household, explaining to Marjorie's younger sister that "Dr. Navidson is both a man of science and a good Christian. Our Bishop Ford recommended him highly."[8]

In addition to demonstrating the challenges posed to patriarchal authority, these novels also emphasize the threat posed by the allegedly possessed pubescent female herself. Her anger at the world, as well as at her captors, is fearsome, but it is her testimony regarding the danger and harm that patriarchal systems have done to her that poses the real danger, causing a crisis of faith in those who hear it. Before such a menace, whether feminine or demonic, can spread, and "contaminate" the world, priests and psychiatrists are employed to avert madness and establish order once again. This is done not only by expelling the demon, but wholly discrediting the woman in whom the demon resides. The priest and/as a psychiatrist contain the menace by re-emphasizing their complex masculine authority, thus returning the human female to her pre-pubescent, docile state.

In this sense, the women themselves are the demonic element within the stable, patriarchal worlds of the novel; Susan questions her father's authority over her and their household, Regan emphasizes her mother's lackluster parenting and highlights her biological father's absences, while Marjorie's physical outbursts and verbal rages punctuate her father's inability to control both her and their family's destiny. Whenever demonic possession is said to have occurred in these novels, there is never a moment when the demon is described as actually entering the women. Instead, it is explained as being a part of them, or one with them, and the instigator of the female characters' rebellion. The line between misbehavior and possession is never drawn or defined, and as a result, it is nearly impossible, throughout each of these works, to see the demarcation between the demon's power and the adolescent girls' outbursts and rebellion against the authority figures that surround her. In many ways, the possessed female embodies the feminist killjoy described by Sara Ahmed; when these young women speak up, the "violence of what was said or the violence of provocation goes unnoticed," and instead, it is the female character "who is viewed as 'causing the argument,' who is disturbing the fragility of peace."[9] These novels of exorcism often go one step further, and almost entirely disregard the woman causing the argument, instead ascribing her voice, her outbursts, and her rage, to that of the male demon. The solution, both within the world of the book and within the world outside it, is containment of the possessed woman through the actions of her father or the priest (also a Father), and the removal of that will to rebel, regardless of its source.

In *The Case Against Satan,* for example, 16-year-old Susan is presented as a quiet, dutiful, innocent young teenager, the daughter of a lonely widower who is bewildered by her behavior and language. In discussing his decision to bring her to the attention of the local priests, Mr. Garth states, "I don't mind telling you I was pretty nervous. The way she'd been behaving was beginning to get me down."[10] At the same time, she is described as an uncontrollable seductress whose toes are "lacquered a shrieking red," indicating her hidden hungers and depravity.[11] Susan's morbid fear of entering a church are interpreted by Father Gregory and Bishop Crimmings as symptoms of demonic possession, but, more personally, her violent, sexualized threats are interpreted as a threat to themselves, their social stature, and the general order of their world. Having detained Susan without her clear consent and tying her to a bedframe, the two priests begin the exorcism ritual on the demon allegedly inside her. Here, the demon, assumed to be Satan himself, and who is coded as male throughout the story, is given a voice and agency, while Susan herself is reduced to a retching "creature on the bed."[12] Susan's regression is marked by her making animalistic sounds, her behavior mimicking the wild, primitive behavior of an allegedly hysterical woman. This image will be repeated and emphasized in Blatty's text, as well. Any intelligent conversation and observations are attributed to the demon; the priests and Susan's father assert that no child of her age is capable of educated, intellectual thought, especially one as disturbed as Susan.

In both *The Case Against Satan* and *The Exorcist*, the central conflict of the story is not the young woman's suffering, but instead a priests' crisis of faith, not only in the powers of faith or psychology, but in their own superiority and authority. As Carol J. Clover notes, the primary conflict in the book is the threat to the authority and rationality of men: Susan's expressions of suffering "however theatrical its manifestation, is largely accessory."[13] This struggle is made even more wrenching when the demon inside Susan alleges that her trauma is the result of surviving multiple instances of sexual assault by her father. This revelation sets up yet another crisis of faith in the assembled priests, not because of Susan's victimization, but because her testimony casts doubt upon another male authority figure in their world.

It is at this point that the real conflict in the story emerges as Father Gregory is forced to confront a challenge to the masculine authority that has governed his world. Susan's begging to be heard and believed, and realizing that her words may very well be true is as frightening to Father Gregory as the presence of a demon inside her. The showdown in question between Father Gregory and the demon inside Susan takes place while Susan's father is pounding on the door:

"The man who tried to rape her—" Gregory held up the crucifix. "Tell me his name!"…

"If I tell you…" Her face was a putty mask being stretched and kneaded grotesquely by an unseen hand. "If I tell you the truth now, will you believe me?"

She had confused him. Would he believe a demented girl? Would he believe the

Father of Lies? And why believe one statement and not others? The pounding at the door was now a steady hysterical tempo.

"*Will—you—believe me?*" The question was torn from her bowels.

Not wanting to stop at this stage, playing along with her, Gregory said, "Yes, yes. Was it Father Halloran? Speak!"...

"This is the truth. It was he—he who knocks—"

"What?"

"He who pounds so long and hard on your door," she groaned. "He it is—whose name—you desire."[14]

When questioned by the priests who are attempting to "cure" her, Mr. Garth refutes Susan's claim, exclaiming "It's a lie ... don't believe her ... she's a filthy little liar."[15] The use of the word "filthy" not only refers to Susan's defilement by demonic possession, but also reminds us of her possible defilement by her father, even as he attempts to reject such accusations. Father Gregory's dilemma, then, is as much whether to accept a young female who speaks against her father as it is to believe in an adversary who speaks against God. In this sense, as in the descriptions of Susan's aberrant behavior, the demon and his female host are conflated into a single threatening, destabilizing entity:

> It was never as if he lacked faith or doubted the existence of God. The idea of God sustained him.... No, it is not difficult to believe in God—the very flesh reaches out for such belief—but for an intelligent man of the twentieth century to wipe from his mind the centuries of ridicule that have been heaped on the Devil, for him to take the Devil seriously, as seriously as he takes God; that is difficult.[16]

Eventually, the priests are successful in their attempts to exorcise the demon and "cure" Susan, which thoroughly renews Father Gregory's faith, both in his religion and in the psychology he has consulted throughout the text. The restoration of masculine authority in its complex and overlapping power allowed Father Gregory to assert at the book's finale, "I must believe.... Do you understand? I must believe that the Devil himself was in that girl and that we routed him. *None* of the evidence is unequivocally supernatural, and yet I believe it was."[17] His last interaction with Susan takes place after she has been moved to an orphanage managed by one of the priests she attacked during her period of illness or affliction. Thanks to his intervention, Susan is once again a dutiful and childlike figure, eager to do missionary work with the Church. In a final exchange, Father Gregory suggests to her that "some young *male* med student might try to change your mind" about becoming a doctor, and "if he does—don't fight too hard."[18] The proof of Susan's possession was her inability to submit to male authority, and the proof of her cure is her acceptance of that authority over both her mind and her life.

Regan MacNeil, the subject of exorcism in Blatty's *The Exorcist* is similarly presented as a dutiful, obedient, almost sycophantic child, whose first real symptoms of possession manifest as rebellion against masculine authority, both in her language to her father and when she refuses to let a doctor examine her for physical symptoms of illness. Dr. Klein's analysis and prognosis as delivered to Mrs. MacNeil emphasizes that it is Regan's rebellious behavior that is a cause of concern as much as the strange physical symptoms that manifest in and around her:

> "It's sometimes the symptom of a type of disturbance in the chemicoelectrical activity of the brain. In the case of your daughter, in the temporal lobe, you see ... so I think I'd like to give her an EEG."
> "What's that?"
> "Electroencephalograph. It will show us the pattern of her brain waves. That's usually a pretty good indication of abnormal functioning."
> "But you think that's it, huh? Temporal lobe?"
> "Well, she does have the syndrome, Mrs. MacNeil. For example, the untidiness; the pugnacity; behavior that's socially embarrassing; the automatism, as well. And of course, the seizures that made the bed shake."[19]

When these modern scientific options prove unhelpful, psychology and religion become conflated, with Klein describing Regan's symptoms as "hysterical" and evidence of her "primitive" nature:

> "An outside chance, since possession is loosely related to hysteria insofar as the origin of the syndrome is almost always autosuggestive. Your daughter must have known about possession, believed in possession, and known about some of its symptoms, so that now her unconscious is producing the syndrome. If that can be established, you might take a stab at a form of cure that's autosuggestive. I think of it as shock treatment in these cases" [...]
> "Name it, for God's sake! What is it?"
> "Have you ever heard of exorcism, Mrs. MacNeil?"[20]

It is into this image of domestic chaos, represented by a helpless single mother, that the figure of the Catholic priests, Fathers Karras and Merrin, arrive to re-instate both traditional sanity and gendered order. Once again, when confronted with Regan/Pazuzu's outbursts, the challenge to traditional authority terrifies and challenges the men; Karras' concern for Regan extends to keeping her alive and monitoring her pulse, but little else. As the demon notes, "You care nothing at *all* for the *pig. You care nothing!* You have *made her a contest between us!*"[21] In this contest for masculine superiority, Regan's suffering, and the reality of this control on her life, goes wholly ignored. Indeed, Merrin's insight into the purpose of possession implies that the demon's goal is to force the male observers to recognize their failings and primitive natures, rendering them as helpless and hopeless as the female victims of possession must themselves feel: "I think the point is to make us despair; to reject our own humanity, Damien: to see ourselves as ultimately bestial; as ultimately vile and putrescent; without dignity; ugly; unworthy."[22] Although Merrin is unable to see any connection between himself, Damien, and Regan, his insight asks for pity and understanding, just as Regan has throughout the text.

Much like Susan in *The Case Against Satan,* the notion that Regan might be dealing with grief or anger at her parents' divorce, or any form of subconscious psychological condition is suggested. Her breakdown exposes the rifts and disorder inherent in her life, including her mother's lack of maternal skills and potential alcoholism. In the throes of the exorcism, Regan/Pazuzu screams at Chris, "See the *puke!* See the murderous bitch! ... Are you pleased? It is *you* who have done it! Yes, *you,* with your career before *anything,* your career before your *husband,* before *her* ... your *divorce!* Go to priests, will you? Priests will not help!"[23] During the same tirade, she also calls out the lies told by her makeshift, dysfunctional family represented by the live-in servants Karl and Willie, as well as Father Karras' own troubled relationship with his mother: "Yes, we *know* of your kindness to *mothers,* dear Karras!"[24] Over and over during these outbursts and revelations, Karras and Merrin order all the others in the house not to listen and to ignore Regan, regardless of the truth of her statements. Again, Regan's outbursts often represent the voice of truth in the story, exposing the pain she endures within her family and the greater world. Those words, however, are attributed to the demon Pazuzu, and her agency goes generally ignored.

In *The Exorcist,* both Damien and Lancaster Merrick serve as the voice of reason and patriarchal blockades to the madness of women. This is clear not only in the physical restraint of Reagan during her period of possession, and Karras' comforting of Chris, but is alluded to throughout the text in relation to other characters, as well. For example, in their final conversation together, Detective Kellerman tells Father Karras about his aunt. As he explains it:

> "She was terrified—*terrified*—for years of my uncle. The poor woman, she never dared to say a world to him—*never!*—much less to ever raise her voice. So whenever she got mad at him for something, right away, she'd run quick to the closet in her bedroom, and then there in the dark—you won't believe this!—in the dark, by herself, with all the clothes hanging up and the moths, she would curse—she would *curse!*—at my uncle and tell him what she thought of him for maybe twenty minutes! ... She'd come out, she'd feel better, she'd go kiss him on the cheek."[25]

In this description, the apparently irrational, maddening rage of Kellerman's aunt is contained by the closet, a symbolic representation of his uncle's paternal control. The aunt remains "healthy" in Damien's estimation, because her rage and rebellion are contained. Patriarchal authority is maintained by her hiding in the closet, and not spewing her rage and her physical desires, violent or sexual, in front of others, as Regan does. This is confirmed when Damien replies: "And I'm your closet now?"[26] He and Merrin both serve as guards against Regan's outbursts, and their faith, in their God and each other, is strengthened as a result.

Following her exorcism Regan is shown reduced again to childhood helplessness, clutching two stuffed animals, and requiring the assistance of an adult to pack a suitcase. The danger she posed through her adult-like insight, her uncontrollable outbursts, and her physical strength have all been subdued. Her regression to childlike innocence is ultimately confirmed when she places a chaste kiss on Father Dyer's cheek. Like Susan Garth, the young woman who was full of intimate knowledge and the truth about others' corporeal desires (such as Sharon's lust for Father Karras), Regan's return to innocence, and her mental containment as a result of the exorcism is hailed as a triumph of faith and reason. Meanwhile, her mother accepts the gift of Father Karras' St. Christopher's medallion, a symbol that she, too, has accepted the masculine authority of the church, at least on some level, in her life and that of her daughter.

Paul Tremblay's *A Head Full of Ghosts* offers an intriguing post-modern approach to the exorcism novel that questions the assumptions of female instability and systems of male authority, even as it demonstrates their importance and influence. Tremblay even adds another layer of patriarchal knowledge and awareness in the form of a television reality show, run by men, who frame the story of Marjorie's exorcism in order to convey a specific narrative. The analysis of the television show provided in the text further demonstrates how Marjorie's agency and lived experience is almost totally silenced. Hired actors portray the Barrett family in re-enactments, with an older, more sexually mature actress literally placing words in Marjorie's mouth. When she is described by her sister or depicted on screen, she is dressed in a sports bra, in clothing that is too small, or ill-fitting, each article of clothing emphasizing her changing body and her changing mind. As the description of the show observes, "[W]hen we finally see the surveillance-style video of *real* Marjorie sitting in a room, across from an unnamed interviewer, wearing her soccer team sweatpants and sweatshirt, flipping her hair away from her face revealing her tired (haunted?) eyes, we're afraid for her and we're afraid of her."[27] Additionally, Mrs. Barrett is reframed and interpreted through the male gaze of the camera such that she also conforms to the image of the emotionally unstable woman, isolated from reason and faith. As Merry, the youngest Barrett daughter, recalls, the production team "painted her as the Doubting Thomas of the family, which she was. But they also made her seem like she was on the verge of an emotional breakdown.... I'm convinced they employed more than a little creative editing to her interviews. On the show she became the character who was inarticulately denying reality."[28] Indeed, Merry herself is only painted as trustworthy (by both the cameras and within the world of the book) because of her age and her childlike behavior.

Even as the text challenges the authority of patriarchal order and religious dogma throughout the text, from Mr. Barrett's unemployment and feeble leadership to Father Wanderly's weak handshake, doctors and priests still represent the highest authorities on Marjorie's condition and salvation. Indeed, faced with constant threats to their authority, male authorities, the medical, religious, and technological unite, magnifying their power and enforcing the idea of Marjorie's instability and untruthfulness with a vengeance. Mr. Barrett justifies involving the Church in Marjorie's condition by describing an alleged breakdown she suffered while they were alone in the car. The exchange between Marjorie's parents emphasize that the Church is yet another form of patriarchal control which Mr. Barrett turns to when his own control begins to fail in the face of Marjorie's outburst. That such an action makes sense to him and not Mrs. Barrett further emphasizes how systems of patriarchy reinforce each other in the face of the threat Marjorie poses:

> "I—I didn't know what to do. She was going…" Dad stopped.
> "Go ahead, say it. Crazy. Right? Your daughter was going crazy. So why not stop at church? Makes perfect sense to me."
> "Marjorie was freaking out and I was crying … and she was laughing at me, growling, making animal noises, telling me that I wanted to do all kinds of sexual things to her, Sarah. My baby girl saying that stuff to me…. And the church was on the way, it was right there, so I just stopped."[29]

Later, Father Wanderly, his psychologist-assistant Mr. Barrett, and the television producer all reinforce each other's authority by questioning and condemning Marjorie's knowledge of the rite of exorcism, her own body, and the works of H.P. Lovecraft. Together, they agree that "a girl like her can't speak as eloquently as she did."[30] Marjorie's words are discounted at the very moment when they might provide insight into the real nature of her suffering. The use of several unreliable narrators throughout the text make it even more difficult to parse the truth of her lived experience in the text.

Tremblay's novel emphasizes the utter breakdown of patriarchal authority: the psychologist departs, the church is ultimately unable to save Marjorie or her family, and the television crew abandons them after the failed exorcism. Nevertheless, with generations of masculine psychological theory on which to draw, and decades of patriarchal tropes depicting women as inherently unstable and unbelievable, *A Head Full of Ghosts* does not have to work hard at all to convince the television audiences, or readers, to doubt Marjorie's descriptions of her own suffering. She is rendered untrustworthy by virtue of her existing as a troubled pubescent teenager in a world that continues to accept that young women are inherently dangerous, unknowable, and fearsome in the darkest of ways. Marjorie's exorcism is unsuccessful, ultimately proving the limits of masculine power in the twenty-first century. Whether the demon is too strong for the priests who attempt to contain it, or whether, as is suggested, Marjorie and her mother conspire to outwit the men who are manipulating them, the result is that Marjorie is never returned to the child-like state that Susan and Regan were before her. Merry recalls for us the end of the failed exorcism, as Marjorie launches over a bannister in an apparent attempt to escape everything trying to contain her, from her family to the cameras, to gravity itself: "I remember her there, over and beyond the railing, hanging in the air, in empty space, time frozen like a snapshot. She was *there* and she's been there in my mind ever since. *There* is in the air, past the railing, and above the foyer."[31] In this way, she perhaps is the most fearsome woman in these texts, because she remains unknowable and uncontainable, by men, by medicine, or by reason itself.

In order to fully understand why horror novels scare us and linger in our memory as they do, it is critical to tease out the real-world concerns and themes, as well as the sources of order and power that can allay those fears. In exorcism novels, the history, both scientific and religious of masculine control and cultural anxieties over the irrationality and potential instability of pubescent and mature women is often translated into a terror of other-worldly possession; a fear which can be vanquished only through the mas-culine powers of the church and Western medicine. To "heal" a possessed woman is to rebalance the threatened and unstable real-world patriarchy, as well as to overlook the harm that such actions may have on the patient herself, or the world in which she must inhabit—on the page or off it.

NOTES

1. Joe. R Landsdale, "Interview: Robert R. McCammon," *The Twilight Zone Magazine,* 10 (1986), accessed July 1, 2018, https://www.robertmccammon.com/interviews/tz_interview. html.

2. "Reviews: Differences in the Nervous Organization of Man and Woman: Physio-logical and Pathological, by Harry Campbell, M.D.," in *The New York Journal of Gynaecology and Obstetrics,* 2(2) February 1892, 133.

3. See Charles E. Rosenberg, "Contested Boundaries: Psychiatry, Disease, and Diag-nosis," *Perspectives in Biology and Medicine,* 49(3) 2006, 407–424.

4. Betty A. DeBerg, *Ungodly Women: Gender and the First Wave of American Funda-mentalism* (Minneapolis: Fortress Press, 1990), 27.

5. Kristin Kobes Du Mez, "The Beauty of the Lillies: Femininity, Innocence, and the Sweet Gospel of Uldine Utley," *Religion and American Culture: a Journal of Interpretation* 15(2) 2005, 223.

6. A.D. Starkey, "The Roman Catholic Church and Violence Against Women," in *Reli-gion and Men's Violence Against Women,* ed. Andy J. Johnson (New York: Springer, 2015), 182.

7. Ray Russell, *The Case Against Satan* (New York: Penguin Classics, 2015 reprint), 11.

8. Paul Tremblay, *A Head Full of Ghosts* (New York: William Morrow, 2015), 158.

9. Sara Ahmed, *The Promise of Happiness* (Durham: Duke University Press, 2010), 65.

10. Russell, 17.

11. *Ibid.*, 33.

12. *Ibid.*, 99.

13. Carol J. Clover, *Men, Women, and Chainsaws; Gender in the Modern Horror Film* (Princeton, NJ: Princeton University Press, 1992), 85.
14. Russell, 101–2.
15. *Ibid.*, 110.
16. *Ibid.*, 44.
17. *Ibid.*, 137.
18. *Ibid.*, 134.
19. William Peter Blatty, *The Exorcist* (New York: Harper Collins, 2013; reprint), 108.
20. *Ibid.*, 191–2.
21. *Ibid.*, 347.
22. *Ibid.*, 351–2.
23. *Ibid.*, 349–50.
24. *Ibid.*, 350.
25. *Ibid.*, 364.
26. *Ibid.*
27. Tremblay, 100–1.
28. *Ibid.*, 188.
29. *Ibid.*, 58.
30. *Ibid.*,179.
31. *Ibid.*, 231.

Bibliography

Ahmed, Sara. *The Promise of Happiness*. Durham, NC: Duke University Press, 2010.

Blatty, William Peter. *The Exorcist*. New York: HarperCollins, 2013; reprint.

Campbell, Harry. "Reviews: Differences in the Nervous Organization of Man and Woman: Physiological and Pathological.," *The New York Journal of Gynaecology and Obstetrics* 2, no.2 (February 1892): 133.

Clover, Carol J. *Men, Women, and Chainsaws; Gender in the Modern Horror Film*. Princeton, NJ: Princeton University Press, 1992.

DeBerg, Betty A. *Ungodly Women: Gender and the First Wave of American Fundamentalism*. Minneapolis: Fortress Press, 1990.

Du Mez, Kristin Kobes. "The Beauty of the Lillies: Femininity, Innocence, and the Sweet Gospel of Uldine Utley," *Religion and American Culture: A Journal of Interpretation* 15.2 (2005): 209–243.

Landsale, Joe R. "Interview: Robert R. McCammon" *The Twilight Zone Magazine* (10) 1986. Accessed July 1, 2018. https://www.robertmccammon.com/interviews/tz_interview.html.

Rosenberg, Charles E. "Contested Boundaries: Psychiatry, Disease, and Diagnosis." *Perspectives in Biology and Medicine* 49.3 (2006): 407–424.

Russell, Ray. *The Case Against Satan*. New York: Penguin Classics, 2015; reprint.

Starkey, A.D. "The Roman Catholic Church and Violence Against Women," in *Religion and Men's Violence Against Women*, edited by Andy J. Johnson, 167–95. New York: Springer, 2015.

Tremblay, Paul. *A Head Full of Ghosts*. New York: William Morrow, 2015.

"Not a Bedtime Story"

Investigating Textual Interactions Between the Horror Genre and Children's Picture Books

Emily Anctil

Scary stories and tales of horror are some of the most memorable texts consumed by children. Whether it be R.L. Stine's significantly popular *Goosebumps* (1992–present) books, the folktale and urban legend retellings of Alvin Schwartz and Stephen Gammell's *Scary Stories to Tell in the Dark* (1981–1991) series, or novels and novellas such as Zilpha Keatley Snyder's *The Headless Cupid* (1971) and Neil Gaiman's *Coraline* (2002), children's horror has proved itself to be a celebrated and abundant subgenre of books for youth. A commonality between many of the books that make up this category of children's literature is that they are written for older children, ranging from children that are beginning to read by themselves to those that are beginning to read longer novels. For example, both *Goosebumps* and *Coraline*, prominent children's horror books that have spawned similar books as well as TV and movie adaptations, are targeted at children aged eight and over.[1]

A consequence of this focus on older children's horror literature is that scary stories for very young children are often overshadowed and excluded from discourse about children's horror. Although scary books targeted at children ranging from three to six have important differences from horror books written for older children, they can still contain qualities that put them in conversation with other texts in the horror genre for older children, teenagers, and adults. Juvenile picture books in particular have great potential to refer back to both horror literature and horror film, as picture books are hybrid art forms that make use of both textual time and visual space. The relationship between words and pictures presented in picture books has been

128

suggested to be filmic in nature,[2] and even the word "picture book" itself suggests hybridity: without a space or hyphen, picture book embodies the combination of the visual and textual.[3] This text-image relationship presented in picture books allows for the communication of meaning through multiple sign systems that intersect with each other, providing a literary experience that is both like reading a book and watching a film.[4] Because horror as a cultural practice and genre is so strongly reflected in both horror literature and horror film,[5] picture books provide ample opportunity for the analysis of horror elements in scary stories for very young children.

The Dark (2013), written by Lemony Snicket and illustrated by Jon Klassen, and *Is That You, Wolf?* (2012), written and illustrated by Steve Cox, are two children's picture books that reflect elements of horror literature and film through the use of literary and artistic techniques. In particular, these books utilize the visual primary metaphors, storytelling techniques, and conventional motifs of horror writing and filmmaking. *The Dark*, about a young boy named Laszlo who is beckoned by an anthropomorphized darkness into the basement of his large house, makes use of visual metaphors often seen in horror film, particularly "EVIL IS DOWN"[6] and "EVIL IS DARK,"[7] to create a sense of fear and foreboding. Snicket and Klassen also incorporate various images associated with the Gothic, a mode of literature and film that has strong ties to both children's literature and genre horror.[8] *Is That You, Wolf?* is a movable book about a pig named Brave Little Piglet who believes that there is a dangerous wolf hiding on the farm. As Brave Little Piglet checks various hiding spots for Wolf throughout the story, Cox uses genre contextualization as well as tactile elements on the pages to create suspense, eventually ending the book in a sudden, jump scare-like pop-up. This essay argues that *The Dark* and *Is That You, Wolf?* hold recognizable characteristics of horror literature and film in their "shadow text," a concept suggested by children's literature scholar Perry Nodelman in his work on children's books.[9] According to Nodelman, shadow text consists of a coded meaning that can be found in all works of children's literature, a meaning that exists by virtue of the fact that adult authors of children's books have a broader repertoire of knowledge than their implied child readership.[10] This suggests that the genre horror elements in *The Dark* and *Is That You, Wolf?* exist in the implications surrounding their simplified stories; the books are coded visually and textually with elements created by horror-literate adults. It can be inferred that the horror elements discoverable in these books are strong enough to locate them as horror texts, despite the fact that they are written for young children.

Although it may seem hard to find horror in contemporary books for children ages three to six, storytelling for young children this age commonly contained horror prior to the 20th century. In her work on fear in picture books, Jackie E. Stallcup suggests that many 18th- and 19th-century texts written for children used horror and violence in order to scare young readers into remaining obedient to adults.[11] By depicting children undergoing violent and horrifying punishments for disobedient acts, authors used horror and fear to maintain control over children who questioned adult authority.[12] Yet popular ideas about children and parenting have changed markedly since the 19th century. Stallcup suggests that in terms of contemporary picture books, modern adults prefer to write and publish books that *alleviate* fear in children.[13] These modern fear-alleviating texts put emphasis on the ultimate comfort of the child and often tell stories of children overcoming scary situations.[14] However, despite the fact that these books seem to contain little horror, Stallcup suggests that some fear-alleviating books still use horror in a subtle and sanitized fashion; instead of scaring children outright, some of these books use scary situations to evoke a sensation of fear before events of the story allow the fear to be dissolved.[15] Stallcup argues that books like this recall 18th- and 19th-century texts that use fear to control children, as many times in these contemporary stories the child protagonist finds safety and security in the arms of adults instead of facing their fear independently.[16] Whatever the undercurrent of adult power and control in these books may be, it is clear that horror and the evocation of fear are still present in some contemporary picture books for young children.

When it comes to frightening elements that connect children's picture books back to recognizable elements of the horror genre, it must be noted that although children may feel some of the effects of horror while reading these stories, genre elements are almost exclusively created and perpetuated by adults. Because adults have deemed horror texts, particularly horror films, inappropriate for children, the typical aesthetic and narrative elements of these texts are outside the repertoire of knowledge of most young consumers. Nodelman, in his work *The Hidden Adult: Defining Children's Literature* (2008), suggests that literature for children is defined partially by the existence of hidden elements like these.[17] Shadow text, according to Nodelman, consists of a secondary, coded meaning that exists in all literature for children.[18] This shadow text exists as a consequence of the fact that authors of children's books are almost exclusively adults; very few, if any, children write and publish literature for other children to read.[19] Thus, adult sensibility and perception affect every part of the creation of books for children.[20] In terms of elements of genre, it follows that any patterns, tropes, archetypes, or other typical characteristics of genre that adult authors write into children's books would be located inside shadow text, as the implied child reader does not yet have the breadth or depth of genre literacy needed to identify them. This is especially true when considering the horror genre, as children are not often introduced to these particular texts at a very young age.

There are a number of reasons that picture books are a compelling choice for analysis in this context. Nodelman suggests that the more simplified children's stories become, the more shadow text they are able to hold.[21] The short, simple text of a picture book therefore provides abundant opportunity for the study of shadow text. Another reason to look at picture books in this context is the fact that they are so closely tied to other forms of multimodal storytelling, particularly film.[22] Because horror as a cultural practice and genre is so strongly reflected in horror film,[23] the semiotic ties between picture books and film allow for a more complex and nuanced understanding of how horror elements are discoverable within texts for children. Finally, it is important to note the intended audience of juvenile picture books as they are published today. Children of a certain age range are the obvious audience for such texts, but there is another implied audience: the adults that will be reading these books to children. From a publishing standpoint, it does a picture book well to appeal to the sensibilities of both adults and children.[24] Adults are the gatekeepers of access to children's picture books in almost every respect, from the creation of the texts to their consumption. The hidden adult knowledge in picture books is therefore extensive; looking at picture books allows for a thorough analysis of recognizable horror elements in literature for young children.

As discussed previously in this essay, some of the dynamics of fear-alleviating picture books are suggested by Stallcup. *The Dark* is a fear-alleviating picture book that functions partially in the way that Stallcup describes. The story follows Laszlo, a young boy who is afraid of the dark that lives in his basement. When the light bulb in Laszlo's nightlight burns out one night, the dark enters Laszlo's room and speaks to him. It says, "I want to show you something,"[25] and Laszlo follows it throughout the house and down into the basement. Once there, the dark leads Laszlo to a rarely opened chest of drawers. Following the dark's instructions to open the bottom drawer, Laszlo reaches in and finds a new light bulb for his nightlight. After this interaction, Laszlo never experiences fear of the dark again.

The Dark functions as a fear-alleviating narrative picture book, but it contains numerous elements that connect it with horror film and literature as well. Along the lines of Stallcup's description, this book uses scares in order to mount suspense until any fear generated by the situation is dissolved at the end of the story.[26] However, unlike the books Stallcup looks at in her work, *The Dark* has a conspicuous lack of adult figures, and safety at the end of the book is found not in the arms of adults but in Laszlo's realization that darkness and light exist in a necessary balance. The absence of Laszlo's parents allows him to move through the story independently, but it also contributes to the book's sense of mounting anticipation; the reader is aware that Laszlo is going to deal with whatever waits for him in the basement alone. An absence of adults also allows for a heightened sense of danger. Laszlo's parents are unable to come to his rescue should the dark actually be planning to hurt him, and the reader is not made aware that Laszlo is not going to be hurt until the very end of the story. This noticeable lack of adult figures and safety recalls horror films starring young adults. According to horror scholars Pamela Craig and Martin Fradley, parents and authority figures are often ineffectual, detrimental, or completely absent altogether in contemporary American horror film starring children and teens.[27] Laszlo's isolation in this book allows him to forge ahead like a youthful horror protagonist, unaided by parental guardians.

Snicket and Klassen also use primary metaphors often seen in horror film to create a sense of danger and unease in the illustrations. On the cover of *The Dark*, Laszlo is pictured at the top of the basement stairs, looking downward, with one hand on the basement door. Light spills forward from behind him but stops at the third step down, everything else in the image is swallowed in darkness. Laszlo's small figure against the doorway and the stairs creates a sense of vulnerability; he is tiny and seemingly defenseless in the large space of the illustration. This vulnerability is strengthened by the use of two primary metaphors that scholar Bodo Winter has identified in horror filmmaking: EVIL IS DOWN and EVIL IS DARK. According to Winter, both EVIL IS DOWN and EVIL IS DARK are metaphors that have their origins primarily in the experience of space and environment. For example, he points to the fact that many children experience fear of darkness[28] and that negative emotions are associated with assuming lower positionality, such as the action of lowering one's head.[29] Winter argues that because of the negative feelings associated with low positionality and darkness, both EVIL IS DOWN and EVIL IS DARK are used generously in horror film to cause fear and discomfort.[30] The cover of *The Dark* uses these primary metaphors in this way as well, and the use of these metaphors contextualizes the book as a story that is meant to scare the reader. The basement stairs and Laszlo's gaze create downward trajectories while darkness shrouds the bottom of the stairs and the rest of the space. Laszlo's implied journey into the darkness at the bottom of the staircase here seems particularly dangerous and scary because of these visual techniques.

Snicket and Klassen continue to make use of EVIL IS DOWN and EVIL IS DARK throughout the rest of the picture book, as well. In terms of vertical positionality, Laszlo's bedroom is illustrated to be at the top of his large house, with at least two large staircases between him and the basement. This is meaningful; Laszlo must descend from top to bottom in order to meet the dark where it lives, moving downwards with an increased sense of fear. This effect is compounded by the use of EVIL IS DOWN in individual illustrations. On the thirteenth opening of the book Laszlo is seen pointing his flashlight down a large staircase that takes up both verso and recto in a full-bleed image. He is again seen descending the stairs into the basement in a similar fashion on the fifteenth opening. The downward trajectory of Laszlo's flashlight beam on these pages draws the reader's eye in a falling line from left to right. This visual representation of the movement from the top floor to the bottom floor of the house thus contributes to the book's mounting suspense with EVIL IS DOWN.

The text of the book also puts emphasis on Laszlo's descent. Snicket often repeats words like "downstairs" and "down" in the book's dialogue. For example, many of the dark's instructions to Laszlo include directions to descend: "'No, no,' said the dark. 'Downstairs.'"[31] Later, the dark tells Laszlo to come "down here."[32] As Laszlo gets closer and closer to the bottom floor of his house, the sense of fear created in the story is bolstered by the repetition of these words that evoke a sense of motion from top to bottom.

EVIL IS DARK is also present throughout the narrative. As Laszlo makes his descent towards the basement, he shines his flashlight beam in the direction the dark instructs him to go. This creates a strong visual contrast between darkness and light in the image, a chiaroscuro that puts emphasis on EVIL IS DARK and the void of blackness that the dark creates in the illustration. As Laszlo makes his way throughout the house, the flashlight gives both he and the reader a sense of control; the beam of light can illuminate anything Laszlo chooses. However, when Laszlo enters the basement on the 16th opening, the beam of light from his flashlight disappears. Although Laszlo is seen pointing the flashlight in front of him on verso, no light shines out. He is completely surrounded by darkness, making this space seem alien and unpredictable. This part of the book also constitutes the first time in the story that Laszlo is implied to be right next to the voice speaking to him. On the fifteenth opening the dark says, "come closer."[33] When Laszlo approaches forward on the 16th opening, the dark says, "even closer."[34] By stifling the light from Laszlo's flashlight in the illustration and making the dark seem very close in the text, Snicket and Klassen make it clear that Laszlo has left the area of the house where he was in a position of power. Here in the basement, Laszlo is at the mercy of the dark.

As discussed, EVIL IS DOWN and EVIL IS DARK create feelings of fear and foreboding throughout the text, and these primary metaphors connect the story back to horror filmmaking.[35] Winter argues in his work that primary metaphors like these are reinforced by repetition and continued use, especially when the same people are consuming them more than once, as in instances of genre filmmaking and the consumption of genre film.[36] However, there is also a strong perpetuation of these metaphors that occurs when they are passed from generation to generation: "the fact that [a conceptual metaphor] subsequently becomes expressed in culture, such as in the case of horror movies, means that culture provides a new set of ... correlations for the next generation."[37] In other words, horror-literate adults can pass on frequently used horror metaphors such as EVIL IS DOWN and EVIL IS DARK to younger generations through the genre texts that they create. *The Dark* provides an excellent example of this. Snicket and Klassen utilize EVIL IS DOWN and EVIL IS DARK in this fear-evoking and fear-alleviating children's story, and in doing so they strengthen these primary metaphors and subtly pass them to children through the book's shadow text.

Aside from its usage with primary metaphors, *The Dark* has a connection to Gothic horror. In their introduction to *The Gothic in Children's Literature: Haunting the Borders* (2008), Anna Jackson, Karen Coats, and Roderick McGillis argue that much of contemporary children's literature is significantly Gothic in nature.[38] In particular, children's books often "invoke … specifically Victorian settings."[39] This is true of *The Dark*; both Snicket and Klassen work with certain characteristics of Laszlo's house to make it seem distinctly Gothic. For example, when looking at the illustration, the reader might notice that the house seems vast, spacious, and unusually empty. On the thirteenth opening depicting Laszlo at the top of a large staircase, it can be observed just how large the space of the house is compared to Laszlo's small figure. Klassen also puts particular emphasis on the hardwood flooring and paneling of the house in this illustration. One can imagine the stairs and floor creaking underfoot.

Snicket focuses strongly on the Gothic elements of the house in the text of the book, as well. He describes various features of the space on the fifth opening: "The dark lived in the same house as Laszlo, a big space with a creaky roof, smooth, cold windows, and several sets of stairs."[40] In his essay "The Night Side of Nature: Gothic Spaces, Fearful Times," McGillis suggests that in terms of Gothic houses, "the older and bigger the better."[41] Laszlo's house certainly seems old and big. This is especially observable in its representation on the 14th opening, which depicts Laszlo looking out of one of the house's big windows on verso. In the illustration, Laszlo is only tall enough to see just above the windowsill. Above him, the window stretches to the top of the page and outside the reach of the light created by Laszlo's flashlight. The text reads: "In Laszlo's living room was the biggest window in the house. Laszlo looked out at all the dark outside. Above him the roof creaked, and he closed his eyes. Now the dark was all Laszlo could see."[42] It becomes clear on this page that the house is inherently connected to Laszlo's experience and fear of the dark, and that the setting of the story serves to strengthen this book's connection to Gothic horror and horror in general. Through the incorporation of these elements, Snicket and Klassen imbue *The Dark* with a strong sense of horror that is decodable by genre-literate readers familiar with Gothicism and other, similar aesthetic and textual qualities of horror.

Moving from *The Dark* to *Is That You, Wolf?*, it is observable that picture books can and do appropriate and transform elements of other horror texts in order to evoke and alleviate fear. By point of comparison with *The Dark*, *Is That You, Wolf?* is resolutely *not* a fear-alleviating picture book, as evidenced by the illustrated sign hanging down from the right corner of the cover image. It reads: "BEWARE! Not a Bedtime Story!"[43] This warning locates *Is That You, Wolf?* firmly in the category of books that are meant to evoke fear; the reader gets the sense that this book is not going to alleviate their fear, but instead cause it, promising an exciting and suspenseful reading experience. Another section of text on the bottom left corner of the cover reads: "Check inside the secret pockets if you dare!"[44] The use of "beware" on the illustrated sign and the rhyming of "if you dare" in the text below it recalls *Goosebumps'* famous call to action: "Reader beware—you're in for a scare!"[45] Text like this presents a tempting challenge to child readers. The book dares its audience to interact with it despite its scariness, allowing the contextualization of the book itself to function in much the same way as both *Goosebumps* and adult horror literature and film. The excitement that comes from the knowledge that readers and viewers are going to be purposefully scared makes the text attractive to those that are seeking this kind of experience. It is a kind of promise that all texts in the horror genre make to their consumers: if you read or watch this, you will experience fear. *Is That You, Wolf?* participates in genre horror contextualization in this way.

The book continues to reflect and appropriate elements of horror throughout its story, as well. In terms of scares, *Is That You, Wolf?* provides a markedly different reading experience than *The Dark*. For example, Cox uses tactile elements and further genre contextualization to encourage increased reader immersion. The story of *Is That You, Wolf?* follows Brave Little Piglet, a young pig who believes that a terrifying wolf, called "Wolf" in the story, is hiding somewhere on the farm. The story begins on the first opening with an image of Brave Little Piglet walking along a pleasant country path, the sun descending below the horizon behind him. This calm, peaceful scene provides contrast for the atmosphere of the rest of the book, as the oncoming of night makes the farm seem more and more unpredictable and dangerous as the story progresses. According to Winter, nightfall is a popular example of EVIL IS DARK in horror texts.[46] Winter suggests that the oncoming of night creates fear for a number of reasons, namely the fact that most human-eating predators choose nighttime to hunt.[47] This explanation certainly fits into the story of *Is That You, Wolf?* On the second opening, Brave Little Piglet wonders if Wolf has come to the farm in order to catch and kill the farm's new lamb.[48] Wolf is set up immediately as a predator coming after vulnerable prey. As night falls on the farm, the stakes of the story are significantly raised; the chances of Wolf being able to kill the new lamb are better when he can use the dark to his advantage.

The second opening is also where Brave Little Piglet encourages the reader to interact with the tactile elements of the book for the first time. After wondering about the safety of the new lamb, the narrator mentions that Brave Little Piglet hears something move in the barn.[49] On recto, Brave Little Piglet is illustrated looking at a large haystack, upon which an envelope is built into the physical page of the book. The envelope is oriented upside down, with an open slot at the bottom. Text printed on the envelope reads: "Slide your hand in if you dare.... Wolf may be lurking so BEWARE!"[50] These pockets are the main conceit of Is That You, Wolf? The book encourages the reader over the course of the story to reach into various envelopes to feel what is inside, all the time making it clear that Wolf could be hiding in that particular spot, waiting to attack. Inside the envelopes are fabrics and other tactile articles that, later in the story, become indicative of certain parts of Wolf's body. For example, on the fourth opening, Brave Little Piglet exclaims that you can feel Wolf's feet inside the pocket. However, the fear and alarm of these exclamations are always diffused on the next page, as Brave Little Piglet finds over and over that he's mistaken something harmless for Wolf.

This type of reading experience uses horror in a number of ways. First, each time Brave Little Piglet thinks he has found the Wolf hiding, a sense of urgency and fear is created and strengthened through text and image. In the illustration, Cox emphasizes Brave Little Piglet's fearful expression; he is always looking pensive, curious, or outright afraid, even when the objects he feels inside the hiding spots turn out to be innocuous. His faith that Wolf is hiding on the farm continues throughout the book, despite the fact that all the other animals believe the farm to be safe. When Brave Little Piglet expresses his fear to others, the animals all reassure him with the same phrase: "Don't be silly! ... There aren't any wolves here."[51] Yet Brave Little Piglet persists with his assertion that the farm is in danger. His commitment to the existence of Wolf in the face of the other animals' suspicion gives weight to the impending scares in the story and also recalls the horror films starring youth discussed in Craig and Fradley's work.[52] Brave Little Piglet, like many young horror protagonists, must act without the help or safety provided by his adult guardians.

Cox also emphasizes Brave Little Piglet's fear in the text of the book. For example, he continuously uses the word "cried" to describe Brave Little Piglet's exclamations. For example, on the sixth opening, the narrator says: "'It's Wolf's claws!' he cried."[53] The use of cried in this context puts focus on Brave Little Piglet's alarm and horror at thinking he has finally discovered Wolf. The fear evoked in the text is strengthened by the reader's knowledge that Brave Little Piglet is afraid too.

Second, the strategic repetition of false scares throughout the story provides a good foundation for the one, real scare at the end of the book: a sudden pop-up where Wolf jumps out from inside a tree on the 11th opening.

This sudden scare only comes when Brave Little Piglet is finally convinced that Wolf is nowhere to be found. There is a short moment of safety on the tenth opening when Brave Little Piglet goes to play with his friends, but it is quickly dissolved when the narrator explains that someone is watching him from inside a tree.[54] When the reader turns the page, Wolf jumps out of the tree and all the farm animals, including Brave Little Piglet, run away terrified. This jumpscare-like page presents a climax for the mounting suspense of the story. It also acts as the only ending the book has. The pop-up on the 11th opening is the final page of the story; there is no concluding reassurance that Brave Little Piglet, the new lamb, or any of the characters introduced through-out the book escape Wolf. In fact, it could be presumed that quite the opposite occurs, as Wolf is depicted as far larger and more powerful than any of the animals on the farm. This open ending allows for a secondary, far darker and more disturbing shadow text to emerge from the surface narrative, one that involves the protagonist's demise.

What stands out most about *Is That You, Wolf?* is arguably Cox's decision to use these interactive elements to immerse the reader into the story. Beyond raising the stakes and moving the story forward, the inclusion of the envelopes and the pop-up helps to make this book a horror experience distinct from other scary stories for young children. In his work on children's horror and *Goosebumps*, scholar Patrick Jones observes that there is an important distinc-tion between writing horror for older children and writing horror for younger children. Using *Goosebumps* and Stine's other work for teenagers as an exam-ple, Jones suggests that horror for young children essentially asks the ques-tion, "What if this could happen?"[55] In other words, horror for children tends to focus on supernatural and otherworldly situations in order to lessen the real fear and threat involved. *The Dark* could fit into this description. Horror fiction for older children, however, heightens the threat. Jones suggests that books like these tend to ask the question, "What if this could happen to *you*?"[56] Horror fiction for older children brings the threat home, making it seem more real and therefore scarier to the reader. It is interesting that *Is That You, Wolf?* uses its immersive, tactile elements to subvert this pattern. By encouraging the reader to reach their hand into a place where Wolf is said to be hiding, Cox forces the reader to wonder what would happen if this actually happened to them. *Is That You, Wolf?* is less about the farm and Brave Little Piglet being threatened by Wolf and more about the reader's experience of that threat.

This is also evidenced by the lack of true ending. If the story were truly about Brave Little Piglet and the other animals, the narrative would have likely continued after the climactic jump scare. However, there is no real con-clusion to the story itself; this book is focused primarily on the scares. In this way, *Is That You, Wolf?* is connected even more closely to horror for older children and adults than it is to scary stories for very young children. It does not exist to alleviate fear or to dissolve it. It exists instead to evoke fear in an exciting and interesting way, much like horror literature and film strives to do for older readers and viewers.

The many elements of genre encouraged and communicated in the shadow texts of *The Dark* and *Is That You, Wolf?* thus connect their stories strongly to other forms and texts of horror. Returning to the concept of shadow text, Nodelman suggests that this coded meaning found in children's literature has inherent ties to the adult understanding that all children must eventually become adults,[57] and that as they grow up and mature, children need adults to write books that provide them with the information they need to operate in the world.[58] If books like *The Dark* and *Is That You, Wolf?* hold genre elements in their shadow texts by virtue of the fact that adult authors and illustrators have a broader repertoire of genre knowledge than their readership, it implies the question: what is the knowledge that creators of horror texts for very young children impart to their readers?

Winter's analysis of primary metaphors provides a starting point for the answering of this question. As discussed previously, Winter argues that the creation of horror film perpetuates and strengthens primary metaphors, both reinforcing them in the minds of their returning audiences and creating them in the minds of younger generations.[59] If primary metaphors can be passed to children through horror texts, then some of the most powerful work performed by books like *The Dark* and *Is That You, Wolf?* involves the cultivation of a child reader's genre literacy. Horror is a genre that defines itself by the creation and recreation of archetypes, motifs, aesthetic elements, and storytelling techniques distinct to its texts. Although genre horror as adults know it may be difficult to find on the surface of books for very young children, many of these books do contain qualities that horror-literate readers will be able to identify. These genre elements, existing in the implications surrounding the deceptively simple story of the picture book, could begin a process of learning that allows children the opportunity to make connections between texts, understand the effects of visual and textual storytelling, and appreciate the nuances and intricacies of the horror genre.

NOTES

1. "Goosebumps Series," *Common Sense Media,* last modified January 12, 2018, https://www.commonsensemedia.org/book-reviews/goosebumps-series; "Coraline," *Common Sense Media,* last modified May 19, 2018, https://www.commonsensemedia.org/book-reviews/coraline.

2. Lawrence R. Sipe, "How Picture Books Work: A Semiotically Framed Theory of Text-Picture Relationships," *Children's Literature in Education* 29.2 (1998): 100, https://link-springer-com.ezproxy.library.ubc.ca/article/10.1023%2FA%3A1022459009182.

3. David Lewis, introduction to *Reading Contemporary Picturebooks: Picturing Text* (New York: Routledge Falmer, 2001), xiv.

4. Sipe, "How Picture Books Work," 100–101.

5. Bodo Winter, "Horror Movies and the Cognitive Ecology of Primary Metaphors," *Metaphor and Symbol* 29.3 (2014): 151, https://www-tandfonline-com.ezproxy.library.ubc.ca/doi/abs/10.1080/10926488.2014.924280.

6. Winter, "Horror Movies," 152–153.

7. *Ibid.*

8. Anna Jackson, Karen Coats, and Roderick McGillis, introduction to *The Gothic in Children's Literature: Haunting the Borders*, ed. Anna Jackson, Karen Coats, and Roderick McGillis (New York: Routledge, 2008), 1.

9. Perry Nodelman, *The Hidden Adult: Defining Children's Literature* (Baltimore: Johns Hopkins University Press, 2008), 8.

10. *Ibid.*, 77.

11. Jackie E. Stallcup, "Power, Fear, and Children's Picture Books," *Children's Literature* 30.1 (2002): 125, https://muse-jhu-edu.ezproxy.library.ubc.ca/article/247516.

12. *Ibid.*

13. *Ibid.*, 125–126. Emphasis mine.

14. *Ibid.*

15. *Ibid.*, 132.

16. *Ibid.*, 134.

17. Nodelman, *The Hidden Adult*, 8.

18. *Ibid.*

19. *Ibid.*, 3, 8.

20. *Ibid.*, 150.

21. *Ibid.*, 9.

22. Sipe, "How Picture Books Work," 100.

23. Winter, "Horror Movies," 151.

24. Elizabeth Bullen and Susan Nichols, "Dual Audiences, Double Pedagogies: Representing Family Literacy as Parental Work in Picture Books," *Children's Literature in Education* 42.3 (2011): 214, https://link-springer-com.ezproxy.library.ubc.ca/article/10.1007%2Fs10583-011-9132-5.

25. Lemony Snicket, *The Dark*, illus. Jon Klassen (New York: HarperCollins, 2013), eleventh opening. Please note that the term "opening" hereafter refers to the number of times a reader flips the pages of a picture book reading left-to-right, with cover and endpapers included.

26. Stallcup, "Power, Fear, and Children's Picture Books," 132.

27. Pamela Craig and Martin Fradley, "Teenage Traumata: Youth, Affective Politics, and the Contemporary American Horror Film," in *American Horror Film: The Genre at the Turn of the Millennium*, ed. Steffen Hantke (Jackson: University Press of Mississippi, 2010), 92.

28. Winter, "Horror Movies," 152.

29. *Ibid.*

30. *Ibid.*, 166.

31. Snicket, *The Dark*, twelfth opening.

32. *Ibid.*, fourteenth opening.

33. *Ibid.*, fifteenth opening.

34. *Ibid.*, sixteenth opening.

35. Winter, "Horror Movies," 152.

36. *Ibid.*, 164.

37. *Ibid.*, 165.

38. Jackson, Coats, and McGillis, introduction to *The Gothic in Children's Literature*, 1.

39. *Ibid.*, 4.

40. Snicket. *The Dark*, fifth opening.

41. Roderick McGillis, "The Night Side of Nature: Gothic Spaces, Fearful Times," in *The Gothic in Children's Literature: Haunting the Borders*, ed. Anna Jackson, Karen Coats, and Roderick McGillis (New York: Routledge, 2008), 228.

42. Snicket, *The Dark,* fourteenth opening.

43. Steve Cox, *Is That You, Wolf?* (New York: Barron's, 2012), cover.

44. *Ibid.*

45. "Original Goosebumps," *Goosebumps*, last modified 2018, http://goosebumps. scholastic.com/books/original-goosebumps-1992–1997.
46. Winter, "Horror Movies," 152.
47. *Ibid.*
48. Cox, *Is That You, Wolf?*, second opening.
49. *Ibid.*
50. *Ibid.*
51. *Ibid.*, third opening, fifth opening, seventh opening, and ninth opening.
52. Pamela Craig and Martin Fradley, "Teenage Traumata," 92.
53. Cox, *Is That You, Wolf?*, sixth opening.
54. *Ibid.*, tenth opening.
55. Patrick Jones, *What's So Scary About R.L. Stine?* (Lanham, MD: Scarecrow, 1998), 158–159.
56. *Ibid.*, emphasis mine.
57. Nodelman, *The Hidden Adult*, 31.
58. *Ibid.*, 4.
59. Winter, "Horror Movies," 164–165.

BIBLIOGRAPHY

Bullen, Elizabeth, and Susan Nichols. "Dual Audiences, Double Pedagogies: Representing Family Literacy as Parental Work in Picture Books." *Children's Literature in Education* 42.3 (2011). https://link-springer-com.ezproxy.library.ubc.ca/article/10.1007%2Fs10583–011-9132–5.

Common Sense Media. "Coraline." Last modified May 19, 2018. https://www.commonsense media.org/book-reviews/coraline.

_____. "Goosebumps Series." Last modified January 12, 2018. https://www.commonsense media.org/book-reviews/goosebumps-series.

Cox, Steve. *Is That You, Wolf?* New York: Barron's, 2012.

Craig, Pamela, and Martin Fradley. "Teenage Traumata: Youth, Affective Politics, and the Contemporary American Horror Film," in *American Horror Film: The Genre at the Turn of the Millennium*, edited by Steffen Hantke, 77–102. Jackson: University Press of Mississippi, 2010.

Jackson, Anna, Karen Coats, and Roderick McGillis. Introduction to *The Gothic in Children's Literature: Haunting the Borders*, edited by Anna Jackson, Karen Coats, and Roderick McGillis, 1–14. New York: Routledge, 2008.

Jones, Patrick. *What's So Scary About R.L. Stine?*. Lanham, MD: Scarecrow Press, 1998.

Lewis, David. Introduction to *Reading Contemporary Picturebooks: Picturing Text*, xiii. New York, London: Routledge Falmer, 2001.

McGillis, Roderick. "The Night Side of Nature: Gothic Spaces, Fearful Times," in *The Gothic in Children's Literature: Haunting the Borders*, edited by Anna Jackson, Karen Coats, and Roderick McGillis, 227–241. New York: Routledge, 2008.

Nodelman, Perry. *The Hidden Adult: Defining Children's Literature*. Baltimore: Johns Hopkins University Press, 2008.

"Original Goosebumps." *Goosebumps*. Last modified 2018. http://goosebumps.scholastic. com/books/original-goosebumps-1992–1997.

Sipe, Lawrence R. "How Picture Books Work: A Semiotically Framed Theory of Text-Picture Relationships." *Children's Literature in Education* 29.2 (1998). https://link-springer-com.ezproxy.library.ubc.ca/article/10.1023%2FA%3A1022459009182.

Snicket, Lemony. *The Dark*. Illustrated by Jon Klassen. New York: HarperCollins, 2013.

Stallcup, Jackie E. "Power, Fear, and Children's Picture Books." *Children's Literature* 30.1 (2002). https://muse-jhu-edu.ezproxy.library.ubc.ca/article/247516.

Winter, Bodo. "Horror Movies and the Cognitive Ecology of Primary Metaphors." *Metaphor and Symbol* 29.3 (2014). https://www-tandfonline-com.ezproxy.library.ubc.ca/doi/abs/10.1080/10926488.2014.924280.

Synchronic Horror
and the Dreaming

*A Theory of Aboriginal Australian
Horror and Monstrosity*

NAOMI SIMONE BORWEIN

A curious intersection exists between monster theory, anthropology, and Aboriginal Australian horror literature. The genre of Indighorror, infused with darker myths of the Dreamtime, is swept up in "monster" discourse, which elicits reactionary and pejorative responses from White and Aboriginal Australia. Monster studies has blossomed as a field, mirrored ironically in monster anthropology, which analyzes "nightmarish" figures of the Dreaming[1] depicted in Indighorror fiction, as an echo of reality and history, premised on standard horror and monster theory of Noël Carroll, Jeffrey Jerome Cohen, and others. Indighorror is a branch of Aboriginal Australian fiction where the horror genre is used as a scaffolding to evoke Indigenous epistemology, metaphysics, and myth. The genre has transformed radically since Ngarrindjeri scholar David Unaipon's 1920s story, "Yara Ma Yha Who." Officially called the first Aboriginal Australian horror tale,[2] it is a written translation of a monstrous mythological figure that exists in Dreamtime, as a part of the oral tradition of Indigenous Australia. When it was written, the tale was often viewed as a source of sociological data. Aboriginal fictions into the 1990s continued to be read as "simply being sociological texts."[3] Today the monsters seen in contemporary Indighorror retain echoes of both their mythological origins and the anthropological readings of monstrosity that once constrained them. Hence, there is the need to investigate this complex theoretical foundation and its application, making way for new methodological perspectives. From the cultural and anthropological context in which the genre took form, readers and critics have had an active impact on how it has been read in monster and horror theory. This is clear when starting to critically inspect and then juxtapose interdisciplinary studies of anthropology, and monster and horror theory. Ultimately, this essay develops an Aboriginal Australian theory of horror and monstrosity, as a culturally specific paradigm based on the complex cosmology of the Dreaming, and its often-destructive totemic figures; such a theory can be applied to the fiction that contemporary Aboriginal Australia is creating. The paradox of monstrosity in the Indighorror genre is a facet of the sociological and ethnographic history of its literary tradition in Australia and the power and ubiquity of the Dreaming in the Australian horror tradition.

The content in this essay has been organized to establish the theoretical basis of how modern Indighorror has been read and to build a framework to help understand how it can be read. To develop a non–Western perspective on the material, this essay is structured into three main parts. The first part is an examination of essential cultural context necessary to comprehend an Indigenous-based theory; this part of the analysis incorporates a reading of book covers, historical details, literary antecedents, and Aboriginal epistemology. Through context and paratext, the position of Aboriginal horror is explored in relation to Australian horror. After which, the difference between the Dark Side of the Dreaming and the Dark Side of the Dream, where mythology fosters constructions of fear, monstrosity, and identity, are explicated. The second part of the essay investigates pertinent monster and horror theory. To build a new theoretical approach that acknowledges the Indigenous ontological roots of the genre, this essay analyzes accepted scholarship on monstrosity within monster studies, monster anthropology, and some horror theory as applicable to Australian Aboriginality. This analysis leads to a description of a new mixed methodology or theory of synchronic horror and monstrosity that can be applied to Aboriginal Australian horror fiction, as produced by Indigenous writers from Philip McLaren to Raymond Gates. Note that synchronic horror is a form of horror that uses a non-diachronic order to evoke fear, represent monstrosity, and examine identity, and it expresses a non-sequential ontological system. Synchronic horror can be viewed as a universalist paradigm, but it functions in a similar capacity to the way an Aboriginal horror theory of monstrosity should. This essay reconceptualizes synchronic horror into an Aboriginal way of being and thinking. Thus, the final part of the essay extends part one and two to a textual analysis of self-identifying Aboriginal authors, whose narratives embody a unique, dynamic theory of culturally specific horror and monstrosity.

Context

As a modern genre, Indighorror emerged in the 1980s and 1990s. It is a mode that elicits fear, and contains elements from Aboriginal metaphysics, cosmology, culture, and identity.[4] It is constrained to self-identified Indigenous writers and has evolved substantially from the works of Sam Watson, Alexis Wright, and Mudrooroo to those of Gates, D. Bruno Starrs, Philip McLaren, and even Ambelin Kwaymullina.

To conceptualize the breadth of Indighorror and its place in the Australian horror tradition, consider some horror-themed covers used to market the genre. They establish the iconography and imagery that fuel a definition, which is inherently hybridized between Aboriginal and White Australian context.

Compare two covers of Mudroodroo's vampire novel *The Undying* (1997), circulated twenty years apart: the 2017 cover uses a painting by Declan Apuatimi that evokes slavery and torture with gritty realism, and uses blood-red hues on a black background, while the 1997 cover depicts a dark Dreaming narrative. These two aspects, nightmares of the Dreaming, as myth, and horrorrealism, are binaries entrenched in the genre. Early covers of Wright's *Plains of Promise* (1997) and Watson's *The Kadaitcha Sung* (1990) showcase images that relate to horrorrealism and the Dreamtime, as the hybrid reality of the Aboriginal condition. Other covers such as Kim Scott's *Benang* (2002) and McLaren's *Sweet Water, Stolen Land* (1993) use images of totems, shadow figures around a bonfire at night, and incorporate style from bark painting and photography, blended with various horror tropes and clichés: blood splatters, heavy use of black backgrounds, skeletal forms, and more. Many of these themes persist in recent works that use Indighorror tropes, but with increasingly global paratext, which can refocus White Australian elements in a transnational context. Take, for instance, the cover of Starrs's *That Blackfella Bloodsucka Dance!* (2011), a title reminiscent of Scott's *That Deadman Dance* (2010), uses European vampire iconography through the cross. However the layout resembles a travel guide, again suggesting realism and voyeurism. While, Kwaymullina's *The Tribe* (2012) shows a deformed face on the cover, a primal embodiment of evil, reflecting darker manifestations of totemism and animism. Indeed, this subset of covers suggest the way in which Indighorror is defined in Australia, and starting to be defined in a global arena. Ironically, they also expose some strong components of the genre: a focus on horrorrealism, the violence of assimilation and dispossession, dark aspects of the Dreaming, Aboriginality through mythology, totemism, and animism. They often combine images of monstrosity and Dreaming nightmares with urban and Outback horror motifs. Such elements relate directly to the mechanisms underpinning Indighorror theory, and Aboriginal methodology that is a part of a theory of horror and monstrosity.

The Hellish Antipodes in Aboriginal Horror

The genre of Indighorror has been affected by myriad factors from White and Indigenous Australia. Such influences include the nature and impact of colonialism on Aboriginal literary production and the effects of *Terra Nullius* (1788) that was mythologized into the *Terror of Terra Nullius* which itself was subverted into a Gothic myth by early colonists. *Terra Nullius* was a legal international law doctrine starting in the 17th century, giving colonial powers the right to control empty territory and thereby Britain the rights to the hellish antipodes as a terra incognita. "Monstrosity" in this supposedly "uninhabited land" came to encompass Indigenous mythology, culture, and identity, looming in the hostile and barren Outback and in the horror of early White Australia. The horror of the land is also a strong feature of convict and settler mythology about the harshness of penal Australia where violent conflicts arose between Aborigines and Whites. This fear, embodied by the wilderness as Other, filtered into an Australian horror tradition.

In Aboriginal Australia, factors that have influenced the genre come from three diverse origins: from darker narratives of Indigenous mythology and the Dreaming; horrorrealism seen in depictions of assimilation, dispossession, and urbanization as by-products of colonization; and White colonial and settler context that made Indigenous people monstrosities of the Outback. Aboriginal horror fiction has its origins in orality and the short story form: as the oral myths of the Dreaming, as well as in Unaipon's "Yara Ma Yha Who," which was the first English translation of a Dreaming myth to be written down and published.

Indigenous horror writing can be understood visually; vast arrays of images from street graffiti to covers of horror texts are a powerful cultural paratext to the way Indigenous culture and myth collide as horror in White Australia today. For instance, street art in Melbourne and Newcastle depict the primal horror of an Indigenous child trapped in an urban space. An example can be found in Adnate's 2013 portrait of an Indigenous boy. It depicts striking vertical red and yellow lines against a black backdrop reminiscent of the Aboriginal flag, which is a yellow circle in a rectangle horizontally bisected by one red and one black stripe.

Furthermore, it is necessary to take into account real contemporary cultural context impacting the genre and its production. The following five circumstances affected the ability of Indighorror to be published and circulated until the rise of digital publishing. Equally, these four circumstances added to the proliferation of an ethnographic, monsterized subject:

> 1. Indigenous authorship started in earnest in the late 1960s. Aboriginal writers were essentially only allowed to publish memoir and life

writing, which became their dominant literary mode into the twenty-first century along with "political protest/cultural revival literature."[5] Indighorror was originally marketed within memoir, and later thriller. The genre is still nearly verboten to the Australian publishing industry.[6]

2. The Australian 1967 Referendum finally granted Aborigines the legal status of Australian people, amending a constitution that only protected rights with "respect to the people of any race, other than Aboriginal people."[7] This contextualizes a cultural atmosphere where continued anthropological and sociological readings of a "living fossil," with non-human status, have implications for representations of monstrosity.

3. Censorship laws, and in particular obscenity laws, under the "Restrictions on the Freedom of Expression," in Australia are more draconian than their American and British counterparts. What constitutes "obscenity," and the sort of publications that are censored, is broader, intimating a cultural sensitivity to depictions of horror. For instance in New South Wales the law defines obscenity to include: "(a) tending to deprave and corrupt persons whose minds are open to immoral influences; and (b) unduly emphasising matters of sex, crimes of violence, gross cruelty or horror."[8]

4. Horror writing was outsourced to Britain and America, in different capacities, which damaged the Indighorror market in Australia.[9]

5. There were concerns about the reading of horror within an Australian Catholic society as described in a panel session later published in *Studies in Australian Weird Fiction Volume 1* (2008).

Such cultural context had a powerful effect on the genre. To further complicate matters, since the Australian Golden Age of Literature (*circa* 1900), horror was a palpable part of White Australian literary tradition, as seen in Banjo Patterson and Henry Lawson. These factors seem to diminish an appetite for home-grown horror. Indeed, such conditions contributed to the relatively late rise of horror fiction in Australia, and its lackluster "commercial or critical success."[10]

As a part of that initial horror boom, nationally syndicated magazines surfaced, during a time as previously noted when Aboriginal writing was mainly published as memoir. More pertinently, these magazines showcased the importance of Aboriginal culture and mythology to Australian horror. This is visible in paratext and other editorial decisions, as much as in the writing in these magazines. For example, the first mass-market horror magazine in Australia, *Terror Australis*, included in its first edition a story called "Dreamers" by Beth Yahp, an extension of images and myths seen in Rosa Praed's early short story "The Dreamers."

The cover of the inaugural edition of *Aurealis*, one of Australia's first national horror and sci-fi magazines, use the Aboriginal's flag as a background to emphasize Australian horror and sci-fi tropes: the flag is transformed into an illustration of dusk, a yellow sun or moon in the middle, the black horizon above, and red land speckled with dark rocks; the only inhabitant is a skeletal figure in a breechclout with a staff whose exaggerated features enhance its alien Otherness. Like many Australian horror publications, they incorporate Aboriginal myth and imagery into a White horror tradition, as a manifestation of fear. Other magazines, like *Bloodsongs* and *Dark Animism*, imply shadows of the Indighorror tradition intimated in an Australian context: from the animism of Aboriginal totemism to the term "bloodsongs" as a reference to songlines.

With a point of origin in the Dreaming, hundreds of thousands of years ago,[11] Indighorror is increasingly difficult to disambiguate in the chronology of Australian horror literature set forth by former Australian Horror Writers Association President, Marty Young.[12] However, elsewhere Young implicitly exposes the Indighorror tradition through postcolonial criticism by Gerry Turcotte, Ken Gelder, and Katrin Althans who analyze Aboriginal Gothic horror texts from Unaipon to Mudrooroo, Gates, and on.[13] These authors and scholars will be drawn on in this essay due to their influence on the formation of the modern genre.

The overview offered above describes factors that affected both White Australian and Aboriginal horror. While the Dreaming is a common feature of Australian horror, it also impacts the theory of Indighorror. As will be seen, "The Dreaming" is a mythology and a system, or *way of being* (see section "Dreaming, Totemism, Songlines: A Definition"), but for Australian horror, this myth is a part of a broader aesthetic of the fantastic and the surreal, and a way of exploring fear through a clearly defined Other, and the dream as a national ideal and an uncanny nightmare.

"The Dreaming" and "The Dream"

Dark images of the Dreaming are a part of the horror iconography of Australia. They can be understood as the Dark Side of the Dream, the subversion of national ideals and identities that are an Australian counterpart to the American Dream. Often conflated, there is an important distinction between the Dark Side of the Dreaming and the Dark Side of the Dream. The Dark Side of the Dreaming is a rich fabric of darker myths that help constitute both Indigenous creation stories and the unique metaphysical context of the Aborigine past, future, and present.

The Dark Side of the Dreaming has infiltrated the Australian horror genre, clearly visible in the melding of horrorrealism, and photorealism on covers like *Macabre: A Journey Though Australia's Darkest Fears* (2010) where a skull is superimposed in the skyline over a desolate outback road; this is mirrored in dark representations of the Dreaming and totemic figures based in documentary realism: for example, the documentary *Beyond the Dreamtime* (2011) with blood red totemic imagery. However, such images, through the implied rupture of the Australian Dream, romanticize (in a European Gothic sense) horror and bind it to Aboriginal myth.

Indeed, the Dark Side of the Dream is invested with pejorative and destructive aspects of the Australian Dream, or the horrorrealism that underlies and disillusions that dream, itself a national myth or ideal. This idea is explored by Bob Hodge and Vijay Mishra: "The 'Australian legend,' then, is and has always been the after-image of the Australian nightmare, suppressing Australians' worst fears by representing them in glowing terms as an ideal."[14] The Dark Side of the Dream is what they describe as "the domain of repression," the other "side—the forbidden, supressed and 'unspeakable'" where "another cultural history is played out."[15] Indeed, they conclude with "the shifting meanings of a dream which has always been the Other of Australian culture."[16] This has been the domain of Aboriginal Australian horror literature. In relation to "Generic Horror" and Aboriginality, Alan McKee notes of Hodge and Mishra's study that "[m]any others have stressed the privileged place which Aboriginality holds in the construction of an Australian sense of self."[17] Hodge and Mishra's work is based in literature and postcolonial analysis, yet their examination is illustrative of the national context; it is clearly influenced by Western notions of the uncanny dream, and bares little resemblance to Indigenous epistemologies of Dreamtime.

Consider the word "dreaming," which as McKee notes in "White Stories" has been "consistently popular and consistently misused."[18] As McKee states, "[D]reamings are often linked to fantasies and the subconscious" and are, "misleading."[19] "Dream and dreaming have informed an important part of white constructions of Aboriginality" in the horror genre whereby relevant Western notions of dreams skew the Aboriginal world into a "dream-landscape"[20] of magic, fantasy, mysticism, nightmare, and the surreal. Many horror genres borrow from various forms of mythology, but Aboriginal mythology has an epistemological framework based in reality that functions as a social order and system, making it particularly interesting for theoretical exploration.

Dreaming, Totemism, Songlines: A Definition

"Dreaming" is an English mistranslation of the Aboriginal words for a concept that bears little resemblance to Western dreams. Often it is viewed as a "complex of meanings" or "enormous spider-web of meaning"[21] in Western thought, or as Mudrooro describes it, the "ancient invisible web of songlines" that traces the Dreaming and its narratives across the land.[22] The Dreaming (known as the Jukurrpa alcheringa, or djugurba) is as Jeannie Nungarrayi states an "all-embracing concept that provides rules for living, a moral code, as well as rules for interacting with the natural environment"; the Dreaming is not "something that has been consigned to the past," it is a part of every day reality.[23]

Indeed, "Aborigines do not perceive space as distance,"[24] nor time as linear. For that reason, time functions differently in such a system. The Dreaming is not timeless; it embraces time "everywhen."[25] In Aboriginal context, space and time are not bound by binary associations. For instance, totems are embodiments of ancestral beings that also represent one's identity (moitey) and association to society (or "mob").

Although these notions may seem uncanny, in a Freudian sense, from the perspective of Aboriginal cosmology and culture it is a concrete part of everyday existence where Self and Other are intertwined. This is distinct from a Western idea of fear, which requires an initial separation between Self and the object of fear. Fear in Aboriginal epistemology is fundamentally always a fear of a conglomerate Self. This blurring of categories is a part of a unique manifestation of Aboriginal totemism and animism that is integral to the Dreaming. Fuelled by blood and heredity, they function as an exchange system of ancestral beings and contemporary identity, taboo, law, and punishment.[26]

Mythic figures from the Dreaming have monstrous qualities like the Pangkarlangu or bogeyman/ogre; the Wati Nyirunya or sorcerer; Mamu or the Baby Guzzlers; the Yawk Yawk Maidens akin to sirens; the Namorroddos as vampiric wind; and the Kurdaitchi, known as the executioner(s).[27] These figures can be understood as manifestations of, or a warning against, the violation of the totemic system, and a departure from the moral and social code of the Dreaming.

Indeed, violent aspects of the totemic system are embedded in the Dreaming and its myths, and correspond to physical, human, and sacred worlds. Totemic figures that are associated with objects in the natural world such as trees, birds, or wind are often embodiments of Indighorror figures, with simulacra in Western tradition. These totems become analogs of possessed objects in Western horror. Within Indighorror, these concepts build a terror and fear through transgressions of the mechanisms or workings of the Dreaming itself. This will be further developed in the sections "Monstrosity, Anthropology, Horror and Monster Theory" and "Fiction Examples: Theory at Work." The concept of Dreaming horror can be extended by looking at the origins of monstrosity and its relationship with anthropology and horror.

Monstrosity, Anthropology, Horror and Monster Theory

The central image of horror proliferated, and reacted against, saw Indigenous culture and figures as monstrous elements of an anthropomorphic landscape that sought to devour and destroy convicts and settlers alike, or to make them barbarous as if by contamination. White fears of monstrosity were fed by Indigenous myths, such as the story of the Bunyip, perceived as a "monstrous sea-calf."[28] Monsters in this context were based on two sets of images: horrorrealism and colonial representations of Gothic horror. The former is constituted by such things as raging bushfires, as part of a vast pitiless outback, and the latter, the bleak romantic melancholy of the antipodes, versus mythic Indigenous monsters and the primordial wilderness. In early colonial literature, these images were tinctured by the horror of Edgar Allan Poe and H.P. Lovecraft as recorded by Marcus Clarke's *Australia Tales* in 1896: "What is the dominant note of Australian Scenery? That which is the dominant note" of Poe's "Weird Melancholy."[29] In both horrorrealism and Western horror, Indigenous figures and their culture are often represented as having monstrous qualities, a facet of their Otherness. This extended to anthropological readings of their monstrosity. Conversely, these readings have come to impact Indighorror production.

Mudrooroo, who self-identifies as Indigenous, writes novels that are filled with Dreaming monsters, and his vampire trilogy is marketed as standard Gothic horror in an international market. Mudrooroo's fiction, criticism, and theory of Maban Reality (or the dark hybrid reality representative of the Dreaming) describes horror figures reflecting the menace of technology through Social Darwinism, for example in his essay on Maban Reality:

> Thus, if we seek to read the more occult or other realities of this period, we find that scientific discourse is the mode that these authors use in seeking to capture them. The use of scientific discourse extends far into the realm of the weird here used in the sense of the eerie and the uncanny, thus proof of the existence of werewolves and vampires is sought in the discourses of natural science[30]

By this he connects classic horror figures to Aborigines through ethnographic methods. In the aforementioned critique, anthropology is a subtext to Mudrooroo's horror.

Monstrosity and Anthropology

Reading monsters in anthropology through interdisciplinary studies is increasingly popular, and important for understanding the critical position of Aboriginal horror. Lisa Hopkins comments in *Gothic Studies* (2000) that monstrosity and anthropology were "intimately and troublingly connected in the nineteenth-century mind."[31] However, today they are still deeply connected in the Australian Indigenous context and tied to horror studies.

This tendency is clearly visible in the following example: The Department of Anthropology at the University of Sydney presented a 2017 Anthropology Symposium called *Living with Monsters*. The intersection between horror, Gothic, and Anthropological studies is overt. Not surprisingly, the convener of the symposium was Dr. Yasmine Musharbash, co-editor of *Monster Anthropology*—a text analyzed in the section "Monster Anthropology and Horror Theory." The keynote speaker was Jeffrey Jerome Cohen, Professor of English, and editor of *Monster Theory*. General speakers at the conference included Gothicists, previously presenting at international Gothic conferences. *Living with Monsters* was interdisciplinary in nature. The symposium combined the anthropology of monstrosity and ethnographic methods to the field of monster studies. It delved into "local monsters," exploring mythic Indigenous horror figures like Mamu.[32]

While Aboriginal monsters feature prominently in new studies of anthropology, there is a conspicuous lack of discussion about Australia and Aboriginal Australian writing and monstrosity in the monster theories of Alexa Wright, Stephen Asma, Carroll, Judith Halberstam, Cohen, and others. On broader horror and fear in Indigenous literature of Australia, there is a gap; on Aboriginal Australian horror methodologies, there is an absence.

Critics like Cohen and Amit S. Rai explore generalized non–Western metaphysics in monster studies and theory, even though they do not delve into Aboriginal Australian figures and ontology. Consider the use of the non-diachronic by Cohen. Diachronism for Cohen refers to a binary order-providing system for understanding monster identity and its relationship to culture. He states in the preface to *Monster Theory* that diachronic order "does not—cannot—exist," arguing against a unified theory of monsters.[33] Cohen notes further in "Monster Culture (Seven Theses)" the monster's "refusal to participate in the classificatory 'order of things.'"[34] Through non-diachronic order, he implicitly points towards a synchronic theory of horror and monstrosity. However, his use of non-binary theory is remote from Aboriginal metaphysics. Additionally, Rai explores a non-diachronic mechanism through "monstrosity and ontology," "tied to the lived experience of duration, which is always a qualitative multiplicity, a 'suddenly' that has no measure, and a relation that exceeds its terms."[35] But, Rai's generalized metaphysics of monstrosity borrows from seminal poststructural theorists like Jacques Derrida, Gilles Deleuze, Jacques Lacan, and Michel Foucault, whom are staples of monster analysis. Ultimately, the theory he uses to construct his argument and his ontological approach is based on a Western praxis. Such an epistemological framework leaves an absent lacuna, a fluxing monster with no core, but the theoretics of Aboriginal monsters do not involve an absent center, because of their unique ontological reality, constituted by Dreamtime. In effect, the theories by Cohen and Rai are not transferrable; they cannot be used to read the nuances of Aboriginal horror fiction monsters.

Monster Anthropology
and Horror Theory

While there remains a conspicuous lack of discussion about Australia and Aboriginal Australian writing and monstrosity in monster theory, writing on Aboriginal monstrosity is readily available in current anthropological texts. Horror projected onto Indigenous mythological creatures is a central aspect of *Monster Anthropology* (2014), edited by Musharbash and Geir Presterudstuen, creates monster theory out of horrific creatures of the Dreaming.

Monster Anthropology indexes figures from the mad Burnt Woman to the kurdaitchi (executioner). They are rooted in the horrors of the real, but theoretically explored alongside zombies, vampires, ghosts, and ogres. The volume purports to "invert longstanding Eurocentric discourses both in anthropology and monster studies"[36] and relies on theories by Cohen, Halberstam, Asma, and Carroll for the construction of a universal monster methodology.

Indeed, the editors of the volume apply Carroll's *Philosophy of Horror* (1990), alongside other criticism of horror and monster reality. But, they do not explore Carroll's analysis of "Ethnicity, Race, and Monstrosity" in "minorities," which draws on horror theories of the grotesque through "the comic and the horrific" and monstrosity as "a violation" of the "concept of the human" condition.[37] The inherent horror of anthropology for Aboriginal Australian identity arises because Aborigines have been represented as monstrous subjects to be studied, and under the auspice of colonial and ethnographic objectives, forced into horror realities. Musharbash posits in the introduction that "monster studies and anthropology produced different understandings of monsters' realities," and by extending Carroll, indicates that fear experienced in the apprehension of horror "about fictional monsters" is qualitatively different,[38] when applied to anthropological figures because the latter becomes real. It is suggestive of current trends towards horrorrealism and hyperrealism. The use of horror in the volume is distinctly a part of horror and its theory. They note "the horror genre" is capable of "incorporating or assimilating general social anxieties into its iconography of fear and distress" citing Carroll's *Philosophy*[39] and extend this to monsters in Europe and America.[40] In the volume, Musharbash notes that in "embodying contemporary horrors, other monsters … adapt and maintain their monstrous presence (their ability to seem 'real') across time."[41] Horrorrealism is premised on a "continuum between symbolic structures and lived experience" through "anthropology [that] can make significant contributions toward contemporary understandings of monsters in monster studies," and an inbuilt instability between transformations of monstrosity.[42] However, they define their universal monster paradigm based on readings of Indigenous myth through corollary: "[M]onstrousness is marked through monstrous bodies, which do not neatly fit into the classificatory schema of the respective people they haunt"; they are "culturally specific," emphasizing the meaning of "local monsters,"[43] but applying non-localized theory.

For *Monster Anthropology*, monstrosity is defined through Aboriginal Australian Dreaming figures often found in Indighorror texts. They "resemble but differ from the human form": Mahnaz Alimardanian presents the ghost of the Burnt Woman.[44] These Dreaming figures "have bodies in-between human and animals": Ure Eickelkamp explores the polymorphous Mamu, and John Morton the Arrentye.[45] They can "have monstrous bodies according to different category subversions": Joanne Thurman analyzes the Minmin, beings of embodied light that transgress categories between animate and inanimate.[46] Such "monsters" feature prominently in Indighorror, manifested in different contexts by the landscape in which they are embodied.

This analysis of *Monster Anthropology* underscores the fact that such Indighorror monsters are accepted as part of interdisciplinary monster discourses within anthropology, but largely omitted from monster studies, and avoided within horror theory. Regardless, in the edition, Musharbash notes that Morton "asks the critical question: 'Why should the Dreaming contain such nightmarish things?'"[47] Morton's "answer arises out of analysis of the interconnect-edness between the monstrous" and the Aboriginal Australian "ways of being in the world."[48] Musharbash hints at a Dreaming epistemology she does not reproduce in her theory. It is imperative to apprehend the onto-logical scaffolding of the Dreaming and Songlines to accurately represent Aboriginal Australian monsters and create a working theoretical model for Indighorror.

Monster Theory from the Dreaming

To analyze Indighorror, it is necessary to further incorporate Aboriginal ontological frameworks into a theory of monstrosity. Consider Robert Lawlor's description of Aboriginal totemism and animism through animal and human relationships in Dreamtime[49] It allows one to understand the construction of monstrosity in an Indigenous context. Monstrosity is con-stituted by three aspects. External bodily forms and behaviors of animals[50] in Indighorror and in dark myth are terrifying; they can be monstrous. The psychology and emotions of humans[51] translates into the horror apprehended, or the individuals monstrous intent. External human form[52] and this physicality, through various notions of difference, can be monstrous. Ancestors are constituted by human and animal forms, and could transform between them. As physical manifestation took shape through the Dreamtime, the original forming of the earthly environment, where "excessive power of the ancestors became destructive, causing constant conflict, bloodshed, and confusion."[53] These monstrous qualities visible in Dreaming narratives were absorbed into the land. Monstrosity is thus the result both of totemic manifestations on the land, and animistic transformations wrought by ancestral potencies.

The mechanism by which these figures exhibit what may be viewed as monstrosity in an Aboriginal context is the result of an "individual's imperfections … sustained by energies from the spirit of the species that makes up" their totem identity.[54] Monstrosity is still essentially about identity, but identity is not singular. For example, eating the flesh and blood of an individual's moiety or totem animal is akin to cannibalism, as a representation of breaking natural order. Lawlor notes that after colonialism the "Aborigines say that the earthly atmosphere is now saturated with dead spirits," as the pollution of their spiritual and physical world.[55] These images and mechanisms of exchange are visible in Indighorror texts examined in "Fiction Examples," where they are utilized to heighten suspense and fear.

Revisiting "Synchronic Horror"

Having laid the groundwork to allow for a non–Western understanding of Aboriginal ontology through the analysis of cultural context and epistemology, it is now possible to examine a theory of Indighorror and Aboriginal "monstrosity." Thus, this section is a detailed description of a culturally specific theory of monstrosity and horror that can be further applied to Indighorror fiction.

First let us address a few questions from a theoretical standpoint, placing previous definitions of horror and theory into a critical and methodological framework.

What is Indighorror? To clarify, Indighorror is a horror fiction subgenre in which Aboriginal Australian culture, mythology and cosmology are used within a mode that in its broadest sense creates fear or terror. It has been described by Raymond Gates as a metaphysical way of being within a horror framework,[56] and D. Bruno Starrs as a hybrid genre where the Aboriginal subject is always left in a state of instability. For Starrs, the Aboriginal fantastic is a representation of Dreaming metaphysics placed in a Western nomencla-ture.[57] Indighorror is represented by two types of horror, (1) the scions of horrorrealism perpetrated by a colonial context, and its aftermath, and (2) the darker aspects of mythological narratives of the Dreaming and songlines. For Indighorror, subject and object are interconnected, multifaceted, and tied to land. Notions of death, as well as the animate and the inanimate are cyclical. The implications for monster and horror theory are vast.

What theory applies to Indighorror? In order to read Indighorror, culturally-specific theory is useful to understand tropes of horror. In each culture, "the horror genre is capable of incorporating or assimilating general social anxieties into its iconography of fear."[58] But, monstrosity is culturally-specific. Horror theory should carefully incorporate non–Western episte-mologies, as in Aboriginal methodologies.

What is Synchronic Horror? Extending Cohen's non-diachronic order of monster theory as described in the section "Monstrosity and Anthropol-ogy," and reinterpreting the notion of a non-binary order in terms of Dream-time epistemology, I juxtapose Lawlor's synchronic ontological system derived from Aboriginal totemism and animism, with an analysis of Dream-ing methodology. Applied to Aboriginal-based horror, "synchronic logic" is a product of "several relational principles operating simultaneously."[59] These are based on a logic system of analogy and multiplicity that stems from Dreaming knowledge. Synchronic horror becomes a useful term to explain the complex multivariable space of Dreaming horror and monstrosity recon-stituted through dynamic exchange. In this essay, synchronic horror is used to describe a Dreaming, Indighorror-based theory.

Consider the following diagram in two parts, A and B, which reflect synchronic horror and monstrosity in an Aboriginal framework.

The following numbers correspond to Figure 2.

1. Ontological or cosmological source of horror and monstrosity, which is in effect the invisible motion of the Dreaming that relates to its creation—the spiritual or metaphysical realm.

2. Physical manifestation of horror. Union of land and subject: where repressed aspects of culture, nature, Dreamtime stories, are inscribed on earth's topography, still reflecting dark spiritual potencies and terrorizing forms of the ancestors (e.g., in totems; the Kurdatchi, etc.), leaving the footprints of destructive and sometimes malevolent gods.

3. This represents the totality of both the dots and the land on which they are refracted and constructed into physical manifestations of monstrosity through constituent parts or *yuti* as the visible, perceivable world.

4. Lacuna at center of unions (set A, B, C) is the monstrous identity exposed at a given moment due to various horror contexts and relying on the intersection of elements in 2 and 3. In the "theory of Indighorror" part of the diagram, sets A, B, and C represent land (A), subject (B), and sky(C) as part of identity formation. In the "Process by which horror and monstrosity are actualized" part of the diagram, sets A, B, and C represent different visions of monstrosity arising from

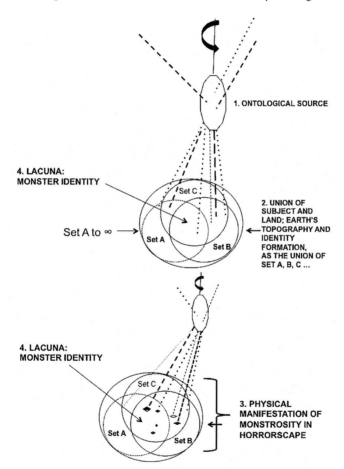

Figure 2. The top diagram represents the theory of Indighorror whereas land (Set A), subject (Set B), and sky (Set C) continuously blend in different ways to become the monstrous identity that produces horror. The bottom diagram represents the process by which horror and monstrosity are actualized. In this physical manifestation, Set A, B, and C represent different visions of monstrosity: physical space (land/totem/identity), spectral horrors, and lens of the viewer respectively.

mutations of the physical space (A) (land/totem/identity), to demented characters (B), to spectral horrors (C) dependent on the lens or perspective of the viewer. The referents that construct monstrosity as aspects of subjectivity, or monster identity are always present, stressing the chance for mistranslation of fear and horror in Aboriginal context. The symbol for infinity in fact translates into constant mutlifoliate couplings, or manifestations of monstrosity in the physical world, that do not rely on a linear expansion of time.

This points to not only a Dreaming-based theory but one in which both Western and non–Western aspects can be understood in relation to each other.

Fiction Examples: Theory at Work

This section constitutes an application of the theoretical model developed, based on Dreaming mechanism and totemic elements as monstrosity, tied to landscape and subject, taking examples of Aboriginal Australian horror fiction and Indighorror tropes from writers such as Wright, McLaren, Starrs, Watson, Mudrooroo, Scott, as well as speculative fiction with strong horror elements from Kwaymullina. These texts clearly expose a contemporary, working theoretical model in which Aboriginal metaphysics and culture replace the myth and fantasy of Western horror.

Wright uses the Aboriginal myth of the Burnt Woman constructed through a fusion of Indigenous dark myth and colonial horror. It is a myth of a deformed feminine figure. In Wright's work, the Dreaming is a living, monstrous representation of this horror, manifested through the Burnt Woman. A murderous and diseased totemic system attacks the foreign or White Australian element that infected it. The infected Dreaming continues to be represented by authors from Watson to Starrs.

That Blackfella Bloodsucka Dance! depicts a mixed-race vampire based partly on Bram Stoker and partly on Dreamtime. Here, Starrs describes a monstrous totemic system in a land that is infiltrated by evil entities of the "underworld."[60] He uses nature symbolically to explore what the West views as an underworld in contrast with the space frequented by ancient spirit beings who came up from the bowels of the earth, finding their way into totemic forms like trees or rocks: "All these Australian landscapes …contain … vaguely tenable memory … waiting, like a dormant, genderless virus."[61] The book ends cyclically, with a similar sentence: "waiting, waiting, waiting, like a dormant, genderless virus," extended to the mechanisms of the Dreaming "each night the Weelow and the Garrawi take flight into new dreams."[62] Yet the "Dreaming" as "the dark elements" of "fantasy would not expire, they fought for acknowledgement and supremacy," and "the monstrous conception responsible for all this tale's mayhem struggled on."[63] The poisoning of the Dreaming is itself a representation of monstrosity, which clearly exposes the dynamic nature of identity and land in Aboriginal horror fiction, or what Starrs calls Aboriginal Fantastic.[64] Clearly visible is the synchronic mechanism of horror created by the hybridization of ontological systems that define the genre.

Unlike Wright, Starrs, or Watson, the Dreaming system Scott employs is not so much poisoned as mutilated. Scott's *Benang* is a stark example of Dreaming mechanisms used to build horror, here primarily emphasizing the harsh reality of the Indigenous condition. The title of the story is a word that translates into thread or line, suggesting the songlines. Through the novel it develops a negative and horrific connotation. The novel starts with brutal colonial oppression, but Scott brings the narrative back to the Dreaming. As with the other texts, such junctures create multifaceted and multicultural violence such as real acts of violence such as physical and sexual abuse. These are followed by moments of Dreamtime: "They saw a dark silhouette drifting across the windows ... the figure in silhouette as it rose"[65]; the narrator "hovered in the air just above everyone's head .... It was frightening. What is he? I heard them say."[66] The staging of scenes between real violence and the mythic augurs of death and destruction evokes the Aboriginal Strange. Totems still herald danger and death: "And, deep in the chill night, ending the song, the curlew's cry. Death bird, my people say."[67] Other totems like the Great Dingo in the sky creating a "howling ... nightmare sound"[68] linked to the graphic maiming of animals in a car crash. The effect is clearly unsettling to narrator, reader, and Aboriginal community. Overall, this use of mythic horror allusions runs concurrently, much like Dreaming. But, it takes a subsidiary position to violent representations of realistic horror of Aboriginal communities, or settings where "[h]aving survived genocide" all that was left was to "try to comprehend what led to this oh-so-near-death?"[69] The exchange of the Dreaming is palpable, through spirits looming in the sky and totemic figures maimed on the highway.

In *Scream Black Murder* (1995), McLaren criminalized and technologized the Dreaming, or as in his novel, *Sweet Water, Stolen Land* made surreal and absurd. *In Sweet Water*, what could be viewed as "surrealism"[70] or even innuendo outside an Aboriginal context, represents horror aspects of the Dreaming and synchronic logic. For example, through a vengeful spirit, "the sketch had her soul trapped in it and now it was being released. It smiled at him as if to say: *we know*, Karl, you cannot hide from us."[71] This representation of transformation, with its dynamic transfer of signifiers, places aspects of a Western horror tradition into an Indighorror framework. The tradition of horrorrealism is accentuated by McLaren's use of imagery and themes from the Myall Creek Massacre. In *Scream Black Murder*, again horrorrealism is a premise for the thriller, but through the "criminal dreaming" its synchronic logic is instrumental in dissecting the mind of a monster through the criminal dimensions of the Dreaming.[72] In relation to Figure 1, the ontological source has changed, the constituent elements of monster identity (for an Indighorror subject) also change, almost themselves becoming simulacra of identity, thus equally, and by definition, monstrous.

Gates' "The Little Red Man" is a contemporary horror genre short story that contains and transforms the mythic figure into a horror monster, and incorporates scientific discourse through the totemic fig, juxtaposing Aboriginal metaphysics and Western scientific discourse through botany.

Some modern speculative writing by Aboriginal authors explores similar horror themes with cultural specificity. In *The Tribe #1* (2012), Kwaymullina clearly illustrates how a Dreaming-based Aboriginal theory works when applied to horror. The text self-reflexively inspects the nature of the Dreaming and horror in a Western and Indigenous context: The author implicitly asks: Is the horror real? Is it Western or is it Indigenous? Her horror is a reaction to the hybrid state. It is manifested by the merging of the Dreaming world (Aboriginal) and the non–Dreaming world (Western), a disjunct between the two ways of being or epistemological structures. The Dreaming and the songlines, which become "labyrinthine passages" actualized through a waking dream state,[73] created through sleepwalking and dreams that are connected to totemic and animistic elements, become surreal and urbanized and thus monstrous. The book explores death, and in doing so, the clash of these two cultures, as a paradox is heightened. The Dreaming becomes a way of understanding surrealism, reality, horror, death, and monstrosity. This horror is about not knowing what is reality. The capitalization in "When I Walked" suggests the Aborigine "Walkabout," where "I moved through the world in an unconscious state, seeing everything as part of a super-intense dream."[74] An object in the dream appears "as some kind of wily monster, holding me in jaws filled with long teeth like the bars on the window."[75] Kwaymullina also depicts the monster subject (serpent), which is a totemic figure. The "Serpent," who is bound to human form, the man, who in actuality is the "reality-bending" embodiment of the great rainbow serpent in the sky, part of Aboriginal mythology: "The Serpent strolled forward … he was broad shouldered, green eyed, and—apparently—somewhat paranoid" with "some kind of reality-bending ability."[76] It accentuates the monstrosity of actions that terrified the tribal figure: "the massive snake slid upwards" and seemingly tries to drown her.[77] But by attempting to murder her, the snake suggests it "was helping" to free her from a surreal and nightmarish world through transformation.[78]

The novel brings together the horror and uncertainty of waking, dreaming, and death. In relation to Figure 1, Kwaymullina's use of d/Dreaming states amplifies the constant flux of unions that constitute subject, and fragments the linear perceived association to land, because the reader never knows where the subject is in time and space—contravening the Western temporal-spatial construct. In doing so, it breaks Western understandings of binary association, or diachronic order, and allows for an understanding of multiplicative or synchronic logic seen in Aboriginal methodology. The monster lacuna is filled with the everything and where of the Dreaming but transformed by Western horror. Ironically, this is an important feature of Indighorror texts, which like most horror fiction, seek to understand cultural anxieties through the genre.

Each example in this section highlights the unique mythological structure of Aboriginal Dreamtime, which creates a specific kind of horror subgenre. The methodology explored above is suited only to this literature. Uniformly, the Dreaming is either infected or mutilated by the inclusion of foreign bodies. It acts both as a governing system and a living changing entity. Monstrosity is often represented in two set ways: firstly, through poisoning or mutilation, which impacts the totemic representations of monsters and land or through horror realism derived from the colonial condition, and secondly, where the monstrosity of the Other represents the Whites. As a result of both representations, there are remnants of the anthropological horror of Aboriginal culture. To recapitulate, in Indighorror, the monster-subject interacts with, and is formed by the unions visible within the lacuna by a constantly fluxing ontological or cosmological source. This source is itself hybridized by Aboriginal methodology and also altered by Western intrusions, like genre form itself, blending within that state of being. The horror is a product of both. Yet, the monstrosity of the Dreaming, that has always existed, can manifest in either a Western or an Aboriginal sense depending on the elements of the lacuna that are most dominant. That is to say, that the monstrosity is across a non-binary composition of Western and Aboriginal horror. A synchronic theory of the Dreaming is a mixed methodology, rewriting Western theoretical practice with Indigenous concepts of horror and reality.

In conclusion, curious intersections exist between monster theory, anthropology, and Indighorror that suggest a concrete aesthetic and theoretic tendency in the treatment and application of Aboriginal Australian horror. The tripartite analysis offered in this essay builds a conceptual and literary vision for an Aboriginal theory of monstrosity and horror. The cultural history of Aboriginal horror is swept up in studies of monstrosity and read through anthropology, where terrifying and macabre figures of Indigenous myth are made real; as in Musharbash and Presterudstuen's edition, real horrors are amplified in the broader literature through misconceptions of Aboriginal epistemology. In Indighorror fiction explored in this essay, combinations of horror conventions and synchronic Dreaming mechanisms, as a distinct deviation from concepts by Lawlor or Cohen, create a unique setting and subject. From Gates to McLaren to Kwaymullina, authors draw on a constellation of horror figures and settings that have dual origins in the narratives of the Dreaming and the broader Aboriginal Australian horror tradition. In Indighorror, aspects of Aboriginality, monstrosity, and identity subvert anthropological caricatures.

NOTES

1. John Morton, "A Murder of Monsters: Terror and Morality in an Aboriginal Religion," in *Monster Anthropology*, ed. by Yasmine Musharbash and Geir Presterudstuen (New York: Palgrave, 2014), 75.

2. Marty Young, "Appendix," in *Macabre*, ed. Angela Challis and Marty Young (Edgewater, Western Australia: Brimstone Press, 2010), 676–667.

3. Mudrooroo, *Indigenous Literature of Australia: Milli Milli Wangka* (South Melbourne, Victoria: Hyland House, 1997), 93.

4. Raymond Gates, "Beyond Unaipon: Part 1," *AWAYE!*, Australian Broadcasting Corporation, last modified June 21 2014. http://www.abc.net.au/radionational/programs/awaye/beyond-unaipon3a-part-1/5527076.

5. Maureen Clark, *Mudrooroo: a Likely Story* (Brussels, Belgium: Peter Lang, 2007), 23.

6. Gates, "Beyond Unaipon."

7. "The 1967 Referendum," Australian Government, Section 51, p. xxvi.

8. "Restrictions on the Freedom of Expression," *Australian Law*, 1967, Section 164.

9. James Doig, "The Australian Horror Novel Since 1950s," in *Sold by the Millions: Australia's Bestsellers*, ed. by Toni Johnson-Woods and Amit Sarwal (Newcastle upon Tyne, UK: Cambridge Scholars Press, 2012), 112–113.

10. Doig, "Australian Horror Novel," 122.

11. Young, "Appendix," 670.

12. *Ibid.*, 670–671.

13. Marty Young, "Australia's Short Horror Story: An Introduction" in *Macabre: a Journey Through Australia's Darkest Fears*, ed. Angela Challis and Marty Young (Edgewater, Western Australia: Brimstone Press, 2010), 9–21.

14. Bob Hodge and Vijay Mishra, *The Darkside of the Dream* (Sydney, NSW: Allen & Unwin, 2012), 217.

15. *Ibid.*, 204.

16. *Ibid.*

17. Alan McKee, "The Generic Limitations of Aboriginality: Horror Movies as Case Study," *Australian Studies* 12.1 (1997): 115.

18. McKee, "White Stories, Black Magic: Australian Horror Films of the Aboriginal," in *Aratjara: Aboriginal Culture and Literature in Australia*, ed. Dieter Riemenschneider and Geoffrey V. Davis (Amsterdam, Netherlands: Rodopi Press 1997), 201.

19. *Ibid.*, 201–202.

20. *Ibid.*

21. WEH Stanner, *The Dreaming & Other Essays* (Collingwood, AUS: Black Inc Agendas, 2010).

22. Mudrooroo, *Writing from the Fringe* (South Yarra, Melbourne: Hyland House, 1990), 127.

23. Judith Christine Nicholls, "Grounded Abstraction: The Work of Dorothy Napangardi," in *Dancing Up Country: The Art of Dorothy Napangardi* (Sydney, NSW: Museum of Contemporary Art, 2002), 60.

24. Robert Lawlor, *Voices of the First Day: Awakening in the Aboriginal Dreamtime* (Rochester, VT: Inner Traditions, 1991), 41.

25. Stanner, *The Dreaming*, 57, 80, 105.

26. Lawlor, *Voices*, 49–50.

27. Morton, "A Murder," 75.

28. Marcus Clarke, *Australian Tales* (Melbourne, AUS: A. & W. Bruce, 1896), 1.

29. Clarke, *Australian Tales*, 1.

30. Mudrooroo, *Literature*, 91.

31. Lisa Hopkins, "Monstrosity and Anthropology," *Gothic Studies* 2.3 (2000): 267.

32. Living with Monsters, "Living with Monsters," *The University of Sydney Anthropology Symposium 2017*, last accessed January 10, 2019, https://anthropologylivingwithmonsters.wordpress.com/.

33. Jeffrey Jerome Cohen, "Preface," in *Monster Theory*, ed. Cohen (Minneapolis: University of Minnesota Press, 1996), ix.

34. Jeffrey Jerome Cohen, "Monster Culture (Seven Theses)," in *Monster Theory*, ed. Cohen (Minneapolis: University of Minnesota Press, 1996), 5–6.

35. Amit S. Rai, "Monstrosity and Ontology," in *Monster Culture in the 21st Century*, ed. Marina Levina and Diem-My T. Bui (New York: Bloomsbury, 2013), 15.

36. Yasmine Musharbash, "Introduction" in *Monster Anthropology* (New York: Palgrave, 2014), 16.

37. Noël Carroll, "Ethnicity, Race, and Monstrosity: The Rhetorics of Horror and Humor," in *Engaging the Moving Image* (New Haven, CT: Yale University Press, 2003), 89, 92.

38. Musharbash, "Introduction," 6.

39. Noël Carroll, *The Philosophy of Horror* (London: Routledge, 1990), 207.

40. Musharbash, "Introduction," 13.

41. Yasmine Musharbash, "Monstrous Transformations," in *Monster Anthropology*, ed. Yasmine Musharbash and Geir Presterudstuen (New York: Palgrave, 2014), 53.

42. *Ibid.*, 8.

43. *Ibid.*, 11–12.

44. *Ibid.*, 57.

45. *Ibid.*

46. *Ibid.*

47. *Ibid.*, 12.

48. *Ibid.*

49. Lawlor, *Voices*, 329.

50. *Ibid.*

51. *Ibid.*

52. *Ibid.*

53. *Ibid.*, 328.

54. *Ibid.*, 333.

55. *Ibid.*, 343.

56. Gates, "Beyond Unaipon."

57. D. Bruno Starrs, "Writing Indigenous Vampires: Aboriginal Gothic or Aboriginal Fantastic?" *Journal of Media and Culture* 17.4 (2014): 1.

58. Carroll, *Philosophy*, 207.

59. Lawlor, *Voices*, 317.

60. D. Bruno Starrs, *That Blackfella Bloodsucka Dance!* (Saarbrücken, Germany: Just Fiction Edition, 2011), Kindle edition, loc. 56.

61. *Ibid.*, loc. 52.

62. *Ibid.*, loc. 3191.

63. *Ibid.*, loc. 3116, 3143.

64. Starrs, "Writing," n.p.

65. Kim Scott, *Benang* (London: Routledge, 2002), 109.

66. *Ibid.*, 12.

67. *Ibid.*, 8.

68. *Ibid.*, 411.

69. *Ibid.*, 446.

70. Philip McLaren. *Sweet Water, Stolen Land* (St Lucia, QLD: U of Queensland P, 1993), 178.

71. *Ibid.*
72. Philip McLaren, *Scream Black Murder* (Pymble, NSW: HarperCollins, 1995), 142.
73. Ambelin Kwaymullina, *The Tribe #1* (Somerville, MA: Candlewick Press, 2012), Kindle edition, loc. 2497–2498.
74. *Ibid.*, loc. 630–632.
75. *Ibid.*, loc. 630–632.
76. *Ibid.*, loc. 1449–1461.
77. *Ibid.*, loc. 1085.
78. *Ibid.*, loc. 1112–1125.

Bibliography

Asma, Stephen. *On Monsters: An Unnatural History of Our Worst Fears*. Oxford University Press, 2009.
Australian Government. "The 1967 Referendum."
Australian Law. "Restrictions on the Freedom of Expression," 1967, Section 164.
Carroll, Noël. "Ethnicity, Race, and Monstrosity: The Rhetorics of Horror and Humor," in *Engaging the Moving Image*, New Haven, CT: Yale University Press, 2003. 88–107.
_____. *The Philosophy of Horror*. London: Routledge, 1990.
Clark, Maureen. *Mudrooroo: A Likely Story*. Brussels, Belgium: Peter Lang, 2007.
Clarke, Marcus. *Australian Tales*. Melbourne: A. & W. Bruce, 1896, 1.
Cohen, Jeffrey Jerome. Monster Culture (Seven Theses)," in *Monster Theory*, edited by Cohen, 3–25. Minneapolis: University of Minnesota Press, 1996.
_____, ed. "*Monster Theory*". Minneapolis: University of Minnesota Press, 1996.
Doig, James. "The Australian Horror Novel Since 1950s," in *Sold by the Millions: Australia's Bestsellers*, edited by Toni Johnson-Woods and Amit Sarwal, 112–127. Newcastle upon Tyne: Cambridge Scholars Press, 2012.
Gates, Raymond. "Beyond Unaipon: Part 1." *AWAYE!*, Presented by Daniel Browning. Australian Broadcasting Corporation. Last modified June 21, 2014. http://www.abc.net.au/radionational/programs/awaye/beyond-unaipon3a-part-1/5527076.
_____. "The Little Red Man," in *Dead Red Heart*, edited by Russel B. Farr, 379–395. Australia: Ticonderoga Publications, 2011.
Halberstam, Judith. *Skin Shows*. Durham, NC: Duke University Press, 1995.
Hodge, Bob, and Vijay Mishra. *The Darkside of the Dream*. Sydney, NSW: Allen & Unwin, 2012.
Hopkins, Lisa. "Monstrosity and Anthropology." *Gothic Studies* 2.3 (2000): 267–273.
Kwaymullina, Ambelin. *The Tribe #1*. Somerville, MA: Candlewick Press, 2012, Kindle edition.
Lawlor, Richard. *Voices of the First Day: Awakening in the Aboriginal Dreamtime*. Rochester, VT: Inner Traditions, 1991.
Living with Monsters. "Living with Monsters." *The University of Sydney Anthropology Symposium 2017*. Last accessed January 10, 2019. https://anthropologylivingwithmonsters.wordpress.com/.
McKee, Alan. "The Generic Limitations of Aboriginality: Horror Movies as Case Study." *Australian Studies* 12, no.1 (1997): 115–138.
_____. "White Stories, Black Magic: Australian Horror Films of the Aboriginal," in *Aratjara: Aboriginal Culture and Literature in Australia*, edited by Dieter Riemenschneider and Geoffrey V. Davis, 193–210. Amsterdam, Netherlands: Rodopi Press 1997.
McLaren, Philip. *Scream Black Murder*. Pymble, NSW: HarperCollins, 1995.
_____. *Sweet Water, Stolen Land*. St. Lucia, QLD: University of Queensland Press, 1993.
Morton, John. "A Murder of Monsters: Terror and Morality in an Aboriginal Religion," in *Monster Anthropology*, edited by Yasmine Musharbash and Geir Presterudstuen, 75–92. New York: Palgrave, 2014.
Mudroorooo. *Indigenous Literature of Australia: Milli Milli Wangka*. South Melbourne, Victoria: Hyland House, 1997.
_____. *Writing from the Fringe*. South Yarra, Melbourne: Hyland House, 1990 127.

Musharbash, Yasmine. "Introduction: Monster, Anthropology, and Monster Studies," in *Monster Anthropology*, edited by Musharbash and Presterudstuen, 1–24. New York: Palgrave, 2014.

_____. "Monstrous Transformations," in *Monster Anthropology*, edited by Musharbash and Presterudstuen, 39–56. New York: Palgrave, 2014.

Musharbash, Yasmine, and Geir Henning Presterudstuen. *Monster Anthropology*. New York: Palgrave, 2014.

Nicholls, Christine Judith. "'Dreamings' and Place—Aboriginal Monsters and Their Meanings." *The Conversation*. Last modified April 29, 2014. https://theconversation.com/dreamings-and-place-aboriginal-monsters-and-their-meanings-25606.

_____. "Grounded Abstraction: The Work of Dorothy Napangardi." In *Dancing Up Country. The Art of Dorothy Napangardi*, 60–67. Sydney, AUS: Museum of Contemporary Art, 2002.

Rai, Amit S. "Monstrosity and Ontology." In *Monster Culture in the 21st Century*, edited by Marina Levina and Diem-My T. Bui, 15–21. New York: Bloomsbury, 2013.

"Restrictions on the Freedom of Expression." *Australian Government*, Section 164.

Scott, Kim. *Benang*. London: Routledge, 2002.

_____. *That Deadman Dance*. Australia: Picador, 2010.

Stanner, WEH. *The Dreaming & Other Essays*. Collingwood, AUS: Black Inc Agendas, 2010.

Starrs, D. Bruno. *That Blackfella Bloodsucka Dance!* Saarbrücken, Germany: Just Fiction Edition, 2011, Kindle edition.

_____. "Writing Indigenous Vampires: Aboriginal Gothic or Aboriginal Fantastic?" *Journal of Media and Culture*, 17 no.4 (2014): 1–3.

Szumskyi, Benjamin. *Studies in Australian Weird Fiction, Volume 1*. Mandurah, Western Australia: Equilibrium Books, 2008.

Unaipon, David. "Yara Ma Yha Who," in *Legendary Tales of the Australian Aborigines*, edited by Stephen Muecke and Adam Shoemaker, 217–219. Carlton Victoria, AUS: Miegunyah Press, 2006.

Watson, Sam. *The Kadaitcha Sung*. Ringwood: Penguin, 1990.

Wright, Alexa. *Monstrosity*. London: I.B. Tauris, 2013.

Wright, Alexis. *Plains of Promise*. St. Lucia: University of Queensland Press, 1997.

Young, Marty. "Appendix," in *Macabre: A Journey Through Australia's Darkest Fears*, edited by Angela Challis and Marty Young, 670–671. Edgewater, Western Australia: Brimstone Press, 2010.

_____. "Australia's Short Horror Story: An Introduction" in *Macabre: A Journey Through Australia's Darkest Fears*, edited by Angela Challis and Marty Young, 9–21. Edgewater, Western Australia: Brimstone Press, 2010.

_____. "Colonial Ghosts and Modern Terrors: An Overview of Australian Horror Fiction," in *Reading Down Under: Australian Literary Studies Reader*, edited by Amit Sarwal and Reema Sarwal, 456–472. New Delhi, India: SSS Publications, 2009.

"Gelatinous green immensity"

Weird Fiction and the Grotesque Sublime

Johnny Murray

The recent critical and popular acclaim accorded to authors such as Caitlín R. Kiernan, Jeff VanderMeer and China Miéville testifies to the surging vitality of the weird, a radically hybrid strain of fiction combining aspects of various non-realist genres and modes such as horror, science fiction, fantasy, and the Gothic. Miéville, a leading critic as well as practitioner of the weird, describes it as a "generically slippery macabre fiction [which] has had a colossal impact across work in all media, with under-investigated generically problematizing implications."[1] Elusive in form as well as content, the weird seems to possess an innate resistance to definition. It remains an uncertain, inchoate category in spite of its increasing prominence, and is still apt to be confused or conflated with other categories, threatening its viability as a critical term in its own right. This essay will endeavor to clarify the concept of the weird by focusing on the cognitively destabilizing phenomena at its core. Specifically, it will demonstrate how the representation of such phenomena in weird fiction can be understood as involving a commingling of the aesthetic notions of the sublime and the grotesque.

The sublime refers to that which exceeds comprehension, things too vast or obscure or transcendent to perceive or understand completely. The grotesque involves physical transgression and ambiguity, things which refuse discernment as discrete, nameable objects. "The sublime surpasses reason toward the abstract," suggests Istvan Csicsery-Ronay Jr., whereas "the grotesque surpasses reason toward the concrete."[2] The weird merges these diverging tendencies in a singular blend that might be termed "the grotesque sublime," a distinctive fusion which characterizes such notably weird entities as H.P. Lovecraft's (in)famous Cthulhu.

The term "weird" traces back to the fiction of certain late Victorian and early 20th century authors such as Arthur Machen, Algernon Blackwood, William Hope Hodgson, Clark Ashton Smith, and especially Lovecraft. Much of this fiction was initially published in cheap pulp magazines such as the now-legendary *Weird Tales* (founded in 1923). In 2011, the sustained potency of the weird was showcased in a massive anthology edited by Ann and Jeff VanderMeer titled *The Weird: A Compendium of Strange and Dark Stories*, which includes stories by over one hundred different authors from the past century or so.[3] In 2014, Undertow Publications launched *Year's Best Weird Fiction*, "a dedicated volume of the year's best weird writing."[4] The "newly revitalized term"[5] has even infiltrated relatively mainstream magazines such as *SciFiNow*, which featured an article called "A Beginner's Guide to Weird Fiction" in a spring 2016 issue.[6]

Penguin Classics released several collections of Lovecraft's stories between 1999 and 2004, while in 2005 he received the imprimatur of a prestigious Library of America edition of his work.[7] Volumes of fiction by Blackwood, Machen and Smith were published by Penguin Classics in 2002, 2011 and 2014 respectively.[8] The rekindled interest in the weird attested by these reprints has been evidenced in recent critical works as well. The 2005 *Routledge Companion to Science Fiction* includes an important chapter on the weird by Miéville.[9] In 2013's *New Critical Essays on H.P. Lovecraft*, David Simmons notes the "growth of critical interest in Weird literature."[10] In 2016's *The Age of Lovecraft*, Carl Sederholm and Jeffrey Weinstock characterize the current cultural climate as one in which "the themes and influence of Lovecraft's writings have bubbled up from the chthonic depths of 1930s pulp writing to assume an unexpected intellectual and cultural influence."[11]

In spite of all of this renewed attention, the weird remains a "nascent critical classification"[12] rather than a fully-fledged one. Its tentative, undetermined status seems to stem partly from its hybridity, which aggravates already-vexed questions of taxonomy surrounding genre fiction. The weird fuses aspects of other genres and modes, and as Brian Attebery notes, "genre criticism is rife with boundary disputes and definition wars."[13] In S.T. Joshi's monograph on weird fiction, he contends that "recent work in this field has caused an irremediable confusion of terms such as horror, terror, the supernatural, fantasy, ghost story, Gothic fiction, and others."[14] Whether or not the confusion is indeed irremediable, the difficulties involved for literary criticism remain formidable.

In terms of its subject matter, the weird deals with cognitively destabilizing phenomena, things "beyond human comprehension,"[15] which presents further challenges for critical analysis. "The weird concerns liminal things, in-between states, transgressions always on the verge of turning into something else," asserts Roger Luckhurst; "It is hard to define because it focuses on the horrors of the hard to define."[16] If definition depends on discernable boundaries, the weird, by trafficking in that which collapses or explodes such boundaries, itself tends to elude definition.

Given these difficulties, it may be productive to approach the weird as a kind of *fuzzy set*. Fuzzy sets differ from classical sets in that they are defined not by boundaries but by centers.[17] Rather than hinging on strict in-or-out assessments, membership in a fuzzy set entails a degree of "family resemblance"[18] to prototypes formulated from the most salient characteristics of the set. Different perspectives on a given fuzzy set may reveal different prototypical features, establishing new areas for analysis and enriching the overall conception of the set. Employing such an approach, this essay aims to clarify the concept of the weird by explicating certain characteristics which are essential to it at its most prototypical.

In their introduction to *The Weird*, the VanderMeers suggest that the weird involves "the pursuit of some indefinable and perhaps maddeningly unreachable understanding of the world beyond the mundane."[19] Miéville characterizes the weird in comparable terms, asserting that "the focus is on *awe* and its undermining of the quotidian" and that "weird writers are in a lineage with those religious visionaries and ecstatics who perceive an unmediated relationship with numinosity."[20] The concept of numinosity referred to by Miéville was developed by the theologian Rudolf Otto in his 1917 treatise *The Idea of the Holy* to indicate the non-rational, non-ethical aspect of the sacred or divine, that which is beyond the grasp of reason, beyond comprehension. In Otto's formulation, the numinous is "the 'wholly other,' something which has no place in our scheme of reality but belongs to an absolutely different one, and which at the same time arouses an irrepressible interest in the mind."[21] The weird concerns just this sort of "wholly other." In weird fiction, characters and readers are brought into contact with the radically alien, the inconceivable, the indescribable, "that for which we have no name."[22]

But how do authors of the weird attempt to convey such incomprehensible otherness? There would seem to be a paradox involved in any attempt to represent the presence of meaning exceeding that which can be comprehended, to communicate the existence of things beyond what can be perceived by the senses or revealed by reason. As Beth McDonald asks, "How [are we] to reconcile the linguistic construction of an experience of the numinous with the idea that the numinous, by definition, is indescribable?"[23] In Blackwood's story "Sand," for instance, the protagonist Felix Henriot is brought to "the edge of knowing unutterable things."[24] Such contact with the ineffable, however fleeting, is fundamental to the weird's appeal. Yet to impart this to the reader would seem to require expressing what is inexpressible. How then do works of weird fiction confront this paradox? How does the weird deal with what Otto calls "the unutterableness of what has been yet genuinely experienced"?[25]

The notion of intuition may provide a clue here. As William James observes in *The Varieties of Religious Experience* (1902), "it is as if there were in the human consciousness *a sense of reality, a feeling of objective presence*, a *perception* of what we may call 'something there,' more deep and more general than any of the special and particular 'senses' by which the current psychology supposes existent realities to be originally revealed."[26] Humans seem to possess a capacity to become aware of even that which they do not entirely sense or understand. The numinous may linger outside the scope of rational cognition, but nevertheless it can be *intuited*, however imperfectly. "While it admits of being discussed," writes Otto, "it cannot be strictly defined. [...] In other words our × cannot, strictly speaking, be taught, it can only be evoked, awakened in the mind."[27] In dealing with the numinous phenomena at the heart of the weird, reception is crucial. Weird texts are overloaded with affective markers such as *horror, awe, terror, fascination, repulsion*, and so forth, highlighting the wonder evoked by things "beyond all human ken."[28]

Brian Attebery proposes that "the concept of wonder [...] may best be understood as an alternative formulation of the idea of estrangement."[29] In the influential 1917 essay "Art as Technique," Victor Shklovsky coined the term *"ostraneniye"* (or "making strange") to indicate a fundamental source of the power of art: namely, its capacity to "remove objects from the automatism of perception."[30] A work of art, perhaps by definition, compels one to *pay attention*, and Shklovsky asserts that it does so primarily by a process of defamiliarization or estrangement. When something is rendered unfamiliar, one is forced to attend to it with heightened awareness. In his essay "On Fairy-Stories," J.R.R. Tolkien calls such enhanced attention "recovery of freshness of vision," and he associates it particularly with non-realist genres and modes such as fantasy.[31] Non-realist texts depict what should be impossible, rendering reality itself strange and obliging one to alter or abandon one's habitual ways of perceiving and conceiving the world. Strangeness begets wonder, unshackling one from routine and convention.

"To wonder," writes Ian Bogost, "is to suspend all trust in one's own logics, be they religion, science, philosophy, custom, or opinion."[32] Such loss of ontological and epistemological faith is a key effect of contact with the weird. As one of the characters in Machen's "Novel of the White Powder" puts it, "my old conception of the universe has been swept away, and I stand in a world that seems as strange and awful to me as the endless waves of the ocean seen for the first time."[33] Those who encounter the weird are utterly despoiled of their orientation and grounding in the world. According to Csicsery-Ronay Jr., this kind of "liberation from the mundane" possesses an "established pedigree in art, in two related ways of feeling and expression: the sublime and the grotesque."[34] Weird fiction, intensifying the estrangement, *merges* the sublime and the grotesque in a singular and potent fusion.

The sublime as a concept in western aesthetics dates back to Longinus's first century tract "On Sublimity." Longinus characterizes the sublime as a kind of rhetorical "grandeur" that evokes "amazement and wonder" and "exerts invincible power and force and gets the better of every hearer."[35] During the Enlightenment, the rediscovery and dissemination of Longinus's text among European thinkers sparked a vibrant discourse on the sublime that provided a useful counterbalance to the then-dominant cultural emphasis on reason, and sublimity came to be understood as pertaining to experiences of nature as well as art. Edmund Burke describes the sublime in his 18th century work *A Philosophical Enquiry into the Origin of our Ideas of the Sublime and Beautiful* (1757) as a quality of things that cannot be grasped in their entirety, things such as mountains and oceans, infinity and eternity. When one encounters something too vast or obscure or transcendent to perceive or comprehend fully, one's "mind is so entirely filled with its object, that it cannot entertain any other, nor by consequence reason on that object which employs it."[36] The result, according to Burke, is "astonishment; [...] that state of the soul, in which all its motions are suspended, with some degree of horror."[37]

Astonishment and fear are quintessential responses to the weird as well, attesting to the sublimity of weird phenomena. Giles Angarth, the protagonist of Smith's "The City of the Singing Flame," experiences "an awe with which something of actual terror was mingled" when gazing upon the titular city, which "soared to confront the heavens" with "massive towers and mountainous ramparts of red stone [...] such that the Anakim of undiscovered worlds might build."[38] Faced with the sublime, asserts Thomas Weiskel, "discourse breaks down, and the faculties are checked or suspended: a discontinuity opens between what can be grasped and what is felt to be meaningful."[39] As Angarth declares in Smith's tale, "there are no words to convey the incomprehensible wonder of it all."[40] And yet the experience of sublimity *is* somehow communicated in such stories, as readers attuned to it can attest. John Milbank contends that "the sublime can best be defined as that *within* representation which nonetheless *exceeds* the possibility of representation."[41] In its very ineffability, the sublime engenders the kind of intuitions described by James as "states of insight into depths of truth unplumbed by the discursive intellect."[42] As Philip Shaw puts it, "sublimity refers to the moment when the ability to apprehend, to know, and to express a thought or sensation is defeated. Yet through this very defeat, the mind gets a feeling for that which lies beyond thought and language."[43] Such a feeling for things "beyond the power of words to classify"[44] is fundamental to the weird, which strives to disclose a radical otherness that is unthinkable and unspeakable in ordinary terms. "The whole experience whose verge we touched was unknown to humanity at all," proclaims the narrator of Blackwood's "The Willows," "It was a new order of experience, and in the true sense of the word *unearthly*."[45]

Yet the weird does more than offer sublime glimpses of the absolutely alien; it forces one to *confront* such alterity, often, as Miéville phrases it, "right up tentacular in your face."[46] "The Weird," observes Miéville, "punctures the supposed membrane separating off the sublime, and allows swillage of that awe and horror from 'beyond' back into the everyday. [...] The Weird is a radicalized sublime backwash."[47] In its (un)earthly manifestations, its infusion of the transcendent into the material, the weird becomes not just sublime but *grotesque* as well.

The grotesque involves hybridity, ambiguity, things which resist clear-cut definition. Like the sublime, the grotesque as an aesthetic category dates back to antiquity, and its valuation has tended to vacillate over the ages. The Roman poet Horace famously disparaged grotesque imagery in "Ars Poetica," likening it to "a sick man's dreams."[48] In the 20th century, Mikhail Bakhtin aligned the grotesque with the emancipatory impulses of carnival, describing it as "a phenomenon in transformation, an as yet unfinished metamorphosis, of death and birth, growth and becoming. [...] It is not a closed, complete unit; it is unfinished, outgrows itself, transgresses its own limits."[49] Grotesque phenomena refuse discernment as discrete objects, destabilizing one's conventional methods of making sense of the world. Peter Stallybrass and Allon White characterize the grotesque as "a boundary phenomenon of hybridization or inmixing, in which self and other become enmeshed in an inclusive, heterogeneous, dangerously unstable zone."[50] Hybrid, metamorphic, transgressive, the grotesque subverts the very logic of identity, undermining fundamental principles of scientific reason.

Grotesque imagery abounds in weird fiction. At the climax of Machen's "The Great God Pan," the human form, the very foundation of conventional notions of physical identity, is inexplicably divested of its integrity: "the firm structure of the human body that I had thought to be unchangeable, and permanent as adamant, began to melt and dissolve."[51] Smith's "The Double Shadow" features a similar transmutation: "the face was no longer in its entirety the face of a man, but was become a loathly fluid amalgamation of human features with a thing not to be identified on earth."[52] Lovecraft's stories teem with grotesque monstrosities, such as the "hybrid winged things" in "The Festival" which "no sound eye could ever wholly grasp, or sound brain ever wholly remember,"[53] and the "teratologically fabulous" Wilbur Whately in "The Dunwich Horror," whose chest "had the leathery, reticulated hide of a crocodile," while below the waist his "skin was thickly covered with course black fur, and from the abdomen a score of long greenish-grey tentacles with red sucking mouths protruded limply."[54]

Such phenomena in weird fiction serve to evoke a kind of "hideous fascination," as Smith phrases it in "The Vaults of Yoh-Vombis."[55] Heady admixtures of attraction and repulsion are typical of the grotesque, which "appears to us in paradoxical guise," according to Wilson Yates, and "elicits from us paradoxical responses."[56] As with the sublime and the numinous, reception is key. "No definition of the grotesque can depend solely upon formal properties," asserts Geoffrey Galt Harpham, "for the elements of understanding and perception [...] play such a crucial role in creating the *sense* of the grotesque."[57] The grotesque's subversive impact on one's perceptual and conceptual machinery tends to fascinate and disturb simultaneously, inducing a powerful yet ambivalent reaction. In Hodgson's "The Hog," the protagonist Carnacki expresses this aptly upon beholding the titular monstrosity: "It was extraordinary, and at the same time, exquisitely horrible and vile."[58]

Weird fiction brims with the slimy and the tentacular, highlighting a vital aspect of the grotesque: its gross physicality. "The grotesque reaches down deep into visceral experience," writes Frances Connelly. "It counters the disembodied abstraction of the sublime with a power that is felt and expressed through the body."[59] According to Bakhtin, an "essential principle [of the grotesque] is degradation, that is, the lowering of all that is high, spiritual, ideal, abstract; it is a transfer to the material level, to the sphere of earth and body."[60] This sort of "degradation" has particular relevance for weird fiction, for in the weird, the sublime itself is brought to "the sphere of earth and body" and rendered grotesque.

The weird phenomenon at its most distinctive involves a *fusion* of the sublime and the grotesque. The acclaimed weird author Thomas Ligotti observes that "a familiar storyline is that of a character who encounters a paradox *in the flesh*, so to speak, and must face down or collapse in horror before this ontological perversion—something which should not be, yet is."[61] Impossible and incomprehensible, transcendent yet intransigently corporeal, the weird phenomenon manifests in and as what might be termed the grotesque sublime. If, as Connelly suggests, "grotesque horror is an inversion of sublime rapture,"[62] the weird subverts this inverse relationship, invoking horror *and* rapture in a heady simultaneous blend. The result is an "ecstatic horror," as the narrator of Smith's "The Devotee of Evil" phrases it, an "abominable rapture."[63]

In Hodgson's "The Hog," Carnacki confronts a "dreadful unknown Horror"[64] which appears in the world in a gargantuan fleshly form: "I saw it pale and huge through the swaying, swirling funnel of cloud—a monstrous pallid snout rising out of that unknowable abyss."[65] In Blackwood's "Sand," Henriot witnesses a "monstrous host" of colossal figures materializing from the tiny desert sands: "Careering over the waste of Desert moved the army of dark Splendours, that dwarfed any organic structure called a body men have ever known. [...] The outlines reared higher than the pyramids, and towered up to hide whole groups of stars."[66] In Lovecraft's *At the Mountains of Madness* (1936), scientific explorers in the Antarctic ascend a "terrifying line of more than Himalayan peaks"[67] to discover architectural ruins of "infinite bizarrerie, endless variety, preternatural massiveness, and utterly alien exoticism,"[68] in the labyrinthine depths of which lurks "a terrible, indescribable thing [...]— a shapeless congeries of protoplasmic bubbles, faintly self-luminous, and with myriads of temporary eyes forming and unforming as pustules of greenish light."[69] In Lovecraft's "The Call of Cthulhu," a ship's crew encounters a thing of "gelatinous green immensity"[70] in the middle of the Pacific Ocean: "The Thing cannot be described—there is no language for such abysms of shrieking and immemorial lunacy, such eldritch contradictions of all matter, force, and cosmic order. A mountain walked or stumbled. God!"[71] In each of these instances, elements of the sublime and the grotesque are commingled in ways that are distinctively and characteristically weird.

If the "study of genre brings us face to face with boundaries,"[72] as Deborah A. Kapchan and Pauline Turner Strong declare, the weird offers particularly acute challenges to such study. Approaching the weird as a fuzzy set lacking rigid boundaries allows its prototypical features to be analyzed while acknowledging its elusive resistance to definition. The aim is not to close off debate, but to further it. In positing the grotesque sublime as a paradigmatic element of weird fiction, this essay seeks to fortify the viability of the weird as a critical category with shared meaning and utility.

NOTES

1. China Miéville, "Weird Fiction," in *The Routledge Companion to Science Fiction*, ed. Mark Bould, Andrew M. Butler, Adam Roberts, and Sherryl Vint (London: Routledge, 2009), 510.

2. Istvan Csicsery-Ronay, Jr., "On the Grotesque in Science Fiction," *Science Fiction Studies* 29 no. 1 (2002): 79.

3. See *The Weird: a Compendium of Strange and Dark Stories*, ed. by Ann VanderMeer and Jeff VanderMeer (London: Corvus, 2011).

4. Michael Kelly, foreword to *Year's Best Weird Fiction: Volume One*, ed. Laird Barron and Michael Kelly (Toronto: Undertow, 2014), 8.

5. Steffen Hantke, "From the Library of America to the Mountains of Madness: Recent Discourse on H.P. Lovecraft," in *New Critical Essays on H.P. Lovecraft*, ed. David Simmons (New York: Palgrave Macmillan, 2013), 142.

6. See Jonathan Hatfull, "A Beginner's Guide to Weird Fiction," *SciFiNow* 119, May 2016, 96–97.

7. See H.P. Lovecraft, *The Call of Cthulhu and Other Weird Stories*, ed. S.T. Joshi (London: Penguin, 1999); H.P. Lovecraft, *The Thing on the Doorstep and Other Weird Stories*, ed. S.T. Joshi (London: Penguin, 2001); H.P. Lovecraft, *The Dreams in the Witch House and Other Weird Stories*, ed. S.T. Joshi (London: Penguin, 2004); H.P. Lovecraft, *Tales*, ed. Peter Straub (New York: Library of America, 2005).

8. See Algernon Blackwood, *Ancient Sorceries and Other Weird Stories*, ed. S.T. Joshi (London: Penguin, 2002); Arthur Machen, *The White People and Other Weird Stories*, ed. S.T. Joshi (London: Penguin, 2011); Clark Ashton Smith, *The Dark Eidolon and Other Fantasies*, ed. S.T. Joshi (London: Penguin, 2014).

9. See Miéville, "Weird Fiction."

10. David Simmons, "H.P. Lovecraft: The Outsider No More?" in *New Critical Essays on H.P. Lovecraft*, ed. David Simmons (New York: Palgrave Macmillan, 2013), 5.

11. Carl H. Sederholm and Jeffrey Andrew Weinstock, "Introduction: Lovecraft Rising,"

in *The Age of Lovecraft*, ed. Carl H. Sederholm and Jeffrey Andrew Weinstock (Minneapolis: University of Minnesota Press, 2016), 3.

12. Simmons, "H.P. Lovecraft: The Outsider No More?" 3.

13. Brian Attebery, *Strategies of Fantasy* (Bloomington: Indiana University Press, 1992), 11.

14. S.T. Joshi, *The Weird Tale* (Holicong, PA: Wildside Press, 1990), 2.

15. Smith, *The Dark Eidolon and Other Fantasies*, 160.

16. Roger Luckhurst, introduction to *The Classic Horror Stories*, by H.P. Lovecraft (Oxford: Oxford University Press, 2013), xvi.

17. See Eleanor Rosch, "Principles of Categorization," in *Cognition and Categorization*, ed. Eleanor Rosch and Barbara B. Lloyd (Hillsdale, NJ: Lawrence Erlbaum Associates, 1978), 35–7.

18. See Ludwig Wittgenstein, *Philosophical Investigations*, trans. G.E.M. Anscombe (New York: Macmillan, 1953), 31–2.

19. Ann VanderMeer and Jeff VanderMeer, introduction to *The Weird: a Compendium of Strange and Dark Stories*, ed. Ann VanderMeer and Jeff VanderMeer (London: Corvus, 2011), xv.

20. Miéville, "Weird Fiction," 510–11.

21. Rudolf Otto, *The Idea of the Holy*, trans. John W. Harvey (Oxford: Oxford University Press, 1958), 29.

22. Arthur Machen, "The Great God Pan," in *Late Victorian Gothic Tales*, ed. Roger Luckhurst (Oxford: Oxford University Press, 2005), 232.

23. Beth E. McDonald, *The Vampire as Numinous Experience: Spiritual Journeys with the Undead in British and American Literature* (Jefferson, NC: McFarland, 2004), 3.

24. Blackwood, *Ancient Sorceries and Other Weird Stories*, 303.

25. Otto, *The Idea of the Holy*, 37.

26. William James, *The Varieties of Religious Experience: a Study in Human Nature* (London: Longmans, Green and Co., 1928), 58.

27. Otto, *The Idea of the Holy*, 7.

28. Smith, *The Dark Eidolon and Other Fantasies*, 6.

29. Attebery, *Strategies of Fantasy*, 16.

30. Victor Shklovsky, "Art as Technique," in *Russian Formalist Criticism: Four Essays*, ed. and trans. Lee T. Lemon and Marion J. Reis (Lincoln: University of Nebraska Press, 1965), 13.

31. J.R.R. Tolkien, *Tree and Leaf* (London: George Allen & Unwin, 1964), 52.

32. Ian Bogost, *Alien Phenomenology, or What It's Like to Be a Thing* (Minneapolis: University of Minnesota Press, 2012), 124.

33. Machen, *The White People and Other Weird Stories*, 79.

34. Istvan Csicsery-Ronay, Jr., *The Seven Beauties of Science Fiction* (Middletown, CT: Wesleyan University Press, 2008), 146.

35. Longinus, "On Sublimity," in *Classical Literary Criticism*, trans. D.A. Russell, ed. D.A. Russell and M. Winterbottom (Oxford: Oxford University Press, 1989), 143.

36. Edmund Burke, *A Philosophical Enquiry into the Origin of Our Ideas of the Sublime and Beautiful*, ed. by Adam Phillips (Oxford: Oxford University Press, 1990), 53.

37. *Ibid.*

38. Smith, *The Dark Eidolon and Other Fantasies*, 56.

39. Thomas Weiskel, *The Romantic Sublime: Studies in the Structure and Psychology of Transcendence* (Baltimore: Johns Hopkins University Press, 1976), 21.

40. Smith, *The Dark Eidolon and Other Fantasies*, 63.

41. John Milbank, "Sublimity: The Modern Transcendent," in *Transcendence: Philosophy, Literature, and Theology Approach the Beyond*, ed. Regina Schwartz (London: Routledge, 2004), 212.

42. James, *The Varieties of Religious Experience*, 380.

43. Philip Shaw, *The Sublime* (London: Routledge, 2006), 3.

44. Lovecraft, *The Thing on the Doorstep and Other Weird Stories*, 83.

45. Blackwood, *Ancient Sorceries and Other Weird Stories*, 50.

46. China Miéville, "On Monsters: Or, Nine or More (Monstrous) Not Cannies," *Journal of the Fantastic in the Arts* 23.3 (2012): 381.

47. Miéville, "Weird Fiction," 511.

48. Horace, "On the Art of Poetry," in *Classical Literary Criticism*, trans. T.S. Dorsch (London: Penguin, 1965), 79.

49. Mikhail Bakhtin, *Rabelais and His World*, trans. Helene Iswolsky (Bloomington: Indiana University Press, 1984), 24, 26.

50. Peter Stallybrass and Allon White, *The Politics and Poetics of Transgression* (London: Methuen, 1986), 193.

51. Machen, "The Great God Pan," 228.

52. Smith, *The Dark Eidolon and Other Fantasies*, 130.

53. Lovecraft, *The Call of Cthulhu and Other Weird Stories*, 116.

54. Lovecraft, *The Thing on the Doorstep and Other Weird Stories*, 223–4.

55. Smith, *The Dark Eidolon and Other Fantasies*, 110.

56. Wilson Yates, "An Introduction to the Grotesque: Theoretical and Theological Considerations," in *The Grotesque in Art and Literature: Theological Reflections*, ed. James Luther Adams and Wilson Yates (Grand Rapids, MI: Eerdmans, 1997), 2.

57. Geoffrey Galt Harpham, *On the Grotesque: Strategies of Contradiction in Art and Literature* (Aurora, CO: The Davies Group, 2006), 17.

58. William Hope Hodgson, *Carnacki the Ghost-Finder* (London: Tandem, 1972), 187.

59. Frances S. Connelly, *The Grotesque in Western Art and Culture: The Image at Play* (Cambridge: Cambridge University Press, 2012), 154.

60. Bakhtin, *Rabelais and His World*, 19.

61. Thomas Ligotti, *The Conspiracy Against the Human Race* (New York: Hippocampus Press, 2011), 16.

62. Connelly, *The Grotesque in Western Art and Culture: The Image at Play*, 134.

63. Smith, *The Dark Eidolon and Other Fantasies*, 29.

64. Hodgson, *Carnacki the Ghost-Finder*, 178.

65. *Ibid.*, 209.

66. Blackwood, *Ancient Sorceries and Other Weird Stories*, 346.

67. Lovecraft, *The Thing on the Doorstep and Other Weird Stories*, 271.

68. *Ibid.*, 289.

69. *Ibid.*, 335.

70. Lovecraft, *The Call of Cthulhu and Other Weird Stories*, 167.

71. *Ibid.*

72. Deborah A. Kapchan and Pauline Turner Strong, "Theorizing the Hybrid," *The Journal of American Folklore* 112.445 (1999): 243.

Bibliography

Attebery, Brian. *Strategies of Fantasy*. Bloomington: Indiana University Press, 1992.

Bakhtin, Mikhail. *Rabelais and His World*, translated by Helene Iswolsky. Bloomington: Indiana University Press, 1984.

Blackwood, Algernon. *Ancient Sorceries and Other Weird Stories*, edited by S.T. Joshi. London: Penguin, 2002.

Bogost, Ian. *Alien Phenomenology, or What It's Like to Be a Thing*. Minneapolis: University of Minnesota Press, 2012.

Burke, Edmund. *A Philosophical Enquiry into the Origin of Our Ideas of the Sublime and Beautiful*, edited by Adam Phillips. Oxford: Oxford University Press, 1990.

Connelly, Frances S. *The Grotesque in Western Art and Culture: The Image at Play*. Cambridge: Cambridge University Press, 2012.

Csicsery-Ronay Jr., Istvan. "On the Grotesque in Science Fiction," *Science Fiction Studies* 29.1 (2002): 71–99.

_____. *The Seven Beauties of Science Fiction*. Middletown, CT: Wesleyan University Press, 2008.

Hantke, Steffen. "From the Library of America to the Mountains of Madness: Recent Discourse on H.P. Lovecraft," in *New Critical Essays on H.P. Lovecraft*, edited by David Simmons, 135–56. New York: Palgrave Macmillan, 2013.

Harpham, Geoffrey Galt. *On the Grotesque: Strategies of Contradiction in Art and Literature*. Aurora, CO: Davies Group, 2006.

Hatfull, Jonathan. "A Beginner's Guide to Weird Fiction." *SciFiNow* 119, May 2016, 96–97.

Hodgson, William Hope. *Carnacki the Ghost-Finder*. London: Tandem, 1972.

Horace. "On the Art of Poetry," in *Classical Literary Criticism*, trans. T.S. Dorsch, 77–95. London: Penguin, 1965.

James, William. *The Varieties of Religious Experience: A Study in Human Nature*. London; New York: Longmans, Green and Co., 1928.

Joshi, S.T. *The Weird Tale*. Holicong, PA: Wildside Press, 1990.

Kapchan, Deborah A., and Pauline Turner Strong. "Theorizing the Hybrid." *The Journal of American Folklore* 112.445 (1999): 239–53.

Kelly, Michael. Forward to *Year's Best Weird Fiction: Volume One*, edited by Laird Barron and Michael Kelly, 7–9. Toronto: Undertow, 2014.

Ligotti, Thomas. *The Conspiracy Against the Human Race*. New York: Hippocampus Press, 2011.

Longinus. "On Sublimity," in *Classical Literary Criticism*, translated by D.A. Russell, edited by D.A. Russell and M. Winterbottom, 143–87. Oxford: Oxford University Press, 1989.

Lovecraft, H.P. *The Call of Cthulhu and Other Weird Stories*, edited by S.T. Joshi. London: Penguin, 1999.

_____. *The Dreams in the Witch House and Other Weird Stories*, edited by S.T. Joshi. London: Penguin, 2004.

_____.*Tales*, edited by Peter Straub. New York: Library of America, 2005.

_____. *The Thing on the Doorstep and Other Weird Stories*, edited by S.T. Joshi. London: Penguin, 2001.

Luckhurst, Roger. Introduction to *The Classic Horror Stories* by H.P. Lovecraft, vii–xxviii. Oxford: Oxford University Press, 2013.

Machen, Arthur. "The Great God Pan," in *Late Victorian Gothic Tales*, edited by Roger Luckhurst. 183–233. Oxford: Oxford University Press, 2005.

_____. *The White People and Other Weird Stories*, edited by S.T. Joshi. London: Penguin, 2011.

McDonald, Beth E. *The Vampire as Numinous Experience: Spiritual Journeys with the Undead in British and American Literature*. Jefferson, NC: McFarland, 2004.

Miéville, China. "On Monsters: Or, Nine or More (Monstrous) Not Cannies." *Journal of the Fantastic in the Arts* 23.3 (2012): 377–92.

_____. "Weird Fiction," in *The Routledge Companion to Science Fiction*, edited by Mark Bould, Andrew M. Butler, Adam Roberts, and Sherryl Vint, 510–15. London: Routledge, 2009.

Milbank, John. "Sublimity: The Modern Transcendent." In *Transcendence: Philosophy, Literature, and Theology Approach the Beyond*, edited by Regina Schwartz, 211–34. London: Routledge, 2004.

Otto, Rudolf. *The Idea of the Holy*, translated by John W. Harvey. Oxford: Oxford University Press, 1958.

Rosch, Eleanor. "Principles of Categorization," in *Cognition and Categorization*, edited by Eleanor Rosch and Barbara B. Lloyd, 27–48. Hillsdale, NJ: Lawrence Erlbaum Associates, 1978.

Sederholm, Carl H., and Jeffrey Andrew Weinstock. "Introduction: Lovecraft Rising," in *The Age of Lovecraft*, edited by Carl H. Sederholm and Jeffrey Andrew Weinstock, 1–42. Minneapolis: University of Minnesota Press, 2016.

Shaw, Philip. *The Sublime*. London: Routledge, 2006.

Shklovsky, Victor. "Art as Technique," in *Russian Formalist Criticism: Four Essays*, edited and translated by Lee T. Lemon and Marion J. Reis, 3–24. Lincoln: University of Nebraska Press, 1965.

Simmons, David. "H.P. Lovecraft: The Outsider No More?," in *New Critical Essays on H.P. Lovecraft*, edited by David Simmons, 1–10. New York: Palgrave Macmillan, 2013.

Smith, Clark Ashton. *The Dark Eidolon and Other Fantasies*, edited by S.T. Joshi. London: Penguin, 2014.

Stallybrass, Peter, and Allon White. *The Politics and Poetics of Transgression.* London: Methuen, 1986.

Tolkien, J.R.R. *Tree and Leaf.* London: George Allen & Unwin Ltd, 1964.

VanderMeer, Ann, and Jeff VanderMeer. Introduction to *The Weird: A Compendium of Strange and Dark Stories,* edited by Ann VanderMeer and Jeff VanderMeer, xv–xx. London: Corvus, 2011.

Weiskel, Thomas. *The Romantic Sublime: Studies in the Structure and Psychology of Transcendence.* Baltimore: Johns Hopkins University Press, 1976.

Wittgenstein, Ludwig. *Philosophical Investigations,* translated by G.E.M. Anscombe. New York: Macmillan, 1953.

Yates, Wilson. "An Introduction to the Grotesque: Theoretical and Theological Considerations," in *The Grotesque in Art and Literature: Theological Reflections,* edited by James Luther Adams and Wilson Yates, 1–68. Grand Rapids, MI: Eerdmans, 1997.

Disease, Viruses and Death in Horror

Night of the Living Dead, or *Endgame*

Jan Kott, Samuel Beckett and Zombies

KEVIN J. WETMORE, JR.

"They give birth astride a grave, the light gleams an instant,
then it's night once more."
—Samuel Beckett, *Waiting for Godot*[1]

"The dead die hard, they are trespassers on the beyond, they must take
the place as they find it..."[2] So begins *Echo's Bones*, Samuel Beckett's zombie
novella that finally saw publication in 2014. *Echo's Bones*, which Fintan
O'Toole, writing in the *New York Review of Books* claims "is deliciously Beckettian: a rejected appendage to an abject failure," was initially written to flesh
out *More Pricks Than Kicks* (1934) and subsequently rejected by the publisher,
Chatto & Windes.[3] Editor Charles Prentice, who initially had requested *Echo's
Bones* to be written in order to increase the size of the contents, called it a
"nightmare" and refused to include it in the collection.[4] Part of the challenge
for Beckett, of course, is that the main characters had all died by the end of
the original, and so Beckett corporeally resurrects Belaqua Shuah for one last
story, a Beckettian "nightmare" that comically, grotesquely concludes in a
graveyard:

> The cemetery a cockpit of comic panic, Doyle stalking and rushing the tombstones,
> squatting behind them in ambush, behaving in a way quite foreign to his nature.
>   So it goes in the world.[5]

Echo's Bones ends in a cemetery, almost as *Night of the Living Dead* (1968,
George Romero) begins in one. Beckett's "Doyle" emerges to attack Johnny
and Barbra (Russell Streiner and Judith O'Dea), a post–Eisenhower Didi and

179

Gogo, come to put a wreath on the grave of a father they no longer remember for a purpose they do not understand. Johnny dies and reanimates in the cemetery while Barbra runs to a farmhouse and holes up with other individuals to wait and pass the night surrounded by the living dead. *Night of the Living Dead* is a positively Beckettian narrative in every sense of the word.

In his transformative collection of essays, *Shakespeare Our Contemporary* (1964), Polish critic Jan Kott saw in Shakespeare's *King Lear* the seeds of Samuel Beckett in an essay entitled *"King Lear, or Endgame."* The essay inspired impresario Peter Brook to direct first a stage version and subsequently a film adaptation of Shakespeare's play, focusing on both the bleak nihilism and grotesque clownshow Kott saw in the text. Three years before Brook's film, however, George Romero co-wrote, directed and produced *Night of the Living Dead*, a horror film that displays a cluster of unexpected affinities with Beckett's canon, most notably *Fin de Partie*—called *Endgame* (1957) in English, with a nod or two towards *Waiting for Godot* (1953). Indeed, *Night of the Living Dead* can be viewed as Theatre of the Absurd as B-horror movie (Theatre of the Absurd here defined as a postwar style of theatre that focuses on the comic aspect of the meaningless of existence and the purposelessness of communication). I propose to read Romero's film through Beckett, seeing in *Night of the Living Dead* a far more sophisticated absurdist narrative that taps into the same zeitgeist that informs Beckett. Far from being the B-movie that could, *Night of the Living Dead* is an absurdist comedy that demonstrates the comic emptiness of America in 1968. When viewed side by side, the affinities are clear between Brook's vision of Kott's *Lear*-filtered-through-Beckett and *Night of the Living Dead*, itself a bleak, unremitting clown show set in an inescapable rural landscape (the farmhouse of the latter is merely an extension of Beckett's tree in *Godot* and the "bare interior" of the home in *Endgame*).[6]

Kott argues that Beckett introduced a new theatre of "the grotesque," the world of which was "closed, and there is no escape."[7] "Tragedy," he notes, "is the theatre of priests, grotesque is the theatre of clowns."[8] *Night of the Living Dead* is not a tragedy, the deaths become ironic—it is a clown show. "In both Shakespearean and Beckettian *Endgames* the *Book of Job* is performed by clowns," writes Kott.[9] *King Lear* and *Endgame* are, in Kott's perspective, meditations on human suffering in which bathos and pathos overlap easily. He also sees both texts as apocalyptic narratives in both senses of the word: hidden things revealed and the end of the world. "The theme of *King Lear* is the decay and fall of the world," proclaims Kott, which puts it in the same category as most apocalyptic and all zombie narratives.[10] In other words, Beckett simply illuminates how to understand the zombies.

Inspired by Kott's reading of the play, Peter Brook directed first a stage version and then a filmed version of *King Lear* as filtered through Beckett.

In Brook's film, as Lawrence Gunter argues, "humanity has alienated itself from its humanness, and Brook reinforces this alienation with his camera."[11] Low angles, close ups of heads surrounded by darkness, Brook creates a world of alienated humans isolated by both the scenario and the camera. So, too, does Romero in *Night of the Living Dead.*

"For Brook," Gunter writes, "*King Lear* is Shakespeare's *Endgame,* a suggestion mirrored in the shot of Lear carrying Cordelia's lifeless body up the beach into a black sky, and it's with a shot that pans from a part of Lear's face to his shoulder to the empty, gray sky, that the film ends."[12] *Night of the Living Dead* ends in the same manner. Ben (Duane Jones), the only one of seven people to survive the night in the farmhouse surrounded by the living dead, is mistaken for a zombie himself by a posse, shot dead and his corpse thrown on a pile of burning refuse next to the farmhouse. He survives everything that happens throughout the eponymous night, only to be shot and killed by the very people tasked with rescuing him, who mistake him for the living dead. His death is meaningless and absurd, ironic and horrifying. The closing credits playing out over grainy photographs in which grey morning sky and smoke from the crematory fire blend into emptiness, just as in Brook's *King Lear.*

Jack Jorgens writes of *King Lear,* "Justice is absent, as the play shows nature shuddering in a nihilist orgasm—evil destroying both itself and the good, leaving behind destruction, emptiness, and men too scarred and stunned to go on living."[13] Noting that he says this about the play, now the film's two elements become clear: first, Jorgen's observation is also a description of every single one of Romero's zombie films. *Night of the Living Dead* sets the pattern for all of Romero's (and indeed many other) zombie films which follow: humans are far more dangerous and evil than the living dead.[14] The dead are slow, they appear tragic, they're, in the words of the sheriff, "all messed up."[15] Harry (Karl Hardman), on the other hand, represents in a more real way the absence of justice. He refuses to help when he hears Barbra screaming above, he fights with Ben for control of the group, and he grabs the gun, rather than help save the group. *Dawn of the Dead* (1978, George Romero) is even more of a "nihilist orgasm": the arrival of the biker gang destroys both itself and the mall, leaving behind meaningless devastation. *Day of the Dead* (1985, George Romero) sees the military and scientists seemingly in a contest over who can destroy the world, both on the micro and macro levels.

Second, the genealogy of this analysis is rather transparent: Shakespeare as understood through Brook and Kott, and learning about *King Lear* from Beckett. Brook's *King Lear* is Shakespeare's narrative, reframed as meaningless action in a bleak void; a clownshow of human suffering: Job as absurd vaudeville turned tragic. Shakespeare's tragedy opens with King Lear giving away his kingdom to his three daughters (the irony, of course, is that the play is about a king who stops being king in scene one) based on how much they love him. His two eldest daughters flatter him and are given a huge part of his kingdom. His youngest daughter explains she loves him as a father, and loves him no less, no more than that, and is banished to France for her honesty. The two wicked daughters begin plotting against their father who is driven mad. Simultaneously, the legitimate son of Lear's advisor, the Duke of Gloucester, is framed by his bastard brother and goes into hiding in disguise as "Mad Tom" while the Duke's bastard and Lear's daughter have Gloucester blinded. They all end up out on a heath in a storm. When the youngest daughter returns from France with an army, a series of battles and plots by the evil siblings follow in which most of the main cast dies, including Lear and all his daughters.

Endgame, the Beckettian play that shaped the perception of King Lear, is set after the end of the world. Some never-identified apocalyptic disaster has ended the world outside. "Outside of here, it's death," one of the characters tells the audience.[16] Four people hide in a claustrophobic, old, broken down house in "gray light,"[17] a "claustrophobic interior."[18] The play introduces Hamm, blind and in a wheelchair, Clov, old and unable to sit, and Hamm's parents, Nagg and Nell, who hide inside garbage bins. The four discuss leaving, killing themselves, and how to fill the time in the house. All four bicker until Clov decides to leave the house, but does not actually go.

Night of the Living Dead actually follows the same Beckettian path. The inhabitants of the farmhouse are all Beckettian clowns, suffering even as they exist and desperately seeking meaningful activity to give them purpose and a sense of being. Yet, all their efforts prove to be for naught. Harry and Helen (Marilyn Eastman), the hate-filled married couple, a middle-class, middle American Nagg and Nell, in the dustbin of the basement, fighting over the future and their dying child. Ben and Barbra, Night of the Living Dead's Hamm and Clov, engaged in what Kott calls, "the suffering nothing"–our fate is to suffer and cry and that proves we are alive.[19] Indeed, Clov looks in on Nagg and tells Hamm, "He's crying"; Hamm responds, "Then he's living."[20] Life is suffering and pain and then we are no more. Barbra is alternatively catatonic and screaming, while Ben fills his time with boarding up the house, finding and watching a television, and planning various escapes that all fail. As with Hamm and Clov, she cannot stand, he cannot endure to sit. They wait for the end in their own ways, often at odds with each other.

Harry and Helen, Nagg and Nell of the basement, also sit at ends with each other. Helen tells Harry, "We may not enjoy living together, but dying together isn't going to solve anything,"[21] and she is completely right. They die together and it solves nothing. Human action or inaction are equally meaningless.

The Beckettian twist Romero provides is that the clownshow continues after the oblivion when the crying ceases. The film concerns itself with humans battling the living dead. Romero's zombies (unlike those of the recent, unBeckettian zombie films and television programs, which are angry zombies), are sad, pathetic clowns. Their facial expressions are that of dimwitted buffoons. They are slow. They are clumsy. They fall down. They bump into each other. Their unlife is similar to their original lives. In the remake of *Night of the Living Dead* (1990, Tom Savini),[22] as a reimagined, feminist Barbara looks from the zombies to those fighting them, "They're us," she pronounces; "We're them and they are us."[23] She does not mean that humans are the raw material for the living dead (although that is true: the living dead are the former living living); rather that in their living death they are continuing a meaningless struggle in a bleak and unforgiving world, and that is, in fact, absurd, ridiculous, and slightly funny. If one is crying, one is living. If one has stopped crying, one is living (dead).

As in Beckett's *Endgame*, a group of individuals are trapped within a bleak place, looking out the windows and arguing among each other. They suffer. As in *Waiting for Godot*, they wait for something that never shows up. They fill their lives and time with activity. One of the most Beckettian lines in *Night of the Living Dead* is when, upon finding and turning on a television, Harry tells the catatonic Barbra, "Now you better watch this and try to understand what is going on!" and the television news program they view is full of misinformation and reporters who do not grasp what is going on.[24]

The opening exchange in *Waiting for Godot* both embodies several themes from *Night of the Living Dead* and implies that Didi and Gogo are living dead as well:

> VLADMIR: I'm glad to see you back. I thought you were gone forever.
> ESTRAGON: Me, too.
> ...
> VLADMIR: (hurt, coldly). May one inquire where His Highness spent the night?
> ESTRAGON: In a ditch.
> VLADMIR: (admiringly). A ditch! Where?
> ESTRAGON: (without gesture). Over there.
> VLADMIR: And they didn't beat you?
> ESTRAGON: Beat me? Certainly they beat me.
> VLADMIR: The same lot as usual?
> ESTRAGON: The same? I don't know.
> VLADMIR: When I think of it ... all these years ... but for me ... where would you be ... (Decisively.) You'd be nothing more than a little heap of bones at the present minute, no doubt about it.[25]

Vladmir thought Estragon was "gone forever" and asserts that he would be "nothing more than a heap of bones" if not for Vladmir. Indeed, Estragon's demise and return from death is also rooted in wordplay in the original

French that does not translate into English (but does in German). Estragon spends the night "in a ditch," but the French and German words for "ditch" are a letter different for their respective words for "grave." In French, ditch is "fossé" and grave is "la fosse"; whereas in German, ditch is "Graben" and grave is "Grab."[26] The linguistic similarities are not present in English, but in the French original (and the German translation) the audience got the play on words, and Estragon's potential status as a dead man. He is living dead. Beckett offers images of those who continue to live, even after they are "gone," those whose condition is both absurd and horrifying. Eventually, in Act Two, Vladmir concludes, "To be dead is not enough for them," referring to everyone who has lived, arguing that we refuse to stay dead, not unlike the "ghouls" and "things" of *Night of the Living Dead.*[27]

Estragon may be dead, having spent the night in a grave, but he moves and talks and suffers and complains about his suffering: everything from his feet to the fact that he was beaten. He is the living dead, an animated corpse, as is Vladmir. Their world is a bleak landscape with a single dead or dying tree. The zombies and the characters in the farmhouse in *Night of the Living Dead* are Beckettian clowns, but the Beckettian clowns in *Waiting for Godot* themselves are a form of zombie.

Tangentially, Beckett's work is the paradigmatic example of the Theatre of the Absurd movement, occurring in Europe after the war. The etymology of "absurd" comes from a phrase meaning "out of harmony."[28] Absurd theatre displays a clownish metaphysical anguish, violent and grotesque, at the inadequacy of rationality. The world does not make sense; but the fault is ours for expecting it to. Absurdism grows out of existentialism; although the latter sees the meaninglessness of existence as inherently tragic, the former finds it hysterical. Sartre, an existentialist forerunner of the absurdists perhaps put it best: hell is other people, as Sartre reminds us, a point proven conclusively and repeatedly in *Night of the Living Dead.*[29]

Further affinities flow forth. Martin Esslin, who coined the term "Theatre of the Absurd," notes that Beckett's characters "are grouped in symmetrical pairs": Hamm/Clov & Nagg/Nell and Didi/Gogo & Lucky/Pozzo.[30] Romero also groups his characters in symmetrical pairs: Barbra begins the film with Johnny, but upon his death is linked with Ben, and not just the alliterative names, which connect them to Harry and Helen. Ben protects Barbra, speaks for her, and shares the longest uninterrupted screen time of any two characters with her. Harry and Helen are a symmetrical pair, their daughter already an absence, banished to the basement. Lastly, Tom and Judy (Keith Wayne and Judith Ridley) form the third pair. All pairs function to limit and impose on both members. In *Endgame*, the dwelling is Hamm's house and he is the only one with access to the food. As noted above, Hamm cannot stand or walk. Clov cannot sit. Clov must feed Hamm or Hamm dies. If Clov leaves, however, both will die, as they will both starve. Every action leads to eventual death. At the conclusion of the play, Clov decides to leave, and, like Vladmir and Estragon in *Waiting for Godot*, does not. The futility of any action overwhelms. He may as well lock himself in the cellar and wait for rescue (which isn't coming) or the end.

Perhaps, in the end, the title of *Night of the Living Dead* refers not to the things, the ghouls, the animated dead, but to the people in the house. They are the living dead, the ones outside the house are the dead, alive. As in Beckett, the narrative is filled with characters not doing what they say they will, or alternately, doing what they swear they won't, for example, Ben's "I'm not going down in that cellar, Cooper."[31] Esslin argues the Theatre of the Absurd ultimately expresses "the tragic sense of loss at the disappearance of ultimate certainties" in the second half of the 20th century.[32] That's also a line that could describe *Night of the Living Dead*.

Daniel W. Drezner states that the post-modern zombie film is not about the zombie, as earlier films such as *White Zombie* (1932, Victor Halperin) or *I Walked with a Zombie* (1943, Jacques Tourneur) were. Rather, the culture has shifted to a focus on the zombie apocalypse: what happens to those still living in a world gone dead.[33] Note: the argument is not being made that Beckett is directly responsible for Romero's film, but Romero does introduce a Beckettian culture of zombies: the ending is here, all shall wait together in this bleak dwelling, arguing, crying and dying, and then shifting from living to living dead. They spend the night in a farmhouse, or a ditch, or a grave; they contemplate suffering even as they suffer; lastly, they die and the whole scenario is both absurd and emblematic of the human condition.

Beckett's worldview lurks behind contemporary zombie culture. As with Doyle in *Echo's Bones*, Beckett now lurks and lurches around the cemetery. There is no evidence that Beckett ever saw Romero's film, nor that Romero ever saw or read Beckett's plays, but the juxtaposition of the two texts reveals a similarity of apocalyptic clown show and ironic nihilism that is both telling of the late 20th century impulses towards the endgame and how American culture understands death. If one reads zombie cinema through Beckett, one is not venturing very far. The converse is also true: if one reads Beckett through zombie cinema, one will find much that is familiar and much that echoes through Hamm's house, past Didi and Gogo's tree, into the graveyard where Doyle, Beckett and Johnny wait.

They're coming to get us, Barbra. Like Godot, they just won't ever get here.[34]

NOTES

1. Samuel Beckett, "Waiting for Godot," in *The Complete Dramatic Works* (London: Faber and Faber, 1986), 83.

2. Samuel Beckett, *Echo's Bones,* ed. Mark Nixon (New York: Grove Press 2014), 1.

3. Fintan O'Toole, "Samuel Beckett: The Private Voice," *The New York Review of Books*, last modified March 19, 2015, http://www.nybooks.com/articles/archives/2015/mar/19/samuel-beckett-private-voice.

4. Mark Nixon, Introduction to *Echo's Bones*, ed. Mark Nixon (New York: Grove Press, 2014), ix.

5. Beckett, *Echo's Bones*, 51.

6. Samuel Beckett, "Endgame," in *The Complete Dramatic Works* (London: Faber and Faber, 1986), 92.

7. Jan Kott, *Shakespeare Our Contemporary*, trans. Boleslaw Taborski (New York: W.W. Norton & Company, 1964), 131, 133.

8. *Ibid.*, 141.

9. *Ibid.*, 158.

10. *Ibid.*, 152.

11. J. Lawrence Gunter, "Hamlet, Macbeth and King Lear on Film," in T*he Cambridge Companion to Shakespeare on Film,* ed. Russell Jackson (Cambridge: Cambridge University Press, 2000), 131.

12. *Ibid.*

13. Jack J. Jorgens, *Shakespeare on Film* (Bloomington: Indiana University Press, 1977), 236.

14. See Kevin J. Wetmore, Jr., *Back from the Dead: Remakes of the Romero Zombie Films as Markers of Their Times* (Jefferson, NC: McFarland, 2011).

15. *Night of the Living Dead,* directed by George R. Romero (1968; Los Angeles: Dimension/Genius Products LLC, 2008), DVD.

16. Beckett, *Endgame*, 96.

17. *Ibid.*, 92.

18. Martin Esslin, *The Theatre of the Absurd* (New York: Penguin, 1961), 62.

19. Kott, 157.

20. Beckett, *Endgame*, 123.

21. *Night of the Living Dead* (1968).

22. *Night of the Living Dead*, directed by Tom Savini (1990; Culver City, CA: Sony Pictures Home Entertainment, 1999), DVD.

23. *Ibid.*

24. *Night of the Living Dead* (1968).

25. Samuel Beckett, "Waiting for Godot," in *The Complete Dramatic Works* (London: Faber and Faber, 1986), 1.

26. My gratitude to Katharine Weiss for sharing this information with me.

27. Beckett, *Godot*, 58; *Night of the Living Dead* (1968).

28. Esslin, 23.

29. Jean Paul Sartre, *No Exit and Three Other Plays* (New York: Vintage, 1989), 45.

30. Esslin, 62.

31. *Night of the Living Dead* (1968).

32. Esslin, 400.

33. Daniel W. Drezner, "Metaphor of the Living Dead, or the Effect of the Zombie Apocalypse on Public Policy Discourse." *Social Research* 81.4 (2014): 835.

34. This essay came out of a course I taught on apocalypse on stage and screen, students seeing in Beckett similarities to apocalyptic narratives in which individuals are trapped, waiting for the end such as *Night of the Living Dead* and its sequels and remakes, as well as such films as *Knowing* and *This Is the End*. My thanks to David Sanchez, my co-teacher on that course.

BIBLIOGRAPHY

Beckett, Samuel. *The Complete Dramatic Works*. London: Faber & Faber, 1986.

_____. *Echo's Bones*. Edited by Mark Nixon. New York: Grove Press, 2014.

Drezner, Daniel W. "Metaphor of the Living Dead, or the Effect of the Zombie Apocalypse on Public Policy Discourse." *Social Research* 81.4 (2014): 825–849.

Esslin, Marton. *The Theatre of the Absurd.* New York: Penguin, 1961.
Gunter, J. Lawrence. "Hamlet, Macbeth and King Lear on Film" in *The Cambridge Companion to Shakespeare on Film.* Edited Russell Jackson. Cambridge: Cambridge University Press, 2000. 117–134.
Jorgens, Jack J. *Shakespeare on Film.* Bloomington: Indiana University Press, 1977.
Kott, Jan. *Shakespeare Our Contemporary.* Translated by Boleslaw Taborski. New York: W.W. Norton, 1964.
Night of the Living Dead. Directed by George R. Romero. 1968. Los Angeles: Dimension/Genius Products LLC, 2008. DVD.
Night of the Living Dead. Directed by Tom Savini. 1990. Culver City, CA: Sony Pictures Home Entertainment, 1990. DVD.
Nixon, Mark. Introduction to *Echo's Bones,* ix–xxii. Edited by Mark Nixon. New York: Grove Press, 2014.
O'Toole, Fintan. "Samuel Beckett: The Private Voice." *The New York Review of Books.* Last updated, March 19, 2015. http://www.nybooks.com/articles/archives/2015/mar/19/samuel-beckett-private-voice/.
Sartre, Jean-Paul. *No Exit and Three Other Plays.* New York: Vintage, 1989.
Wetmore, Kevin J., Jr. *Back from the Dead: Remakes of the Romero Zombie Films as Markers of Their Times.* Jefferson, NC: McFarland, 2011.

Koji Suzuki's *Ring*

A World Literary Perspective

FRAZER LEE

This essay will examine aspects of Koji Suzuki's *Ring* (1991) and its heterogeneous collection of adaptations and spin offs to evaluate how it behaves as a world literary work, according to definitions from three key theorists. These aspects will include the socio-political backdrop of nineties Japan informing the context of the source text and its boundary crossing translation and transition into a worldwide franchise, and the dynamic of male versus female protagonists in the source text and its adaptations.

With the publication of *Ring*, Suzuki spawned a monster that would become even more far-reaching than its monstrous avenger Sadako Yamamura. The first novel in the series sold almost three million copies worldwide and kick-started an enduring franchise. A sequel, *Rasen* (*Spiral*) was published in 1995, followed by *Rupu* (*Loop*) in 1998, a short story collection *Birthday* (1999), and two further novels, *S* in 2012 and *Tide* (2013).

The first screen adaptation appeared in 1995 with *Ringu: Kanzenban* (Chisui Takigawa), a made-for-TV movie that eroticized the interactions of the (often naked) Sadako (Ayane Miura) with the recipients of her vengeance from beyond the grave. Hideo Nakata's *Ringu* followed in 1998, a feature film with excellent production values, along with *Rasen* (George Iida) also in the same year. The latter was far less successful critically than the first, and another sequel, *Ringu 2* (Hideo Nakata) was released in 1999 to far greater acclaim. Several more TV and film sequels and adaptations followed, including *Ring 0: Birthday* (2000, Norio Tsuruta), based upon one of the stories in Suzuki's collection from the previous year, and *The Ring Virus* (1999, Kim Dong-bin), which provided a South Korean take on Suzuki's story. Sadako (rebranded "Samara") crawled out of the silver screen and into the American public consciousness via Gore Verbinski's remake of Nakata's film, *The Ring*

(2000) starring Naomi Watts, and this was quickly followed by *The Ring Two* (2005, Hideo Nakata). The series continues in screen adaptations and spin-offs to date, with *Sadako vs. Kayako* (2016, Kōji Shiraishi) presenting a grudge match in all senses of that term between the female "monsters" from both the *Ring* and the *Grudge* franchises. Other "versus" movies include *Hikiko-san vs. Sadako* (2015, Hisaaki Nagaoka) and *Bunshinsaba vs. Sadako* (2016, River Huang). The latest entries in Sadako's solo series canon are two 3D movies from Japan, *Sadako 3D* (2012, Tsutomu Hanabusa) and *Sadako 3D 2* (2013, Tsutomu Hanabusa), and *Rings* (2017, F. Javier Gutiérrez), which is the third in the Hollywood series of *Ring* re-imaginings. The short film *Rings* (2005, Jonathan Liebesman) bridged the narrative gap between *The Ring* and *The Ring Two* feature films.

There have also been several manga based on Suzuki's story, from *The Ring* (1996) to *The Curse of Yamamura Sadako* in 2000. Two video games have been produced to date: *The Ring: Terror's Realm* and *Ring: Infinity*, both in 2000. It is surprising given the viral nature of Sadako's method of revenge, that there have not been further video game installments related to the franchise. One can speculate that this may be due to the success of other J-horror supernatural video games, such as the *Silent Hill* series (1999–2014), the *Clock Tower* trilogy (1995–2002), and *Fatal Frame* (2003).

An examination of the basic premise for Suzuki's story can assist in explaining the popularity of the franchise as a whole. Director Hideo Nakata summed up *Ring*'s main selling points:

> The key line is very simple. There is a cursed video which can kill very quickly, in seven days exactly, and the three main characters watch the video. How can they get away from the curse? That kind of simple and strong story, it might not be very realistic, but, well VCRs and TVs have become so common in our daily lives, in Japan and other Asian countries, as well as in Europe and America. And of course, Koji Suzuki's ideas are very suitable for popular horror movies, especially for teenagers.[1]

The familial curse is a storytelling concept rooted in the early Gothic literature of Ann Radcliffe and Horace Walpole that can also be found in the works of Edgar Allan Poe (1839's *The Fall of the House of Usher*, for example), and the 20th-century movement such as Melvyn Peake's *Gormenghast* (1950). The fear of new technologies has fueled horror narratives from Mary Shelley's *Frankenstein; or, The Modern Prometheus* (1818) onwards, with technology coming into the home as a source for scares in works such as Tobe Hooper's 1982 film *Poltergeist*, which marries a child abduction story structure to a supernatural device that turns the humble TV set in the corner of the 1980s living room into a portal to Hell. As Nakata outlines in the quote above, the advent of the "be kind, rewind" VCR generation meant that televisions were no longer the mainstay of the shared living space. The notion that VCRs were once cutting-edge tech might be something of a leap to generations that have grown up with smartphones, tablets and A.I. but *Ring* very much began as a nineties phenomenon, after all. During that decade, TV-video combo units could be found flickering late into the night in kitchens and bedrooms and were becoming more affordable to all with the proliferation of "buy now, pay later" deals of 1980s credit card savvy, upwardly mobile consumer culture. Suzuki seized on this as an opportunity to scare readers by simply using what was there, in the most intimate spaces within our homes, asking the question "what if?" *Ring's* what if scenario asks what lengths someone might go to if they watched a cursed videotape and had only seven days to live. Would they pass the curse on to someone else if they could survive by doing so? The moral dilemma of this simple premise—save yourself, but risk harming others—has fascinated countless readers of Suzuki's work, and eager viewers of its adaptations. The act of then recommending the source text, or latest film, to a friend or relative mirrors the viral act of passing along Sadako's curse. As consumers and co-curators of Suzuki's work, audiences are playing out the central concern of the novel.

This "Ring Virus," both fictional and actual, is a key characteristic that makes Suzuki's novel an ideal candidate to be considered as a work of world literature. Pheng Cheah states that world literature refers to the circulation, translation and dissemination of texts—exploring the fresh readings and meanings that emerge as texts enter into new cultures and languages.[2] Cheah describes the production of world literature as world-making, or more specifically an "active process in the world."[3] World literature as world-making "seeks to be disseminated, read and received around the world so as to change that world and the life of a given people within it."[4] Sadako Yamamura's psychic revenge, projected by an awesome act of mental will onto a videotape in a building above her last resting place, is in itself an act of world-making. Suzuki's character seeks to send her rage out into the world, unmaking it and changing it by sheer force of will. The imagery on the disturbing videotape contains clues in the form of characters and tableaux that reveal her tragic backstory, for those who are looking deeper, such as the protagonist Asakawa, who is desperate to shake the curse before it kills him, and then his family. The Ring Virus seeks to be disseminated, read and received around the world, changing that world and the lives of the people touched by it. This effect can be seen on a wider scale on the latest film in the Hollywood *Ring* sequence, *Rings*, where Samara (Bonnie Morgan) is witnessed crawling out of the seatback screens on a transatlantic flight. Suzuki's ever-persistent virus has travelled far beyond a log cabin in Japan. It is now airborne, a localized horror tale, translated, sequel-ized and mutated into in-flight entertainment.

Considering Suzuki as world literature-creator, it is important to observe the form from an authorial perspective. Goethe's highlights a key characteristic of the process: "it is [the] connection between the original and the translation that expresses most clearly the relationship of nation to nation and that one must above all know if one wishes to encourage a common world literature transcending national limits."[5]

There are contradictions in Goethe's approach to the creation of world literature. He promotes new forms but favors the Greek classics, and embraces transnationalism yet also seeks to promote the inherent virtues of German literature. This tension is present in many adapted works that break borders to find global audiences. The process by which localized storytelling becomes globalized story consumption is perhaps rooted in a cultural transaction that takes place within the writer's own practice. The authorial intent to speak to universal themes through the lens of localized culture is the progenitor of particularly world literary material. Goethe underlines the transactional nature of worldwide dissemination of literature, and in the following quotation the process can be discerned by which Sadako has found her way to the Hollywood box office and beyond, into homes across the globe:

> General world literature can only develop when nations get to know all the relations among the nations. The inevitable result will be that they find in each other something likeable and something repulsive, something to be imitated and something to be rejected. This too will contribute to expanding economic relations...[6]

Similarly, Suzuki as a practitioner rejects the "horror writer" label[7] but embraces the cultural exchange, and apparently also the expanding economic relations of book sales figures and substantial movie option deals. Perhaps the initial cultural transaction in the creation (accidental or otherwise) of world literature occurs within the writer. By creating characters and situations that are translatable across cultural divides, as *The Ring* is in its conceptual universality (fear of tech) and contextual simplicity (the Gothic curse), as outlined above, the author sets the work on a path that is open to interpretation and re-interpretation in receptive cultures.

This process of creative transactions and cultural transformation is discussed by Damrosch, in particular how texts gain new meaning as they circulate, a process of translation as transformation. Damrosch defines world literature as "all literary works that circulate beyond their country of origin, either in translation or in their original language."[8] This definition is certainly supported by *Ring*, as the viral nature of Suzuki's story mutates from the first novel in the series to the latest book and film sequels, just as the supernatural videotape of the original story becomes the viral pop-up perpetuated via the Internet in the sequel *Rings*. The rural hotel cabin complete with fitness and leisure complex of the first novel is an undeniably Japanese setting, while cleverly riffing on the secluded log cabin of Western slasher movies, even namedropping one such franchise. Suzuki's prose celebrates the gleaming modernity and originality of the Ballardian spaces within the mountain hideaway, while acknowledging the familiarity via horror genre expectations:

> Asakawa could more or less analyze why he'd been drawn to this modern building, to the point of barging into the restaurant. He found it somehow comforting. All the way here he had been imagining dark, utterly primitive log cabins—the perfect back-drop for a Friday the 13th scenario—and there was nothing of that in this building.[9]

Here, the Gothic imagination is present and at play in the expectations of the protagonist, while the localized Japanese aspects of the setting provide succor to him, albeit briefly, until he watches the haunted videotape.

The mutation of this setting into a North American university campus in *Rings*, another staple of U.S. slasher movies, demonstrates how Suzuki's text gains new meaning as the story continues via a network of creator-interpreters. By looking at the uniquely Japanese roots of Suzuki's tale, this process of translation and transformation can be observed.

Damrosch suggests that world literature is "as much about the host culture's values and needs as it is about a work's source culture"[10] and to consider *Ring's* source culture, it is essential to dial back to the roots of J-horror in Japanese folk horror and its long established theatrical tradition. *Kaidan*, or Japanese ghost tales, refer to *yurei* (ghosts) including *onryo* (avenging spirits) which return to the mortal world seeking revenge either through bodily trauma, or inflict wider impacts upon the human world in, for example, the form of environmental disasters. These folk tale ghosts became film subjects in *Onibaba* (1964, Kaneto Shindo) and *Kwaidan* (1965, Masaki Kobayashi). *Onibaba* (trans. *Demon Hag*) is based on the folk tale of *The Black Mound* (Kurozuka) and offers a reversal of Sadako's story, with a ghost attacking men and throwing them into a deep, dark, round hole. *Kwaidan* is a four-part episodic narrative that includes the tale of "The Black Hair." The long, black hair, flowing white robes, and staring eyes of these avenging female spirits are among the cultural markers found in Suzuki's creation. Wronged women, haunted houses, mother-child bonding, demonic/demonized mothers, and domestic violence at the hands of males are all elements of these stories, including *Ring*. These elements carry over into Butoh dance performance and its spasmodic, convulsive movements are echoed in the broken body of Sadako Yamamura crawling out of the well, through the television screen and into her victims' nightmares. At the intersection of these traditional literary and theatrical forms, and contemporary J-horror cinema, is Nobuo Nakagawa's 1960 film *Jigoku* (*Hell*, aka *The Sinners of Hell*) with its visions of a torturous underworld. Offering a striking departure from traditional *kaidan*, *Jigoku* eviscerated genre norms with visceral imagery that resonated across the decades into operatically violent and gory films such as Kei Fujiwara's *Organ* (1996).

These cultural transactions of genre are married to those of style and tone in Suzuki's work and its translations and adaptations. Stylistically, the imagery and typography contained within Sadako's psychic projections upon the cursed videotape in *Ring* are abstract and, particularly in filmed versions, surreal. The French surrealist Andre Breton defined surrealism as, "Pure psychic automatism, by which one intends to express verbally, in writing or by any other method, the real functioning of the mind. Dictation by thought, in the absence of control exercised by reason, and beyond any aesthetic or moral preoccupation."[11] This definition perhaps describes the content and method of delivery of Sadako's projections. Her mind is in anguish, broken down into a singular desire for revenge and amplified by hatred for those who have wronged her. The language of Sadako's video is one that encapsulates terror and vengeance, its imagery and cryptic text antagonizing the minds of those who bear witness to it. Sadako is an innocent, as is Samara, scrutinized like a lab rat then abused and discarded. But she is also an "evil genius" in the execution of her vengeance from beyond the grave. Her surreal psychic projections enter into the real world and shatter it, as she herself mutates into an artwork-becoming via the videotape, living beyond death in an analogue, then digital, world. "To become truly immortal, a work of art must escape all human limits: logic and common sense will only interfere," said surrealist painter Girgio De Chico, "But once these barriers are broken, it will enter the dreams of childhood visions and dreams."[12]

Tonally, *Ring* places its core focus on naturalism through explorations of the domestic. Work spaces, faculties of study, and the flickering screen of the TV set in the living room are all mainstays of Suzuki's claustrophobic story world. The human drama, and tension of having seven days to live, is heightened by the use of intimate settings that culminate in Sadako's resting place of a claustrophobic well. The investigating characters are sandwiched between its opening and the foundations of the vacation rental chalet above, crushed between the two worlds of the everyday and the unexplained central to the depiction of domestic-slash-paranormal horrors. In Western horror storytelling, William Friedkin's *The Exorcist* (1973) deployed heightened realism, with naturalistic performances, bringing the horror home in all senses and making the fantastical believable.

Echoing Butoh, Regan's "spider walk" (reinstated to the extended "version you've never seen" 2000 cut of *The Exorcist*) pre-empts Sadako's jerky, unnatural movements in *Ring*, and Kayako's crawling abomination in the *Ju-on (The Grudge)* series. A similar pattern of translation can be found in German Expressionism's ecstatic theatrical style, which was transferred into early horror cinema via *The Cabinet of Doctor Caligari* (1920, Robert Wiene) and others. The *chiaroscuro* of German Expressionist cinema informs John Carpenter's *Halloween* (1978), which used highly stylized camerawork, including continuous takes and Steadicam footage, to place the horror of its protagonist and her friends onto day lit suburban streets. The day-time world plays out in stark contrast to the night-time world of trick or treaters and horny (and/or terrified) babysitters in Carpenter's vividly staged sequences.

Ring follows in the disturbing footsteps of these examples, but with the added device of the "film within a film" provided by the cursed videotape. In Ring, domestic terror becomes global fear, a dynamic that is reflected in the sociopolitical backdrop of Japan at the time Suzuki unleashed Sadako upon an unwitting world. The publication of Ring in 1991 and Rasen in 1995, tapped into techno-fear and coincided with threats to the ordered society of Japan from within. Kevin J. Wetmore highlights the impact of doomsday cult Aum Shinrikyo (Supreme Truth) with its devastating sarin gas attack in the Tokyo subway system on March 20, 1995. The gas attack killed 13, injured 54 and affected many thousands more, leaving Japanese society shocked that such a crime could be committed within the confines of ordered society. In a plot twist that could have come from the pages of Suzuki's Ring series, the cult's leader Shoko Asahara used a radio signal (purchased from Russia and broadcast to Japan) to protest his innocence.[13] Membership of this Japanese death cult then rose in Russia, rather like a virus spreading beyond borders a la Sadako's tape and the Ring Virus. Mirroring the trajectory of Sadako's psychic projections, the now international members of Aum Shinrikyo became a diaspora infected by a doctrine of violence. Russia designated the group a terrorist organization and banned it in September 2016. Asahara was executed at Tokyo Detention House along with six other cult members in 2018.

With the elements of genre, style, tone and dramatic context in mind, it is little wonder that the powerful screen adaptation potential of Suzuki's novel became apparent to an industry often influenced by book sales figures. The 1990s saw several successful independent film adaptations of acclaimed novels, with Nakata's Ring joining the ranks of Danny Boyle's Trainspotting (1996), David Cronenberg's Naked Lunch (1991) and Crash (1996) in theaters. Commercial viability of the source text as global entertainment franchise exploded with J.K. Rowling's wizarding worlds and one need only look to the self-publishing popular fiction phenomena of E.L. James's Fifty Shades of Grey (2011) and Andy Weir's The Martian (2011) to see a twenty-first century continuation of this trend.

Joni Iida's role as the adapting screenwriter for Ring: Kanzenban would seem to be a straightforward one—adapt a smash hit book, create a smash hit film—and indeed his work is perhaps the most faithful of all the Ring adaptations to the original source text. Iida went on to direct Rasen the first of the official sequels to Nakata's Ringu, with both films presented as a double bill initially, until it became clear that Rasen was less popular with audiences and another sequel Ringu 2 was green-lit. That the source text has been successful is by no means a guarantee that the film derivation will be equally so. A comparative example from Western cinema is *The Golden Compass* (2007, Chris Weitz), which took Philip Pullman's *Northern Lights* (1995) and somehow drained it of all the ingredients that made the book so popular with its readers. According to story structure analyst and screenwriting guru Robert McKee, "The conceit of adaptation is that the hard work of story can be avoided by optioning a literary work and simply shifting it into a screenplay. That is almost never the case."[14]

McKee also sets out his "first principle of adaptation," namely that "The purer the novel, the purer the play, the worse the film."[15] To date, *Ring: Kanzenban* has not received a commercial release outside of its television broadcast. In a twist that might please Sadako herself, VHS video copies do exist and have been shared by fans of the series via the world wide web. Chisui Takigawa's TV film shares the overwhelmingly male gaze of the source novel, sexing-up Sadako's presence throughout its 95-minute runtime (she appears naked and haloed in light). Most strikingly of all, *Kanzenban* maintains Suzuki's male protagonist Kazuyuki Asakawa, a family man who stumbles upon Sadako's curse and then attempts to shield his family from it. Asakawa is painted in moody, rather selfish tones by Suzuki and the character's erratic behavior often portrays him as dysfunctional. Ken Dancyger describes such dysfunctional male protagonist characters as archetypes in world cinema, "These men are family men, but they are also self-absorbed men, overconcerned with how they are perceived by others, their peers particularly. Because they live too much in their heads and they are ruled by the conflict between desire and duty, they are confused, troubled men."[16] Asakawa fits this definition perfectly. He is at odds with his personal and professional lives, creating the essence of the character drama in the novel. Bizarrely, Asakawa seemingly covers for his (alleged rapist) friend Ryuji Takayama during their investigation into the source of the cursed videotape: Despite being "shocked speechless […] Naturally, Asakawa never told anybody about Ryuji's crime," with the two becoming buddies to the extent that "he and Ryuji could just call each other up anytime to go have a drink—Ryuji was the only one Asakawa had that kind of relationship with."[17]

The two characters already share a secretive darkness, perhaps preparing them for their confrontation with Sadako's malevolent force. It is worth noting that as the novel progresses, its true antagonist becomes the Ring Virus itself, with Sadako its unwitting progenitor due to her smallpox infection and her ability for psychic photography. At the close of the novel, the veracity of Ryuji's account of the crime is left ambiguous, though this does nothing to address his earlier contradictory condemnation of Sadako's physician Nagao Jotaro's actions in raping her and infecting her with smallpox. During Ryuji's interrogation of Jotaro, Suzuki reveals another aspect of his damaged "monstrous feminine": Sadako Yamamura was intersex, a revelation that serves as motivation for Jotaro to then dispose of Sadako in a well, before burying her under rocks. He kills her following a struggle, during which Sadako launches a psychic attack on him. His lust and revulsion are entirely at odds and are driven to fever pitch by his smallpox symptoms. "On the one hand I desired the destruction of her body, but on the other hand I didn't want her body to be marred,"[18] the doctor confesses.

Referring to the cultural transaction within the author of world literary works outlined above, it is worth noting that Suzuki is a renowned author of "better parenting" texts in his native Japan, and in interviews has stated that he enjoys macho pursuits such as riding fast motorbikes.[19] One reading of Asakawa is as the antithesis of Suzuki's apparent comfort with his public and personal personas as both author and parent, and whose primary career as novelist perhaps dictates that he lives "too much in his head."[20]

Returning to McKee, his "second principle of adaptation" is simply, "be willing to invent."[21] Screen adaptations of *Ring* have certainly steered the franchise away from the moral ambiguity of Ryuji's character, omitting his claims of rape assaults and adapting him from something of a wise-cracking misfit into a morose, more introspective character. The source novel sees Asakawa provoked into decisive action as a reaction to the nightmare scenario of his young daughter Yoko inadvertently watching the cursed tape on his wife Shizuka's lap. Suzuki's novel makes Shizuka complicit in the curse upon Yoko, a plot detail that also serves as a subtle extension of the monstrous feminine. In *Ring* adaptations post–*Ringu: Kanzenban*, something significant occurs; the greater threat to the family unit is explored via the dramatic archetype of the single mother who is protecting her child. In Nakata's *Ringu*, Ryuji is recast as the ex-husband of the film's protagonist, television reporter Reiko Asakawa (Nanako Matsushima). A similar dynamic is at play in Verbinski's *The Ring*, with Seattle-based journalist Rachel Keller (Naomi Watts) calling upon her video technician ex-boyfriend Noah Clay (Martin Henderson) for help with her investigation.

Hideo Nakata said of the female characters driving his horror narratives, "I love melodramas. I always feel more related to those female protagonists who are in an agony situation, dealing with genuine love but something becomes an obstacle and she just can't continue."[22] Reiko, in Nakata's *Ringu*, and Rachel in Verbinski's *The Ring*, each face that agony situation when they frantically attempt to offset Sadako's/Samara's curse plaguing them and their offspring. Both these female protagonists are a mirror for Sadako/Samara's monstrous feminine persona, which perhaps represents an explosion of anger in the context of harm done by patriarchies given power and dominance over women. In recent outings for the franchise, Sadako's viral revenge for the terrible crimes of men reflects some of the online "outings" of alleged perpetrators during the recent #metoo and #timesup campaigns on social media platforms. In its translation and transition from novel to screen, the collective "old boys' club" is threatened by the new individualism of the liberated female in Japanese (and other) societies. Traditionally, Japanese society is founded upon collectivism, or what's best for the community as a whole. In Nakata's *Ringu*, the film concludes with Reiko telephoning her father and telling him she needs help for his grandson, who has unfortunately watched the cursed videotape. The implication here is that Reiko will ask her father to view the copy of the tape made by her son in order to save her son's life. It is the ultimate moment of paternalism in that it isn't Reiko who will save the boy, but rather his grandfather. The moment suggests that it is the community's elders who will pay the ultimate price, in keeping with the culture of collectivism.

Conversely, the notion of individualism driving Western society is so prevalent in its mythology, culture and storytelling that the ending of Verbinski's *The Ring* conveys a completely different sentiment. When Aiden (David Dorfman) asks his mother what will happen to the next person who sees the tape, Rachel remains silent, perhaps indicating that the answer to that question is less important than Aiden and Rachel saving themselves. The individual's rights are above all others in this story world. In this shift from collectivism to individualism, translation as transformation can be seen in action via the adaptation processes from *Ringu* to *The Ring*.

These two starkly different takes on the same source material highlight *Ring*'s function as a transnational product in a globalized marketplace. Globalization has long been perceived as a one-directional flow of culture disseminating from America to the rest of the world. The process is not simply a "cultural pillaging" of Japanese studios and their filmmakers by powerful American creative industries. Instead, the advent of the American J-horror remake boom must be understood like many other transnational trends and commodities, as an ongoing process of negotiation and exchange.

A dominance of American culture followed the U.S. occupation of Japan during World War II. While "homegrown" Japanese products still had negative connotations in America, the opposite was not the case with American brands taking on cultural significance for Japanese consumers. The trade route was somewhat reversed in the 1970s, with the export of Akira Kurosawa's 1958 film *Hidden Fortress* into the American consciousness via the silver screen. This particular transactional and transformative process of cultural negotiation and exchange resulted, of course, in *auteur* filmmaker George Lucas's *Star Wars* (1977), still a highly lucrative and ever-present franchise to this day. With it, a cycle of commercial U.S. remakes of visionary Japanese films had begun. In 2002, Dreamworks' remake *The Ring* hit theatres, making $8.3 million in its first two weeks, with receipts of over $129 million domestically, and over $249 million worldwide.[23]

Visual theorist Pennylane Shen writes, "Much like the thematic idea within *The Ring/Ringu*, its existence as a digital commodity speaks to the cyclical process of transnational products on the global market."[24] An example of this cyclical process of negotiation and exchange can be seen when Sadako is exported to the U.S. as Samara, then *Freddy vs. Jason* (2003, Ronny Yu) is imported into the East as *Sadako vs. Kayako*, which has its roots in the *Gamera/Kaiju* movies of Japan. A final layer of influence is at play in the Universal monster mash-ups of *Frankenstein Meets the Wolf Man* (1943, Roy William Neill), and numerous comic entries starring enduring double act Abbott and Costello.

Just as Freddy Krueger from the *A Nightmare on Elm Street* series, or Jigsaw from the *Saw* franchise, have become pop icons in Western culture, so too has Sadako in Japan. Evidence of this is compelling in Sadako's first pitch at a Marines vs. Nippon Ham Fighters baseball game in 2012, a promotional stunt for the latest *Ring* sequel.

Sadako Yamamura is equally at home haunting the baseball field as she is infecting our nightmares, a *bona fide* pop culture phenomenon sourced from a truly world literary text. Suzuki's text operates as world literature by channeling the collective fears of nineties Japan into an enduring horror narrative that continues to provoke a global audience. *Ring* transcends its national limits via processes of translation and transformation and supports Goethe's observation that the worldwide dissemination of literature requires "something likeable and something repulsive, something to be imitated and something to be rejected."[25]

NOTES

1. Tom Mes and Jasper Sharp, *The Midnight Eye Guide to Japanese Film* (Berkeley, CA: Stone Bridge Press, 2005), 260.

2. Pheng Cheah, "What Is a World? on World Literature as World-Making Activity," *Daedalus* 137.3 Special Issue: "On Cosmopolitanism" (Summer, 2008): 28–29, 35–36.

3. *Ibid.*, 35.

4. *Ibid.*, 36.

5. Johann Wolfgang (von) Goethe, "On World Literature (1827)" in *World Literature: a Reader*, ed. Theo D'haen, Cesar Dominguez and Mads Rosendahl Thomsen (London: Routledge, 2013), 14–15.

6. *Ibid.*

7. Randy Kennedy, "Koji Suzuki—Bringing Out the Horror of What He Knows Best," *New York Times*, November 1, 2004.

8. D. Damrosch, "What Is World Literature?" *World Literature Today* 77, 1 (April 2003): 9–14.

9. Koji Suzuki, *Ring*, trans. Robert B. Rohmer and Glynne Walley (London: HarperCollins, 2005), 82.

10. Damrosch, "What Is World Literature?," 9–14.

11. André Breton, *Manifestoes of Surrealism*, trans. Richard Seaver and Helen R. Lane (Ann Arbor: University of Michigan Press, 1969), 26.

12. Terry W. Strieter, *Nineteenth-century European Art: a Topical Dictionary* (Westport, CT: Greenwood Publishing Group, 1999), 142.

13. Kevin J. Wetmore, Jr., "Technoghosts and Culture Shocks: Sociocultural Shifts in American Remakes of J-Horror," *Post Script–Essays in Film and the Humanities* 28.2 (Winter 2008): 72.

14. Robert McKee, *Story: Style, Structure, Substance, and the Principles of Screenwriting* (London: Methuen, 1998), 364–365.

15. McKee, *Story,* 367.

16. Ken Dancyger, *Global Scriptwriting* (Burlington, MA: Focal Press, 2001), 226.

17. Suzuki, *Ring,* 120–121.

18. *Ibid.,* 291.

19. Kennedy, "Koji Suzuki—Bringing Out the Horror of What He Knows Best."

20. *Ibid.*

21. McKee, *Story,* 368.

22. Stella Papamichael, "Calling the Shots: Hideo Nakata," *BBC Movies,* last modified September 24, 2014, www.bbc.co.uk/films/callingtheshots/hideo_nakata.shtml.

23. "The Ring Box Office Data," *The Numbers,* last accessed January 1, 2019, www.the-numbers.com/movie/Ring-The.

24. Pennylane Shen, "It Came from the East—Japanese Horror Cinema in the Age of Globalization," *Gnovis* 9.2 (2009): par. 39, www.gnovisjournal.org/2009/05/13/it-came-east-japanese-horror-cinema-age-globalization/.

25. Goethe, "On World Literature," 14–15.

BIBLIOGRAPHY

Breton, André. *Manifestoes of Surrealism.* Translated by Richard Seaver and Helen R. Lane. Ann Arbor: University of Michigan Press, 1969.

Bunshinsaba Vs. Sadako. Directed by River Huang. 2016. China: Zhonglele Pictures, 2016. DVD.

The Cabinet of Doctor Caligari. Directed by Robert Wiene. 1920. Germany: Eureka Entertainment, 2000. DVD.

Cheah, Pheng. "What Is a World? on World Literature as World-Making Activity." *Daedalus* 137, 3, Special Issue: "On Cosmopolitanism." (Summer, 2008): 26–38.

Crash. Directed by David Cronenberg. 1996. Canada: Sony Pictures, 2000. DVD.

Damrosch, D. "What Is World Literature?" *World Literature Today,* 77, 1 (April 2003): 9–14.

Dancyger, Ken. *Global Scriptwriting.* Burlington, MA: Focal Press, 2001.

The Exorcist. Directed by William Friedkin. 1973. Burbank, CA: Warner Home Video, 2002. DVD.

Goethe, Johann Wolfgang (von). "On World Literature (1827)," in *World Literature: A Reader.* Edited by Theo D'haen, Cesar Dominguez and Mads Rosendahl Thomsen. London: Routledge, 2013: 14–15.

The Golden Compass. Directed by Chris Weitz. 2007. USA: Entertainment in Video, 2008. DVD.

Halloween. Directed by John Carpenter. 1978. Troy, MI: Anchor Bay, 2005. DVD.

Hikiko-san Vs. Sadako. Directed by Hisaaki Nagaoka. 2015. Japan: Interfilm, 2015. DVD.

James, E.L. *Fifty Shades of Grey.* London: Arrow Books, 2012.

Jigoku. Directed by Nobuo Nakagawa. 1960. New York: Criterion Collection, 2010. DVD.

Ju-on. Directed by Shimizu Takashi. 2002. South Korea: Premier Asia, 2004. DVD.

Kennedy, Randy. "Koji Suzuki—Bringing Out the Horror of What He Knows Best." *New York Times,* November, 2004.

Kwaidan. Directed by Masaki Kobayashi. 1965. Japan: Eureka Entertainment, 2006. DVD.

McKee, Robert. *Story: Style, Structure, Substance, and the Principles of Screenwriting.* London: Methuen, 1998.

Mes, Tom, and Jasper Sharp. *The Midnight Eye Guide to Japanese Film.* Berkeley, CA: Stone Bridge Press, 2005.

Naked Lunch. Directed by David Cronenberg. 1991. Canada: StudioCanal, 2004. DVD.

Ochazuke, Nori. *The Curse of Yamamura Sadako.* Japan: Kadokawa Shoten, 2000.

Onibaba. Directed by Kaneto Shindo. 1964. Japan: Eureka Entertainment, 2013. DVD.

Organ. Directed by Kei Fujiwara. 1996. Japan: Terra, 2007. DVD.

Papamichael, Stella. "Calling the Shots: Hideo Nakata." *BBC Movies.* Last modified September 24, 2014. www.bbc.co.uk/films/callingtheshots/hideo_nakata.shtml.

Peake, Melvyn. *Gormenghast.* London: Vintage, 1998.

Poe, Edgar Allan. *The Fall of the House of Usher.* London: Penguin Classics, 2003.

Poltergeist. Directed by Tobe Hooper. 1982. Burbank, CA: Warner Home Video, 2007. DVD.

Pullman, Philip. *Northern Lights.* London: Scholastic, 2001.

Rasen. Directed by George Iida. 1998. Japan: Artsmagic Ltd, 1998. DVD.

The Ring. Directed by Gore Verbinski. 2000. USA: Dreamworks, 2002. DVD.

"The Ring Box Office Data." *The Numbers.* Last accessed January 1, 2019. www.the-numbers.com/movie/Ring-The.

Ring 0: Birthday. Directed by Norio Tsuruta. 2000. Japan: Tartan Video, 2002. DVD.

Rings. Directed by F. Javier Gutiérrez. 2017. USA: Paramount Pictures, 2017. DVD.

Rings. Directed by Jonathan Liebesman. 2005. USA: Dreamworks, 2006. DVD.

The Ring Two. Directed by Hideo Nakata. 2005. USA: Dreamworks, 2005. DVD.

Ringu. Directed by Hideo Nakata. 1998. Japan: Tartan Video, 2002. DVD.

Ringu: Kanzenban. Directed by Chisui Takigawa. 1995. Japan: Amuse, Inc., 1995. VHS

Ringu 2. Directed by Hideo Nakata. 1999. Japan: Tartan Video, 2002. DVD.

The Ring Virus. Directed by Kim Dong-bin. 1999. South Korea: Tai Seng, 2005. DVD.

Sadako 3D. Directed by Tsutomu Hanabusa. 2012. Japan: Well Go USA, 2013. DVD.

Sadako 3D 2. Directed by Tsutomu Hanabusa. 2013. Japan: Intercontinental Video, 2015. Blu-ray.

Sadako Vs. Kayako. Directed by Shiraishi, Kōji. 2016. https://www.shudder.com/movies/watch/sadako-vs-kayako/2754306.

Shelley, Mary Wollstonecraft. *Frankenstein; Or, the Modern Prometheus.* London: Penguin Classics, 2003.

Shen, Pennylane. "It Came from the East—Japanese Horror Cinema in the Age of Globalization." *Gnovis* 9.2 (2009). www.gnovisjournal.org/2009/05/13/it-came-east-japanese-horror-cinema-age-globalization/.

Strieter, Terry W. *Nineteenth-century European Art: A Topical Dictionary.* Westport, CT: Greenwood Publishing Group, 1999.

Suzuki, Koji. *Birthday.* Translated by Glynne Walley. New York: Vertical, 2007.

_____. *Loop.* Translated by Glynne Walley. London: HarperCollins, 2015.

_____. *Ring.* Translated by Robert B. Rohmer and Glynne Walley. London: HarperCollins, 2005.

_____. *S.* Translated by Greg Gencorello. New York: Vertical, 2017.

_____. *Spiral.* Translated by Glynne Walley. London: HarperCollins, 2005.

_____. *Tide.* Tokyo: Kadokawa, 2013.

Takahashi, Hiroshi. *The Ring.* Milwaukie, OR: Dark Horse Books, 2003.

Trainspotting. Directed by Danny Boyle. 1996. UK: Channel 4, 2009. DVD.

Weir, Andy. *The Martian.* London: Del Rey, 2015.

Wetmore, Kevin J., Jr. "Technoghosts and Culture Shocks: Sociocultural Shifts in American Remakes of J-Horror." *Post Script–Essays in Film and the Humanities,* 28, 2 (Winter 2008): 72.

Mapping Digital Dis-Ease

*Representations of Movement
and Technology in Jim Sonzero's
Pulse and Stephen King's Cell*

RAHEL SIXTA SCHMITZ

Where there once was a lonesome monster there now are terrors on a larger scale: instead of the singular villain and a handful of victims, today's horror texts feature zombie masses, deadly pandemics, post-nuclear wastelands, and technologized, global warfare. In short, the apocalypse lurks everywhere. Many contemporary stories use a microbial disease as the cause for world-wide catastrophe. Zombie narratives such as *Resident Evil* video games and films, *The Walking Dead* comics and television shows, or Max Brooks' novels *The Zombie Survival Guide* (2003) and *World War Z: An Oral History of the Zombie War* (2006) explain the rise of the undead by means of a virus. A different set of narratives instead focus on the possibility of the global nuclear holocaust: for instance, both Dmitry Glukhovsky's *Metro* novels and subsequent video game adaptations, as well as the *Fallout* video game series are set in a post-apocalyptic world where atomic warfare has put an end to the world as we know it. *The Matrix* trilogy (1999–2005, the Wachowskis), in contrast, portrays artificial intelligence as the true antagonist of human life. Some stories entwine several such apocalypse-inducing events: in Richard Matheson's *I Am Legend* (1954), modern warfare has facilitated severe dust storms that disseminate a deadly vampire germ on a global scale. Likewise, in Justin Cronin's *Passage* trilogy (2010–2016), it is the U.S. military's attempt to weaponize a vampire virus that causes the world-wide spread of vampirism.

This essay focuses on a different subgenre of apocalypse fiction: narratives of digital "dis-ease." These texts portray a technological disease that is

201

transmitted via modern communication technologies and which affects digital devices and human bodies alike. Through the entanglement of the biological and the technological, such narratives express a profound anxiety or dis-ease regarding life in a digitalized, interconnected, and ultimately chaotic, uncontrollable world. The same devices that are supposed to facilitate communication and community are cast as the cause of a persistent feeling of isolation or alienation, endangering the human subject in the process. Disease hence bears two connotations, signifying both an ailment and an anxiety.

Jim Sonzero's movie *Pulse* as well as Stephen King's novel *Cell*, both released in 2006, are such narratives of digital dis-ease, depicting the large-scale apocalypse brought on by digital communication technologies. In *Pulse*, Internet and cell phone technologies dissolve the boundaries between the worlds of the dead and the living, facilitating a fatal ghost invasion. Every person who encounters a ghost eventually loses their will to live, until they either disintegrate or commit suicide. In *Cell*, a mysterious "pulse" is transmitted through the cell phone networks, turning every person using their mobile phone at the time of transmission into zombie-like, highly aggressive "phoners." Over time, the infected evolve a telepathic hive mind and lure all "normies" to a supposed dead zone in order to transform them as well.

There are multiple parallels between the two texts. For instance, the title of each narrative reveals the intersection of technology and biology central to the tale: while "pulse" can denote both a digital signal and a throbbing heart, "cell" can refer to mobile phones as well as the cells of a body. Additionally, both stories portray urban spaces as places of disease and signal-free dead zones as sanitary. Likewise, each story features a mass of network-like—that is, highly organized and well-coordinated—antagonists instead of individualized villains.

Of course, there are also significant differences between *Pulse* and *Cell*. Whereas Sonzero's film is set a few days before the apocalypse hits full force, King's novel takes the catastrophe as its starting point and hence depicts the protagonists' struggle in a post-apocalyptic world. Consequently, the narratives differ vastly in their depiction of the movement of the disease, its carriers, and healthy survivors: in its opening credits, *Pulse* follows the long-established convention of featuring animated epidemiological maps displaying the spread of disease; *Cell*, on the other hand, deliberately refrains from the use of any such visual aids and ultimately renders the progress of the disease, its victims, and the survivors unmappable. It is this portrayal of movement and its implicit thematization of technology in these two narratives of digital dis-ease that lies at the heart of this essay.

Charting the Territory: Media Anxiety and Digital Dis-Ease

Digital media technologies have been a welcomed topic in horror fiction of the twenty-first century. The fascination with technological innovation is by no means a new development, but has always been a key theme within the genre, as the endeavors of Victor Frankenstein or Henry Jekyll exemplify. As Joseph Crawford points out, narrative media form a particular point of interest within this wider fascination with potentially harmful technologies: Gothic writing evolved from the trope of the "Terrible Text" or "Evil Book," the reading of which would have dire consequences for its often unsuspecting consumer, to "the Evil Play, the Evil Game, or the Evil Videotape."[1] These notions of "evil" media illustrate a central difference of recent texts compared to the early tales of reckless scientists, as it now is technology itself which is infused with agency. Technology thus becomes the Other:

> These plots revolve around the fear that the technology we control will twist around and start to control us. Here, technology exerts a dehumanizing power that will kill us, or enslave us, or make us into mere nodes on a digital grid.[2]

Inspired by the perceived extent to which today's technologies increasingly determine our everyday social relations and even political power structures, such horror fiction envisions the human being as a mere extension of the digital devices that were originally supposed to function at the service of mankind. This particular type of media anxiety is one of three key features of narratives of digital dis-ease, as it hinges upon the intertwining of biology and technology. While these fictions infuse digital devices with a life and will of their own, the human subject is debiologized and reduced to a compilation of data.

A second particularity is that narratives of digital dis-ease envision the detrimental effects of technology on a global scale. Kimberly Jackson interprets anxieties regarding autonomous media technologies in contemporary horror film specifically in relation to a wider obsession with the apocalypse:

> Anxieties about the end of humanity are intimately linked in these films with the perception that technology, particularly media technology, has begun to take on a life of its own and that the human subject is no longer the determining factor in how reality is constructed or experienced. The technologically produced and reproduced image comes to the fore, both as the most threatening media force and as the one that offers the most promise in terms of a new understanding of humanity's place in the world.[3]

Jackson here touches the third characteristic of narratives of digital dis-ease: technology appears both as a danger and as possible salvation. Technology may have created the problem in the first place, but it could also be its solution.

The confluence of media anxiety and the apocalypse in twenty-first century horror arises out of the perception that today's world is highly interconnected: information, innovation, and infection travel fast and far in this brave new world. Aris Mousoutzanis has referred to this development in fiction as the "network apocalypse," which envisions "the impending apocalypse as a result of a major event or accident that escalates due to the connectivity and interconnectedness of different narratives, events, computers, machines or individuals."[4] Furthermore:

The "global network" in particular would be one of the most persistent motifs of the 1990s that has emerged [...] as a paradigm to organize a set of fictions consisting of different interlocking narratives set in different times and places around the globe, involving many characters, often in a constant state of travel and mobility as they find themselves involved in or affected by incidents from a distant time, place or storyline.[5]

While Mousoutzanis specifically focuses on science fiction of the 1990s, the global network remains a key topic to this day. Expanding on his theory, it is here claimed that it is not only characters, but also technologies, diseases, and information that travel through the links established by the global network.

Such a discussion of mobility demands a close reading of spaces, routes, and mappability. It is in particular the relationship between the narrative and its geographical settings as well as the question of what meanings these spaces bear that is of interest here. Fiction has the potential to destabilize and defamiliarize supposedly well-known, real-world geographies. Understanding how geographies are created and mapped in fiction can be the key to uncovering central themes of the narrative.[6] *Pulse* and *Cell*, as is the case with almost all apocalypse fiction, perform such a defamiliarization not only by portraying an eerily empty world in ruin, but specifically a world that no longer functions according to the rules of modern times, as survivors have to depend on mouth-to-mouth communication, printed route atlases, and slower means of travel.

Epidemiological maps as they are used by scientists in order to visualize the movement of a disease are a particular type of cartographical work. They have become a conventionalized standard in films focusing on infectious disease.[7] Priscilla Wald identifies such visual aids as a central element of any outbreak narrative, whether fictional or factual:

Maps of geographical areas, often dotted with pins or, in films, with colored lights, represent epidemiological work in progress [...]. These maps evoke both fear and reassurance. Dots or lines signal a spreading infection, often following the routes of trains, planes, buses, cars, and trucks as they transport carriers and their viruses rapidly around the globe. But the maps also help the epidemiologists solve the puzzle of the disease and thus represent evidence of experts on the case, a materialization of the epidemiological work that generally gets the threat under control.[8]

Epidemiological maps hence reveal the implicit yet omnipresent assumption of any disease narrative: trace, study, neutralize. It is through visualization that the path of a disease can be traced. If its path can be traced, then its carriers and the channels through which it progresses can be studied, while sanitary and unsanitary zones can be identified. Finally, if the disease's means of spread are understood, they can be contained and the threat neutralized. As is discussed in the following section, Sonzero's *Pulse* deliberately draws on these conventions of the epidemiological map in order to set the tone for the film.

"We broadcast to everyone where we are and we think we're safe": Fatal Interconnection in Pulse

An animated epidemiological map makes a brief, yet central appearance during the film's opening credits: while a pulsing soundtrack reminiscent of the beating of a heart plays, images of digital technologies, such as keyboards, web browsers, but also glitches and distortions on computer screens, are juxtaposed with pictures of an animated epidemiological map displaying the spread of an unknown disease throughout all major urban areas in the United States. As these alarming red dots grow bigger, the images of technology become more distorted and more chaotic. It is with this juxtaposition that *Pulse* establishes its subject matter of digital dis-ease at the very beginning.

A central function of such epidemiological maps is the delineation of sanitary and unsanitary zones—that is, places where the infection has not yet gained a foothold and which should hence be protected from contamination, and places which already are lost to disease. Usually, this delimitation hinges upon a "thirdworldification": infected regions are portrayed as poor and primitive, posing a great risk to vulnerable, civilized, and modern spaces.[9] *Pulse* turns this rhetoric on its head: it is precisely those highly urbanized and technologized geographies that become perilous places. The epidemiological maps display urban spaces such as the greater Los Angeles area or New York City as infected spaces. The only chance of escaping the invasion is by relocating to a dead zone, where signal transmission is impossible. Safety is bound to a technological regress, in which survivors can no longer depend on long-distance calls, but instead have to revert back to mouth-to-mouth communication.

Furthermore, by opening with these images of an epidemic, the movie implies that all is already lost at this point: while it may take the characters some time to figure out that virus-like ghosts are invading the world of the living, the cycle of infection is already in full swing by the time they realize this. Like all epidemiological maps, the opening credits therefore exemplify the dismal truth of "the impossibility of ascertaining the precise location of the virus until *after* the fact."[10] *Pulse* hence begins where it ends—with the advent of an apocalypse induced by a digital dis-ease. It was always already too late to stop the epidemic. The movie ends with Mattie (Kristen Bell) and Dex (Ian Somerhalder), the two surviving protagonists, driving through an apocalyptic world in search of the next dead zone. The scene is accompanied by a voice-over by Mattie: "We can never go back. The cities are their's. [...]] What was meant to connect us to one another instead connected us to forces that we could have never imagined. The world we knew is gone, but the will to live never dies. Not for us, and not for them."[11] This final voice-over ties directly to the fatalism established by the epidemiological map at the beginning, acknowledging the inevitability and finality of the apocalypse.

In order to establish the large scale of the ghostly invasion, the animated epidemiological map covers the entirety of the United States. Significantly, these images displaying the movement of the disease across the entire country stand in stark contrast to the almost microcosmic, claustrophobic settings of the remainder of the movie: the entire action is set on an unspecified university campus and its lecture halls; the characters seldom travel farther than to their run-down apartment buildings. Juxtaposing the highly mobile disease as represented in the opening credits with immobile, almost lethargic characters, *Pulse* singles out these settings as closed-off microcosms in which the infection flourishes. The choice of a university campus as its main setting is by no means arbitrary: firstly, it harkens back to the origins of the Internet. While the first initiative to create a distributed, attack-resistant network structure was predominantly a military venture, it is through the intervention of universities such as MIT and UCLA that the Internet became a public commodity fit for large-scale application.[12] In Sonzero's film, however, it is precisely at such a university that the Internet is rendered dangerous—not only to computers, but also to human beings.

Secondly, a campus is predominantly a place of young, tech-savvy people. Almost every shot of the film features some piece of technology; when it comes to the portrayal of the university's students, it is specifically communication technologies such as cell phones, pagers, and computers that are foregrounded.[13] Regardless of where they are or whom they are with, these students are always communicating with each other via digital communication technologies. It is precisely this unquestioning use of technology that becomes their doom, as a stranger (Brad Dourif) explains to Mattie and Dex at a diner: "Do you have any idea of the amount of data that's floating out there? The amount of information we just beam into the air? We broadcast to everyone where we are and we think we're safe?"[14] Every device used by these students constantly transmits its location in the network. It thus becomes an easy task for the ghosts to trace, study, and neutralize each living individual, turning the logic governing all epidemiological work around and against us. Even when it becomes apparent that digital devices are causing the apocalypse, nobody seems to be able to free themselves of them: while leaflets informing people how to stay safe emphasize the importance of shutting down every PC, these flyers were obviously created with the help of a computer and a printer. This same paradox is also already present in *Pulse's* opening credits: the only means of creating such animated epidemiological maps is by using the same devices that enable the infection's spread.

It is by no means arbitrary that the location of the campus is left unspecified. In times of digital media, exact geographical placement becomes almost meaningless. What matters instead is the existence on and location within the communication network. Within this network, the technologized, interconnected university campus becomes a central node. Hence, once the border between worlds begins to leak at this specific campus, the infection spreads throughout the entire network in a short time. Since this is a communication network attacked by a digital dis-ease, the progress of the disease is not restricted by geographical proximity or physical transportation means. Instead, the infection travels through the information highway.

Pulse's ghosts are in themselves representations of a network logic. Kevin Wetmore describes the phantoms as "technoghosts," that is, as "spirits that display the physical properties of electronic or technical media, in other words, their physical appearance involves static, appearing blurry, featuring interference, as if they are being broadcast, rather than haunting, and whose manifestation is both made possible by technology and mediated through it."[15] Neal Kirk specifically reads these technoghosts in terms of their networkedness, claiming the intersection of digital technology and spectrality to be a key development in the contemporary portrayal of ghosts: "from the singular, linear, personal and analogue to ghosts that are digital, multiple, nodular and distributive."[16] In other words, the technoghosts of *Pulse* are not individualized personalities, but identity-less units which together comprise a larger network. This becomes apparent when Mattie is briefly sucked into the phantomworld: as she is grabbed and held in place by numerous hands, the camera zooms out to reveal a sheer endless mass of writhing arms. From a distance, what appears to be chaos turns out to be a highly organized, recognizable structure: a face.

As this highly organized ghost-network infiltrates the world of the living, the campus becomes emptier with each day—yet, students and teachers alike ignore these absences. While the infection continuously spreads, the majority of its potential victims remain immobile and inactive. At first, this appears to contradict Mousoutzanis' formula that, in narratives of interconnection featuring the global network as their topical focus, characters are usually "in a constant state of travel and mobility,"[17] since it is the disease that is in motion rather than people. The immobility of the living, however, is a key strategy in *Pulse*'s representation of digital dis-ease: they are portrayed as lethargic subjects, whose technology-dependency has disabled their sense of survival.

It is only towards the end of the movie, when the world has already entered an apocalyptic stage, that survivors attempt to flee the cities. Mattie and Dex are among the last people to leave the city after their attempt to stop the infection by uploading a computer virus to the university's main server system fails. In a highly symbolic moment, an airplane, the ultimate symbol of modernity, standing for fast, comfortable global travel as well as minute planning, scheduling, and communicating, crashes in the middle of the campus. Perpetuating this symbolism, they drive along an empty highway lined with tents. The era of digital technology, fast communication, and global travel has come to an end. In fact, it is precisely these commodities that have enabled fatal interconnection.

"If we could chart them...": Ultimate Isolation in Cell

In a sense, King's *Cell* picks up where Sonzero's *Pulse* left off: with an airplane crashing in the middle of Boston.[18] The novel's protagonist, Clayton Riddell, is in the city when the mysterious "Pulse" turns every cell phone user into a savage "phoner." While *Pulse* envisions digital dis-ease as a slow, creeping, yet unstoppable threat, *Cell* portrays a crisis that leads to the instantaneous and complete breakdown of society. Already the novel's epigraph foreshadows the full impact of the Pulse:

> Civilization slipped into its second dark age on an unsurprising track of blood, but with a speed that could not have been foreseen by even the most pessimistic futurist. It was as if it had been waiting to go. On October 1, God was in His heaven, the stock market stood at 10,140, and most of the planes were on time [...]. Two weeks later the skies belonged to the birds again and the stock market was a memory. By Halloween, every major city from New York to Moscow stank to the empty heavens and the world as it had been was a memory.[19]

The first paragraph of the story provides further details on the crisis:

> The event that came to be known as The Pulse began at 3:03 p.m., eastern standard time, on the afternoon of October 1. The term was a misnomer, of course, but within ten hours of the event, most of the scientists capable of pointing this out were either dead or insane. The name hardly mattered, in any case. What mattered was the effect.[20]

These two passages describe the signal in terms recognizable from outbreak narratives by offering details on its geographical position and dispersal as well as its spread over time: the first quote establishes a timeframe ("two weeks") as well as a location ("every major city"; "the world"). The second passage further adds to this knowledge ("3:03 p.m., eastern standard time, on the afternoon of October 1"; "within ten hours") while also revealing the symptoms of the Pulse in greater detail: death or insanity.

As is the case with *Pulse*, the novel employs these opening sections to provide a glimpse at the large-scale results of the catastrophic event, only to choose a highly restricted focalization for the remainder of the story. While the initial descriptions of the Pulse are very detailed, the majority of the tale is strikingly devoid of any definite facts. For instance, some characters speculate that the signal may be manmade, either by a terrorist group or "a couple of inspired nutcases working in a garage."[21] Yet, it ultimately remains a mystery where the Pulse truly came from and why. The exact origin, nature, reach of and motivation behind the disease is never revealed. Instead, *Cell* offers an extremely limited viewpoint in which the surviving characters can only rely on their own experiences and observations. The novel particularly foregrounds how the flow of information is disrupted in such a post-apocalyptic scenario: not only is mouth-to-mouth communication significantly slower than the sophisticated pre–Pulse technologies, but it is furthermore highly unreliable. When the group around Clayton travels north on foot in search of his family, they are repeatedly warned by other survivors that the New Hampshire border is closed off and protected by armed survivors; yet, Alice, a young survivor whom the group met in Boston, immediately doubts these rumors: "News doesn't travel that fast anymore. Not without phones."[22] Indeed, the survivors enter the state unchallenged.

The travel of information is further scrutinized soon after this, when the survivors begin to see mysterious signs reading "KASHWAK=NO-FO"[23] scrawled on streets and houses along their route. After some time, they decode the message's meaning: the small town of Kashwak, located in the unincorporated area TR-90, is supposedly a dead zone without cell phone reception. One of the group's members, however, doubts whether this sanitary zone is truly safe:

> "Purely as a sociologist, I began to question those signs," Dan said. "Not how they began—I'm sure the first No-Fo signs were posted soon after the Pulse, by survivors who'd decided that a place like that, where there was no cell phone coverage, would be the best place on earth to go. What I questioned was how the idea—and the graffiti—could spread so quickly in a catastrophically fragmented society where all normal forms of communication—other than my mouth to your ear, of course—had broken down. The answer seemed clear, once one admitted that a *new* form of communication, available to only one group, had entered the picture."[24]

At this point, it is becoming clear to the survivors that the phoners have developed a telepathic hive mind. Significantly, their telepathy enables a form of communication that not only matches, but rather outperforms cellular technology. Thus, these graffiti signs are strategically well-placed, appearing along all routes that survivors navigating this chaotic, post–Pulse world are sure to take. As few normies question their appearance, the signs successfully lure the uninfected to the borders of the dead zone, where they are forcedly exposed to the Pulse.

Already a few hours after the initial catastrophe, the infected exhibit first signs of this telepathy in the form of "flocking" behavior, with large masses of the hitherto savage phoners peacefully marching in tandem. When the flocking begins, Alice recognizes that gathering as much knowledge as possible regarding their antagonists may be key to survival: "If we could chart them, it might matter a lot."[25] Just like Dan's observation regarding the dubious spread of information, this idea of charting the movement of the phoners resonates strongly with the guiding principles of epidemiological work: trace, study, and neutralize. However, while *Cell* engages in the discourse of outbreak narratives,[26] the novel deliberately subverts the convention of providing any visual representation of the spread—be that as a chart created by the characters as Alice proposed, or as an epidemiological map attached to the print novel. In light of the nature of the Pulse, this makes sense: as the apocalypse ensues within seconds, no scientific institution is left to chart the progress of the disease. Epidemiological maps are inherently associated with scientific expertise and global surveillance.[27] This, however, is no longer possible in the post–Pulse world. By denying any reliable information regarding the signal, the novel forces a restricted viewpoint on the reader that matches those of the characters. There is no clinical, omniscient top view on the goings-on, every piece of information is mere speculation based on observations from within ultimate chaos.

Further denying such an omniscient perspective, the novel not only leaves the signal's spread in the dark, but eventually even renders the route of the travelling survivors untraceable. At first, while Clayton is still in Boston, minute descriptions of his position, including street and hotel names, together with the current time of the day are provided. As the signal hits, this iconic setting becomes alien and perilous within moments: car wrecks clog the streets; buildings are consumed by fire; black smoke obscures the sky. It is obvious that, from now on, such metropolises are dangerous, unsanitary zones that should be avoided at all costs. Thus, after leaving Boston, Clayton and his travelling companions shun larger cities and instead hike through increasingly small towns. While this in itself already makes it more difficult for the reader to trace their route, it is highly significant that only some of these towns are real, mappable cities; others are entirely fictional creations. This increasing untraceability resonates with the novel's above-quoted opening paragraphs detailing the temporal progression of the infection. As it is stated there, within ten hours of the initial outbreak scientific institutions have largely broken down and after two weeks the entire world has been severely affected. Significantly, it is approximately two weeks that the group's journey takes. In other words, the breakdown of societies around the globe and the untraceability of the group are parallel developments.

The very notion of mappability as it has been established by modern technology hence comes under attack as the group gradually vanishes off the map of the U.S. Not only is the city of Boston defamiliarized in the novel, but the entire world becomes a strange, unstable geography. *Cell* foregrounds the extent to which our understanding of any geography today is based on information and communication technology. GPS enables constant, global surveillance from outer space; cellular triangulation reveals the exact location of any mobile phone as long as the device has reception. By focusing on the journey of a small group of survivors, King's novel portrays how labyrinthine and insurmountable the world truly becomes once these devices fail: with only printed road atlases for orientation and no possibility of traversing the blocked highways by car, it may take several days to travel a few miles. The breakdown of those communication networks that once established the "global village" further expands these distances. Or, as Clayton realizes shortly after the onset of the signal: "home had never seemed so far."[28] What remains after the Pulse is a feeling of ultimate isolation.

Conclusion

The portrayal of movement and mobility is a central aspect of both *Pulse* and *Cell*, shedding light on how digital dis-ease is envisioned in each narrative. Sonzero's film utilizes the convention of visually representing a spreading disease by means of an epidemiological map, yet, the opening credits are the only instance where this clear top-view is granted. The remainder of the film portrays largely immobile and lethargic characters, while the infection slowly spreads and ultimately envelops them. The underlying logic of the film is one of fatal interconnection enabled by digital, networked technologies: these devices allow not only for quick communication between friends, but can be used by evil forces to trace, study, and neutralize the human subject. Yet, nobody seems to be able to free themselves of these devices: even when she should already know how the ghosts are attacking their victims, Mattie still carries a cell phone around.

Cell, in contrast, portrays an infection that spreads almost everywhere within an instant, and which is therefore an omnipresent threat already from the very beginning. The healthy normies attempt to navigate this dangerous world safely, traveling through the midst of infected phoners. In contrast to

Pulse, King's novel hinges upon a feeling of ultimate isolation. Whereas the infected soon develop their own telepathic communication network, the survivors are reduced to archaic means of movement and information exchange: walking and verbal communication. What were once short distances are suddenly almost insurmountable, week-long hikes, with no possibility of calling ahead or knowing what to expect at the end of the journey.

What connects both *Pulse* and *Cell* is their ambivalent view on technology. On the one hand, communication media outside of human control are the cause of global digital dis-ease. On the other hand, it may be these same devices that can also halt the infection. Even though Mattie and Dex's attempt to restore the borders between the two worlds fails, Dex nonetheless takes the USB stick carrying the virus with him as they flee, indicating that he intends to improve the program. Similarly, when Clayton finally finds his son, he forces him to place another phone call via cell phone, hoping that a second dose of the Pulse will entice his brain to "reboot." In each narrative, it is never revealed whether these attempts are felicitous: both endings lack a clear resolution. Technology, then, may be able to solve all the problems it created in the first place.

NOTES

1. Joseph Crawford, "Gothic Fiction and the Evolution of Media Technology," in *Technologies of the Gothic in Literature and Culture*, edited by Justin D. Edwards (New York: Routledge, 2015), 39.

2. Justin D. Edwards, "Introduction: Technogothics," in *Technologies of the Gothic in Literature and Culture*, edited by Justin D. Edwards (New York: Routledge, 2015), 2.

3. Kimberly Jackson, *Technology, Monstrosity, and Reproduction in Twenty-First Century Horror* (New York: Palgrave Macmillan, 2013), 4.

4. Aris Mousoutzanis, *Fin-de-Siècle Fictions, 1890s/1990s: Apocalypse, Technoscience, Empire* (New York: Palgrave Macmillan, 2014), 94.

5. *Ibid.*, 223. The two narratives discussed in the present paper cannot truly be regarded as network fictions in so far that they themselves are not organized as networks. However, they share the topical focus of the "global network" identified by Mousoutzanis. However, the 2001 Japanese film *Kairo* (Kiyoshi Kurosawa), on which Sonzero's *Pulse* is based, qualifies as a network fiction.

6. Barbara Piatti and Lorenz Hurni, "Cartographies of Fictional Worlds," *The Cartographic Journal* 48.4 (2011): 218–219.

7. Kirsten Ostherr, *Cinematic Prophylaxis: Globalization and Contagion in the Discourse of World Health* (Durham: Duke University Press, 2005), 127. A few examples for this convention are *Outbreak* (1995, Wolfgang Petersen), *Carriers* (1996, Patrick Lynch), *Contagion* (2011, Steven Soderbergh), and *Jurassic World* (2015, Colin Trevorrow).

8. Priscilla Wald, *Contagious: Cultures Carriers, and the Outbreak Narrative* (Durham: Duke University Press, 2008), 37.

9. *Ibid.*, 269.

10. Ostherr, *Cinematic Prophylaxis*, 1. Emphasis added.

11. *Pulse*, directed by Jim Sonzero (2006; Leipzig, Germany: Kinowelt Home Entertainment GmbH, 2007), DVD.

12. Jussi Parikka, *Digital Contagions: a Media Archeology of Computer Viruses* (New York: Peter Lang Publishing, 2007), 238.

13. In line with the stereotypical image of computer literates, *Pulse* additionally portrays

these students as potentially irresponsible individuals who endanger the entire network: it is due to Josh's careless hacking and his malevolent distribution of a virus on his acquaintance Zielger's computer system that the world of the dead begins to leak.

14. *Pulse.*
15. Kevin J. Wetmore, Jr., "Technoghosts and Culture Shocks: Sociocultural Shifts in American Remakes of J-Horror," *Post Script—Essays in Film and the Humanities* 28.2 (2009): 73.
16. Neal Kirk, "Networked Spectrality: *In Memoriam, Pulse,* and Beyond," in *Digital Horror: Haunted Technologies, Network Panic, and the Found Footage Phenomenon,* ed. Linnie Blake and Xavier Aldana Reyes (London: I.B. Tauris, 2016), 55.
17. Mousoutzanis, *Fin-de-Siècle Fictions, 1890s/1990s,* 223.
18. Stephen King, *Cell* (New York: Pocket, 2006), 34.
19. *Ibid., Cell.*
20. *Ibid.,* 3.
21. *Ibid.,* 344.
22. *Ibid.,* 171.
23. *Ibid.,* 234.
24. *Ibid.,* 346.
25. *Ibid.,* 141.
26. For more information on the formula of the outbreak narrative, see Wald, *Contagious.*
27. Wald, *Contagious,* 223.
28. King, *Cell,* 38.

BIBLIOGRAPHY

Crawford, Joseph. "Gothic Fiction and the Evolution of Media Technology," in *Technologies of the Gothic in Literature and Culture: Technogothics,* edited by Justin D. Edwards, 35–47. London, NY: Routledge, 2015.
Edwards, Justin D. "Introduction: Technogothics," in *Technologies of the Gothic in Literature and Culture: Technogothics,* edited by Justin D. Edwards, 1–16. New York: Routledge, 2015.
Jackson, Kimberly. *Technology, Monstrosity, and Reproduction in Twenty-First Century Horror.* New York: Palgrave Macmillan, 2013.
King, Stephen. *Cell.* New York: Pocket, 2006.
Kirk, Neal. "Networked Spectrality: *In Memoriam, Pulse* and Beyond," in *Digital Horror: Haunted Technologies, Network Panic and the Found Footage Phenomenon,* edited by Linnie Blake and Xavier Aldana Reyes, 54–65. New York: I.B. Tauris, 2016.
Mousoutzanis, Aris. *Fin-de-Siècle Fictions, 1890s/1990s: Apocalypse, Technoscience, Empire.* New York: Palgrave Macmillan, 2014.
Ostherr, Kirsten. *Cinematic Prophylaxis: Globalization and Contagion in the Discourse of World Health.* Durham, NC: Duke University Press, 2005.
Parikka, Jussi. *Digital Contagions: A Media Archeology of Computer Viruses.* New York: Peter Lang Publishing, 2007.
Piatti, Barbara, and Lorenz Hurni. "Cartographies of Fictional Worlds." *The Cartographic Journal* 48.4 (2011): 218–23.
Pulse. Directed by Jim Sonzero. 2006. Leipzig, Germany: Kinowelt Home Entertainment GmbH, 2007. DVD.
Wald, Priscilla. *Contagious: Cultures, Carriers, and the Outbreak Narrative.* Durham, NC: Duke University Press, 2008.
Wetmore, Kevin J., Jr. "Technoghosts and Culture Shocks: Sociocultural Shifts in American Remakes of J-Horror." *Post Script—Essays in Film and the Humanities* 28.2 (2009): 72–81.

Afterword

Guardians of the Damned:
Horror Scholarship and the Library

BECKY SPRATFORD

You just read a scholarly collection of literary criticism. It was thought provoking, probing, and enlightening. The essays were about those who have crafted stories of fear, anxiety and monsters and what these feelings of unease say about us as humans, the societies we build, and our interactions with each other and the world around us. The works contained here have clearly made a case for horror and its practitioners to be held to the highest literary standards afforded books in other genres.

However, we are among friends here; it is a safe space. Those who sought out and read this book are sympathetic to the cause. But now it is time for me to tell you a scary story of my own, one that is also nonfiction, and one that illustrates the demons we on the academic side of horror need to battle with, constantly, if we want to survive that is.

My story opens on a plane, on the final day of February 2018. I was on my way to StokerCon in Providence, Rhode Island, to run Librarians' Day, and was sitting next to a well-dressed, proper, senior citizen woman who was reading a very literary tome. Being a librarian who specializes in adult leisure readers, I did what I always do when I encounter someone with a book, I engaged her in a conversation about it. I shared that I was working with a group of librarians to train them how to lead a discussion on this exact title and she shared some of her thoughts about the book. As our conversation about her book wound down, she asked me, "And what is bringing you to Providence?"

And that my friends is where our horror story begins. I think many of you already know what is coming next because you too have experienced it.

"Well," I said, "while I train librarians all over the country to help all types of leisure readers, my specialty is horror. I have written textbooks on the topic and am on my way to run Librarians' Day for the Horror Writers Association as part of their annual StokerCon."

Her response, "Horror?"

"Yes," I answered enthusiastically.

"Oh," and she rolled her eyes, put on her headphones, and that was the end of the time she was going to afford me.

Now this is but a single encounter, but it is not the only time I have experienced this reaction to my professional affiliation with horror. Every time I meet someone new and they ask what I do, I get the exact same response as the one I received from that woman on the plane. They hear that libraries from all over the country hire me to train their staff, that I write reviews and content for professional library journals and databases, but then, they hear that my specialty is horror, and well, we already saw what happens.

The public and even many of my fellow librarians do not think horror is worth their attention. To most people, it lives on the fringes of acceptable academic endeavors. That is why this book and the Ann Radcliffe Academic Conference specifically, from which these thought-provoking essays sprung, is so vital. Together these events and the academic output they inspire prove just how important literary scholarship is, and in fact, how much more vital it is when scholars focus their attention on some of the more popular genres. When we give attention to the stories people read in their leisure time, we learn more about humanity in general. We learn about their tastes, preferences, and desires that happen in their private moments. These are the stories people choose to read when they have free time and want to lose themselves in a good book. These are the tales they seek out whether they will admit it publicly or not. These are the stories that resonate with them the most on a personal level, whether they realize it consciously or not. This is true for all popular genres from romance to mystery and beyond, but specifically when we analyze the literature of supernatural monsters, when we confront our basest fears, this is when we see how authors and their readers are using fiction to wrestle with how we can all be more human.

Let us take just a few of the essays included here as brief examples to underline this point. Any time literary scholars look how fiction is introduced to our youngest readers, such as in "'Not a Bedtime Story': Investigating Textual Interactions Between the Horror Genre and Children's Picture Books" by Emily Anctil, we can make connections as to how stories are framed to the youngest among us and see how that influences people as we become the adults who make the rules that govern society. How we as adults create tales for children says much about what we value in our stories and how we expect them to navigate the world as adults. This line of intellectual study becomes even more evident in essays like "ScatterGories: Class Upheaval, Social Chaos and the Horrors of Category Crisis in *World War Z*" by J. Rocky Colavito which analyzes a novel that clearly speaks to the fears, conflicts, and realities of globalization on Earth in the 21st century. *World War Z* is a novel about humanity and the socio-political civilization we have created more than it is a zombie tale.

Even those who hold horror to a lower rung on the literary ladder see the benefit in essays such as those; works that look at the foundations of us as readers or analyze how we organize our civilizations. However, I would argue that where we all need access to literary scholarship in the genre is illustrated best by the essay in this collection, "Synchronic Horror and the Dreaming: A Theory of Aboriginal Australian Horror and Monstrosity" in which Naomi Simone Borwein takes the argument back to some of the oldest human storytelling traditions, ones that have not been typically studied in "the cannon." This is literary scholarship that probes the depths of the literature of humanity and provides a necessary comparison to the millions of pages of research that has been devoted to the Western viewpoint. We cannot begin to understand who we are as people today unless we have looked at the stories we have told as an entire species all across the world.

But scholars need access to these marginalized works. Who is gathering, cataloging, and preserving these monstrous tales? We barely have access to horror from the Western perspective let alone from all over the world. People have been telling scary stories of the supernatural since the dawn of our species. Fear of the unknown has driven humanity to create supernatural explanations, and monsters have always existed to help keep people in line, following the norms of their particular civilization. There is a treasure trove of scholarship to be found in the genre, but how much has been saved? If the public does not deem horror important enough to turn a critical eye toward it, if everyone reacts like that woman on my plane, then what are we missing?

That's where the library comes in. Librarians as a profession need to stop denigrating popular genres as less worthy of their attention because without the librarian, the gatekeepers of information, without their guidance, without their willingness to gather and safeguard these stories and storytelling traditions, there is no one left to stop it from being lost forever, and that is truly horrific.

That is why the book you just read is so crucial. The Ann Radcliffe Academic Conference and the exceptional research it has produced over the years, is doing the work of reminding us that horror needs to be preserved, so that it can be studied, and so that we can learn more about ourselves as people. By publishing the very best of this research into one book, Michele and Nicholas are doing everyone a great service, especially those of us who ply our trade in horror scholarship; they are showing the world the important critical analysis, for everyone, that is coming out of horror, a genre that most people look down upon.

And this is where I come in, to remind both sides, scholars and librarians, how important it is that we work together. At the library, we need to make sure we do not judge some scholarship as more important than others. We need to help authors do research, identify resources, provide access to primary documents, and generally assist all scholars regardless of their area of specialization. We are gatekeepers, not judges. But more importantly, we need to help preserve the work of all authors, not only the most literary or most normalized. The more voices future scholars have access to the better their scholarship and the more it will help all of humanity understand itself better.

So, librarians, when an author approaches you to house their papers, say yes. Or if you do not have the physical space to house these materials, assist the authors in finding an institution that can, especially when we are dealing with genres and subjects that most people do not respect. Without us, the guardians of the damned, this work will be lost.

But it is not solely up to the librarians. Scholars, you too need to get out there and advocate for yourselves and the important work you do. Those of you reading this book, you are among those who analyze and study horror. You too need to make inroads with your local libraries, both academic and public. You need to advocate for and educate others on the genre to help raise its standing among the larger public. Offer to give lectures, present research, or provide programming to the public that centers around horror and its place in our world, now and throughout our human history. As leaders in the world of horror scholarship, we have to remind people that our work matters. Space needs to be made for all voices and perspectives to be collected in order for it to be preserved for future generations to study.

And books like the one you just read are a great place to start.

Becky Spratford (MLIS) trains library staff all over the world on how to match books with readers through the local public library and runs the critically acclaimed library training blog RA for All *as well as its evil twin,* RA for All: Horror. *She also writes for EBSCO's NoveList database,* Booklist *and* Library Journal. *She is the author of* The Reader's Advisory Guide to Horror, Second Edition *[ALA Editions, 2012] and is currently working on the Third Edition coming out in 2021.*

About the Contributors

Emily **Anctil** holds an MA in children's literature from the University of British Columbia, Canada. Her research interests include child-constructed spaces in narrative picture books, children's horror film and literature, cult cinema in youth culture, and noir sensibility in children's film and fiction. She reviews children's horror books and scary stories online.

James Arthur **Anderson** is a professor at Johnson & Wales University's Miami campus. He earned his Ph.D. from the University of Rhode Island. He is the author of *Out of the Shadows: A Structuralist Approach to Understanding the Fiction of H.P. Lovecraft, The Illustrated Ray Bradbury,* and *The Linguistics of Stephen King: Layered Language and Meaning in the Fiction.*

Elizabeth **Bobbitt** was awarded her Ph.D. in English literature from the University of York in 2018. Her research focuses on Ann Radcliffe's "post-1797" text, posthumously published by Radcliffe's husband in 1826. She is particularly interested in exploring how Radcliffe's later work interrogates Britain's medieval and ancient past.

Naomi Simone **Borwein** has a Ph.D. in English literature from the University of Newcastle, Australia. Her work has appeared in volumes like *Horror Literature Through History* and *The Palgrave Handbook to Horror Literature*; she has research forthcoming in Palgrave Handbooks on *Modern Gothic, Steam Age Gothic,* and *Gothic Dreams.*

Michele **Brittany** is the editor of the Bram Stoker Award for Non-Fiction-nominated *Horror in Space: Critical Essays on a Film Subgenre* (2017) as well as *James Bond and Popular Culture* (2014). She is the book review editor for the *Journal of Graphic Novels and Comics* and the co-chair of the Ann Radcliffe Academic Conference focused on horror studies. She is a member of Horror Writers Association, and her poetry and fiction have been published in various horror anthologies.

J. Rocky **Colavito** is a professor of English at Butler University. He publishes and presents on a broad range of topics, from zombie studies to the *Sharknado* franchise. He is working on a monograph about the seminal '70s television series, *Kolchak: The Night Stalker,* and a collection of short horror stories set in the world of professional wrestling.

Nicholas **Diak** is a pop culture researcher interested in industrial music, Italian genre cinema, sword and sandal films and H.P. Lovecraft studies. He's the editor of *The New Peplum: Essays on Sword and Sandal Films and Televisions Programs since the 1990s* (2017) and has contributed many reviews and essays to a variety of academic anthologies, journals and websites. He is one of the co-creators and co-chairs of the annual Ann Radcliffe Academic Conference.

Gavin F. **Hurley**, Ph.D., is an assistant professor of English at University of Providence in Great Falls, Montana, where he teaches writing and rhetoric. He has published in journals and has contributed to essay collections including *Virtual Dark Tourism* (2018) and *Horror in Space* (2017). He is the author of *The Playbook of Persuasive Reasoning* (2018).

Bridget E. **Keown** received her Ph.D. in history from Northeastern University. Her research focuses on the intersections of gender, trauma and the history of medicine in the early 20th century. She is a contributing writing for the *Nursing Clio* blog.

Frazer **Lee** is a novelist, screenwriter, and filmmaker. His debut novel *The Lamplighters* was a Bram Stoker Award Finalist and his film credits include award winning short films *On Edge, Red Lines, The Stay*, and the acclaimed feature film *Panic Button*. He is Head of Creative Writing at Brunel University, London. His official website is www.frazerlee.com.

Erica **McCrystal** earned her Ph.D. in English literature from St. John's University in New York. Her research interests include Gothic literature and media, Victorian crime fiction, and comic book studies. Her podcast, *Villains 101*, launched in 2017 (www.villains101.com).

Johnny **Murray** is an independent scholar from the rural wilds of central New York. He is the author of the poetry chapbook *Ghost Calling* and co-author/co-designer of the art chapbook *An Abecedarian* (both from Unlock the Clockcase Press). He works for a non-profit philanthropical organization in Boston.

Danny **Rhodes'** short horror tales have appeared in publications on both sides of the Atlantic including Black Static in the UK and Cemetery Dance in the U.S. He is a member of the Horror Writers Association and a mentor on the HWA's Mentor Program. He is the author of *Asboville* (2006), *Soldier Boy* (2009), and *FAN* (2014). He teaches creative and professional writing at Canterbury Christ Church University in the UK.

Rahel Sixta **Schmitz** is a doctoral student at the Justus-Liebig-University in Giessen, Germany. She became a fellow of the International Graduate Centre for the Study of Culture, as well as the international Ph.D. program "Literary and Cultural Studies" in 2015. Her dissertation project focuses on virus metaphors and networked media culture in contemporary Gothic fiction.

John C. **Tibbetts** is an educator, artist, and broadcaster. As associate professor at the University of Kansas, he teaches courses on film history, adaptation studies, criticism, theory, and aesthetics. His book *The Gothic Worlds of Peter Straub* was a finalist for the Bram Stoker Award for Best Non-Fiction. He is writing a book on Marjorie Bowen.

Kevin J. **Wetmore**, Jr., is the author of ten books, editor of eleven more and has written dozens of book chapters and articles. His books include *Post–9/11 Horror in American Cinema, Back from the Dead, The Theology of Battlestar Galactica,* and *Uncovering Stranger Things.* He is a professor at Loyola Marymount University where he teaches about horror theatre, horror cinema, among other topics.

Index